Hollywood Dish

Hollywood Dish

More Than 150 Delicious, Healthy Recipes from Hollywood's Chef to the Stars

Akasha Richmond

AVERY ★ a member of Penguin Group (USA) Inc. ★ New York

AVERY

Published by the Penguin Group
Penguin Group (USA) Inc., 375 Hudson Street, New York, New York 10014, USA •
Penguin Group (Canada), 90 Eglinton Avenue East, Suite 700, Toronto, Ontario M4P 2Y3,
Canada (a division of Pearson Penguin Canada Inc.) • Penguin Books Ltd, 80 Strand, London
WC2R 0RL, England • Penguin Ireland, 25 St Stephen's Green, Dublin 2, Ireland (a division of Penguin
Books Ltd) • Penguin Group (Australia), 250 Camberwell Road, Camberwell, Victoria 3124, Australia
(a division of Pearson Australia Group Pty Ltd) • Penguin Books India Pvt Ltd, 11 Community Centre,
Panchsheel Park, New Delhi–110 017, India • Penguin Group (NZ), Cnr Airborne and Rosedale
Roads, Albany, Auckland 1310, New Zealand (a division of Pearson New Zealand Ltd) • Penguin
Books (South Africa) (Pty) Ltd, 24 Sturdee Avenue, Rosebank, Johannesburg 2196, South Africa

Penguin Books Ltd, Registered Offices:
80 Strand, London WC2R 0RL, England

Most Avery books are available at special quantity discounts for bulk purchase for sales promotions,
premiums, fund-raising, and educational needs. Special books or book excerpts also can be created to fit
specific needs. For details, write Penguin Group (USA) Inc. Special Markets, 375 Hudson Street,
New York, NY 10014.

Library of Congress Cataloging-in-Publication Data

Richmond, Akasha.
Hollywood dish: more than 150 delicious, healthy recipes from Hollywood's chef to the stars.
p. cm.
Includes bibliographical references and index.
ISBN 1-58333-241-3
1. Cookery.   2. Celebrities—California—Los Angeles—Anecdotes.
3. Hollywood (Los Angeles, Calif.)—Social life and customs—Anecdotes.   I. Title.
TX714.R53   2005   2005048169
641.5—dc22

Printed in the United States of America
1   3   5   7   9   10   8   6   4   2

This book is printed on acid-free paper. ∞

Book design by Stephanie Huntwork

While the author has made every effort to provide accurate telephone numbers and Internet addresses at the
time of publication, neither the publisher nor the author assumes any responsibility for errors, or for changes
that occur after publication. Further, the publisher does not have any control over and does not assume any
responsibility for author or third-party websites or their content.

The recipes contained in this book are to be followed exactly as written. The publisher is not responsible for
your specific health or allergy needs that may require medical supervision. The publisher is not responsible
for any adverse reactions to the recipes contained in this book.

Contents

Acknowledgments

natural and organic food would never be where it is today without the pioneering works of the original health crusaders who started more than a hundred years ago. Many thanks to Dr. John Harvey Kellogg, Otto Carque, Paul C. Bragg, Clark Irvine, Harold Hain, John and Vera Richter, Dr. Phillip Lovell, Dr. Henry Bieler, Mildred Lager, T. A. Van Gundy and Dorothea Van Gundy Jones, Adelle Davis, and most of all Gayelord Hauser for making health food glamorous all over the world. Below are just some of the many people who helped me be who I am, and have contributed to the writing of this book.

First to my mom, Judy Litman, for making her own sprouts over thirty years ago, and for keeping it up when friends asked why she was eating "whisker and peanut butter sandwiches"—keep eating those "whiskers," Mom. To my dad, Merle Litman, for always pushing me to be somebody. I miss you more than ever and I am sorry you are not around to see this book.

To Bobby Ayres, for turning me on to Athens Juice Bar and the Health Hut, and for inspiring me to make a better carrot cake. To Cathy Scholl, for getting me to move to the West Coast. Thanks for that letter—you were right! In loving memory of my first yoga teacher, Sahaj, for introducing me to Gurmukh. Thank you, Gurmukh, for encouraging me to learn yoga and to do some cooking at the Golden Temple. Who knew? Many thanks to Yogi Bhajan for teaching me about infusing healing foods into everyday dishes.

There have been many clients in the last twenty years that have inspired me to create beautiful food. A big thank-you to Barbra—cooking for you is such a joy and inspiration. Michael, thank you for treating me like a fellow artist. Pierce and Keely, you're the best. And a special thanks to Billy Bob for inspiring me to create some amazing recipes. There are too many more to mention but I appreciate every one of you.

Along the way there were numerous friends who shared my love of good food and inspired me to be a better chef. Many thanks to Mani Niall, Eddie J. Caraeff, Beth Ginsberg, Lisa and Michael Mesnick, Nancy and Morris Zaslavsky, Claudia McQuillan, Sue Polin, Richard Rosenthal, Staci Valentine, Sat and Andrea Khalsa, and Richard Lasser. Dana Jacobi and Sat Simran also share my love of good food and inspire me, but deserve an extra thank-you for always being there for me and listening. To Anna Getty and Debbie Robbins, for teaching me something I should have already known; I am forever grateful. Thank you to my friend and business adviser Albert Spevak at Ambassador Entertainment for many things, but most of all for teaching me "Don't react." In the advice department, I also must thank Beth Shepard; I appreciate you always.

Thank you to Norman Koplas for the UCLA cookbook writing class and the advice to "write the book that only you can write." I never could have written this book without soyfoods expert Bill Shurtleff. Thank you for sharing your knowledge, love of history, your database, and for teaching me to find the true facts to every story. I can't thank Beth Salmon at *Let's Live* magazine enough for opening up her archives to me—it was like discovering a treasure chest. I really appreciate it. No author can write a book alone, so I am grateful to Jen Joos, Alex Hilebronner, and Julie Janney for all of their help in testing recipes. And to Susan Biegal and Daniel Maskit for the testing party—Daniel, you missed your calling. Lots of appreciation and thanks to those who contributed or inspired recipes for this book: Neil Zevnick, Donna Prizgintas, Eddie J. Caraeff, Mani Niall, Ann Gentry, Nikki Reiss, Gavan Murphy, Beth Ginsberg, Alice Medrich, Nancy Silverton, Alice Irvine, Angja Aditi, Shirley Knight, and Nancy Zyslavsky.

To the companies and organizations that shared their archives and contributed photos and images: Sunkist Growers, Diamond Walnuts, Waring Products, *Let's Live* magazine, Bragg Live Food Products, Eddie J. Caraeff, Rodale, Los Angeles Public Library, Palm Springs Historical Society, Rancho La Puerta, and Sun Maid. An additional thank-you to Mary Rodgers at Waring for the blenders—they do make the best smoothies, and everything else.

To those who shared their stories with me: Alice Irvine, Efrem Zimbalist Jr., Egon Reich, Peter Roy, Gabrielle Barrett, Leo Pearlstein, Damian Paul, Michael Mesnick, Richard Lasser, and especially to Gypsy Boots, the original "California Nature Boy."

To Steve Demos, for believing in me and teaching me how to throw a really good party. Doug Greene, thanks for your advice and encouragement, and for starting New Hope Natural Media. To Sonya Kugler, for always being ready to help out and make it happen. Big kiss to the MOD Squad, Sheryl Roth and Mara Engel, for the positive energy and enthusiasm that make everything so much fun. Thanks to Ellen Feeney and the team at Silk Soymilk for making it all "smooth as silk." And thank you to my friend Doug Block for all the parties and for bringing me to Sundance. Your friendship is so special and you are the life of every party.

To Debbie Levin and Patie Maloney at the Environmental Media Association, for all that you do and for producing the best events. A big thank-you to Katherine DiMatteo and Laura Stravino at the Organic Trade Association for making "all things organic."

I must thank the people who make my food look good all the time: the fabulous Nikki Reiss, the multitalented Sergio Gomez, the always-together

Gavan Murphy, master baker Doug McNatton, and Jack McLaughlin, the sexiest bartender I know. Without all of you, and many more, I could never cater a party.

To Jane Dystel and Stacey Glick at Dystel-Goderich Literary, your guidance was invaluable. Stacey, thanks for putting up with me—I really appreciate it. Thank you to my editor at Avery, Dara Stewart, for pushing me to do more, and for making this a better book.

Last but not least is a big thank-you to the two people who put up with me every day, my daughter, Amrit, and my husband, Alan. Thanks for bearing with me while I wrote this book. I really appreciate your patience.

The Road to Hollywood

INTRODUCTION

I grew up in Hollywood, Florida, a town named, ironically, after its California counterpart. I started cooking from *The Betty Crocker Boys and Girls Cook Book* when I was ten, and moved on to my mom's copy of *The Joy of Cooking*. I come from a family of really good home cooks, so when my mother discovered Adelle Davis, Tiger's Milk bars and brewer's yeast, we thought she had gone nuts. Three years later, when I became immersed in the surf culture of South Florida (greatly influenced by the Beach Boys of California), I too became enlightened to a new way of eating, and started patronizing local health food restaurants like Here Comes the Sun and the Health Hut. I read the *Miracle of Fasting* by Paul Bragg and started juice fasting on fresh tropical juices. My first job at sixteen was at a health food store, the kind that sold more vitamins than food. Since I loved to cook, I started creating my own healthful dishes. My first attempts were complete whole-wheat and honey disasters, and when my boyfriend told me that my carrot cake was a lead brick, I vowed to figure out how to use natural ingredients to make great-tasting food.

Historically, folks have headed to California for a reason—gold, oranges, health, wealth, and fame probably being the top five. Once you arrive, you can't help but fall in love with California, and you will do whatever you can to stay. I headed west for a reason, too. When I heard that the organic foods, beaches, surfers, and yogis were better in California, I decided to head west for college. I had already tried meditation (years after the Beatles' liaison with the Maharishi), and a fateful meeting with Gurmukh (before she became "yogi to the stars") led me to Los Angeles to study yoga and work at the Golden Temple Conscious Cookery, where she was the manager. I, too, was influenced by the yogis and swamis to eat a healthful diet, and my cooking has always included the healing spices of India and other ethnic flavors.

I am fortunate to work privately and cater parties for some of the biggest names in the entertainment business. Some of my favorite memories include going "red carpet all the way" on the Michael Jackson tours, making dinner for Captain Kangaroo, cooking holiday dinners for Billy Bob Thornton, working as a private chef for Barbra Streisand, catering parties for Keely and Pierce Brosnan, and catering events for MTV, the Oscars, and the Emmys. My favorite is the Sundance Film Festival, where I promote organic foods, cater parties, and cook at the ChefDance dinners.

One of my favorite Hollywood events that combines talented chefs, organic foods, and the arts is the annual Environmental Media Awards, where environmentalists such as Keely and Pierce Brosnan, Blythe Danner, Daryl Hannah, and Ed Begley Jr., Amy Smart, and Wendy Malick speak out for a cleaner and safer planet. As the celebrities arrive on the "green carpet" to discuss with the press the virtues of hybrid vehicles, organic foods, and solar panels, the chefs are busy in the kitchen preparing a meal made with natural and organic ingredients.

Actors, chefs, yogis, and exercise experts tend to get along because we are all artists and have a mutual respect for one another's talents. It's not surprising that many aspiring actors have become chefs and television personalities, and many celebrities have opened restaurants, written cookbooks, and become fitness experts. James Beard did it first, when he left the theater to start a catering business during the Great Depression.

I have been collecting vintage cookbooks and cook booklets for more than seven years. About three years ago, I decided to take advantage of the amazing culinary collection at the Los Angeles Central Library. After a couple months of research, I realized there was a story to tell about the history of health and diet in California. I was truly surprised and inspired by what has gone on in the health food world over the last hundred years—and I was only focusing on one city! The beauty of our world today is that all of the California ingredients used in these recipes are available nationwide in supermarkets and natural food stores.

Hollywood Dish is not a diet book, per se. Though some of the recipes are low carb or low fat, this book is more about using good-for-you ingredients in tasty recipes with some interesting historical stories. I've included some of my best recipes that I use when I cater events. They're all chock-full of fresh, wholesome healthy ingredients.

Feel free to change the ingredients in any of the recipes if you have allergies or you just hate figs, walnuts, broccoli, or whatever. Most of my recipes call for ingredients that are readily available in supermarkets and natural food stores. There are a few that you may need to find at Asian or Indian markets and specialty food stores. I have included at the end of the book a resource section with some of my favorite brands, as well as some online sources for harder-to-find ethnic or organic ingredients. I always try and use the freshest ingredients, organic whenever possible, because if you start with quality ingredients, your food is bound to be better.

There are certain ingredients I am more specific about than others, and before you prepare a recipe from this book, I would like to clarify my approach. My big rule of thumb is to read all labels and avoid anything containing artificial additives, sweeteners, flavors, colors, or preservatives, hydrogenated oils (trans fats), nitrites or nitrates, sulfites, MSG, and anything that sounds like a chemical in general. I try and buy as many organic fruits and vegetables as I can, and when the organic ones are out of season, I substitute something else. Some of the information-based websites listed in the Resources have valuable information on why it's better to eat organic fruits and vegetables, and which nonorganic foods are highest or lowest in pesticides.

Many of my recipes call for soymilk. I prefer to use a plain or unsweetened soymilk, especially with savory dishes. If you want to use full-fat or 2 percent cow's milk in place of the soymilk, go ahead—it can be replaced cup for cup—but if you haven't cooked with soymilk, give it a try—I think you'll be surprised. When it comes to other soy products like tofu, tempeh, and miso, I prefer to use organic brands and those free of GMOs (genetically modified organisms).

Most supermarkets carry organic dairy products; if not, look for dairy products that are completely free of rBGH (recombinant Bovine Growth Hormone) and antibiotics. Look for meats and poultry that are free of antibiotics and hormones and use organic if available. The resource section lists a couple of websites with sustainable seafood information. Since the oceans are always changing, I check the Monterey Bay Aquarium website often to find out what the safest seafood choices are.

I use herbs and spices that are nonirradiated and free of caking agents. These can be found at natural food stores and through mail order. Many of the recipes call for kosher salt, which is a pure coarse salt. Kosher sea salt or coarse sea salt can be used instead, but remember that coarse salt has less sodium per teaspoon than fine-grained sea salt, so use less fine-grained salt in the recipe if that's all you have on hand. For baking, I use a fine sea salt. Good-quality coarse sea salt can be found in natural food markets, and kosher salt without caking agents is available in most supermarkets and natural food markets.

I like to use a light blond finely granulated organic sugar for cooking and baking, but you can substitute white sugar and get the same results—it will just be a tad sweeter. Look for some of the specific varieties of honey called for in the recipes in natural food stores, by mail order, or at your local farmers market. You can definitely substitute other types of honey if necessary—they each have a unique taste and will add an additional flavor to any dish. There are so many good-quality chocolates available on the market right now, it's hard for me to choose a favorite, but I do prefer semi- or bittersweet varieties, since they are rich in antioxidants and have a deeper flavor. Some of the recipes call for white spelt flour, which gives great results in all kinds of recipes and is easier for some people to digest than wheat. Unbleached white flour can be substituted for spelt flour, but you may need to use 2 tablespoons more per cup in the recipe, since spelt flour is a bit lighter. When it comes to oils, I use expeller- or cold-pressed oil, since most regular commercial brands are processed with chemical or solvents. Read the labels on vegetable shortenings and margarines to make sure they are trans-fat free and contain no hydrogenated oils.

Cooking is a science and trying new things in the kitchen is part of the process. Don't be afraid to try new ingredients like green tea powder, soymilk, or spelt. If you love cooking as I do, you'll have fun with these recipes, and I hope these stories entertain you as they have me.

The Road to Wellville

Ever since the Hollywood Diet made the cover of *Motion Picture* magazine in 1929, star power has set healthy, nutrition, and lifestyle trends in America. When the Beatles, Mia Farrow, and Donovan visited Maharishi Mahesh Yogi in Rishikesh in 1968, it was reported in *Life, Look,* and the *Saturday Evening Post,* and TM (Transcendental Meditation) was put on the map. No one is a better spokesperson for macrobiotics, yoga, and kabbalah than Madonna, and who wouldn't want to try a raw food diet after seeing what it did for Demi Moore and Donna Karan?

Many celebrities use their fame and life experience to help others by becoming fitness experts. Academy Award–winning actress Jane Fonda shared her Adelle Davis–inspired whole-wheat bread recipe with *Life* magazine in 1962 and started the aerobic exercise craze and video fitness empire in the 1980s. Then there's actress Marilu Henner, who shared with her fans how her health problems and lack of energy led her to give up dairy, and whose best-selling books and Total Health Makeover plan have changed other lives as well. The queen of this domain is Suzanne Somers, best known as Chrissy from the popular 1970s sitcom *Three's Company.* No one can outsell Somers, whose diet cookbooks, food products, and exercise equipment are an empire on the Home Shopping Network.

Throughout Hollywood's history, celebrities and their star power have set the stage for most of the trends that have swept the country, and healthy living trends have been no exception.

Even before Hollywood became the movie capital of the world, thousands came to California for inexpensive land, horticulture, sunshine, and the search for better health. After the Gold Rush of 1848, the legend grew that Southern California's climate could cure diseases like tuberculosis, asthma, and rheumatism. This led to an influx of health seekers and crusaders, which played a role in the agricultural, residential, cultural, and industrial development of Los Angeles and the surrounding areas.

The immigration of German health reformers to Los Angeles at the turn of the century was crucial to the development of the natural foods industry. The German *Naturmenschen* (natural men) and *Lebensreform* (life reform) movements had been popular in Germany since 1883, when health reformers pioneered homeopathy, vitamin therapy, hydrotherapy, nature cures, and raw food diets. Los Angeles became the ideal destination, since fruits grew wild in the Hollywood Hills, land was cheap, and the sun shone year-round. It was a paradise compared to the cold physical and political climate of Eastern Europe.

Since that time, health retreats, natural food companies and markets, chic, hip healthy-eating restaurants, spas, and the like have popped up all over the Hollywood area and have become the *it* places to find Hollywood's insiders.

The film crowd also helped launch America's fitness craze at the famed Muscle Beach in Santa Monica. Jack LaLanne was a regular at Muscle Beach, where thousands came every weekend during the 1930s, '40s, and '50s to watch the musclemen and women lift weights and perform aerobic feats. Many of the performers became well-known Hollywood stuntmen, and many actors got in shape by working out with them. Roy Rogers, Kirk Douglas, and Robert Wagner all worked out at Muscle Beach, where Mae West, Jayne Mansfield, and Jane Russell were frequent visitors. Fitness legend Joe Weider began his career on Muscle Beach and brought Arnold Schwarzenegger to the United States in 1969, when he gave him his start on the sand pumping iron at his Gold's Gym.

Hollywood did not invent exercise or reducing diets; it just glamorized and popularized them like never before. When the 18-Day Diet became the rage in the late 1920s, it was renamed the Hollywood Diet, since it was so popular with the movie crowd. Diets like Gaylord Hauser's 7-Day Elimination Diet, the Beverly Hills Diet, Fit for Life, and the 48-Hour Hollywood Miracle Diet are just a few with Hollywood roots.

When television came into American homes in the late 1940s, it gave Hollywood a whole new way of creating stars, and health crusaders like Jack LaLanne and Paul Bragg gained national recognition with their own shows in the 1950s. Gypsy Boots, who learned his ways from the German *Naturmenschen,* was a regular on Steve Allen's *Tonight Show,* swinging in on a vine and feeding Steve wheatgrass, sprouts, and fresh juices.

Motion Picture magazine features the Hollywood Diet, 1929. On the cover is Sue Carol, star of Girls Gone Wild and the future wife of Alan Ladd.

Hollywood clearly has had a huge impact on our lives, including how we stay in shape. *Hollywood Dish* celebrates Hollywood's history of healthy eating since its beginnings. Long before Hollywood was the movie empire of the world, the area set the standards for healthy living. Once Hollywood's stars fell in love with vegetarian, raw, and macrobiotic foods, and all sorts of healthy meals, soon the rest of the country did, as well. Let's look at and celebrate Hollywood's tradition of healthy eating while enjoying some healthy eating of your own with the recipes that follow. They're so good, you'll never believe they're good for you.

Breakfast at Tiffany's

CEREAL, EGGS, AND OTHER WAYS TO START THE DAY

The American breakfast revolution began in 1863, when Dr. James C. Jackson created the first ready-to-eat breakfast cereal and named it "granula." Jackson made his granula with a whole-wheat flour dough and water and baked it into bricks. The bricks were broken up and baked again to produce small bits that resembled Grape-Nuts. Jackson's granula experiment was the beginning of a new concept in breakfast foods that would eventually change the way many Americans started the day.

In 1876, Dr. John Harvey Kellogg of the Battle Creek Sanitarium—whose patients included Henry Ford, retailers J. C. Penney and S. S. Kresge, actress Sarah Bernhardt, Thomas Edison, President William Howard Taft, aviator Amelia Earhart, and film star Johnny Weissmuller (talk about a celebrity following!)—began to experiment with ready-to-eat cereals. When he named his wheat, corn, and oat cereal Granula, Jackson sued him, so Kellogg changed the name to Granola.

Dr. Kellogg also developed Granose, the first wheat-flake cereal, and Toasted Corn Flakes, the cereal that established corn as a major player in breakfast cereals. Dr. Kellogg's brother Will (known as W.K.), who had helped to develop Granose in 1895, was also instrumental in the pioneering of the "Toasted Corn Flake," which they started packaging in 1906. When W.K. bought him out of the Toasted Corn Flake Company in 1911, the real cereal revolution began, as W.K. wished to promote cornflakes for taste, not just for health.

W.K. promoted his new cereal company in true Hollywood fashion, using pretty girls to promote his Toasted Corn Flakes. In the 1920s, W.K. hired actor and humorist Will Rogers as the company spokesperson, and ads for Corn Flakes in the *Los Angeles Times* featured film starlets promoting Corn Flakes. W.K. began hanging out in Hollywood in the mid-1920s, and soon Hollywood stars like Loretta Young were promoting All-Bran Cereal for dieting. A 1930s booklet entitled *The Modern Figure* includes Young and other actresses sharing weight-reducing tips using All-Bran.

The Kellogg Company also sponsored *Breakfast in Hollywood,* a popular morning radio show that eventually became a movie starring Tom Breneman, Billy Burke (*Oz*'s Glinda the Good Witch of the North), and gossip diva Hedda Hopper. Post Cereal (Grape-Nuts) also sponsored television shows, such as *The Danny Thomas Show* and *The Andy Griffith Show.* Jim Nabors guest-appeared on *Andy Griffith* as Gomer Pyle, and he eventually got his own Post-sponsored show, *Gomer Pyle U.S.M.C.* Comedian Ronnie Schell, who played Pvt./Cpl. Gilbert "Duke" Slater on *Gomer Pyle*, often made frequent appearances on talk shows preparing his "Breakfast in a Blender" with juice, fruit, oat bran, peanut butter, protein powder, and vitamin C. Today, "Breakfast in Hollywood" is anything you want—and much more than cold cereal.

Seared Bananas with Honey Yogurt

Serves 2

*L*ydia Lane, a syndicated beauty columnist for the *Los Angeles Times,* wrote a daily column from 1934 to 1982. Lydia interviewed popular film stars and provided their health and beauty tips to readers. In 1954 she spoke with Grace Kelly, who told Lydia that a doctor who specialized in nutrition cured her health problems. After that, Grace claimed she never forgot the relationship between food and health and always tried to eat balanced meals containing "energy foods." One of her favorite snacks was yogurt and honey.

1 teaspoon walnut or canola oil

¼ teaspoon ground turmeric

2 ripe but firm bananas, cut into ½-inch slices

⅛ teaspoon ground cinnamon

1 cup low-fat or nonfat yogurt

2 teaspoons orange blossom honey

½ teaspoon pure vanilla extract

3 tablespoons chopped walnuts

Heat the oil in a 10-inch skillet over medium heat. Add the turmeric and cook for 30 seconds; it should darken in color. Add the bananas and cook about 45 seconds on each side, just until they sear a bit. Turn off the heat. Sprinkle with the cinnamon.

In a small bowl stir together the yogurt, honey, and vanilla. Add the bananas and top with the walnuts.

Granola Baked Peaches

Serves 3 to 4

In *The Cook Book of the Stars* (1939), Warner Brothers actors such as Olivia de Havilland and Humphrey Bogart lent their likenesses and quotes to recipes throughout the book. Actor Ronald Reagan claimed that baked stuffed peaches were one of his favorites. In 1939, Reagan had already made over a dozen movies, including the classic *Dark Victory,* starring as one of Bette Davis's suitors. Years later, he became president of the Screen Actors Guild, where he met his future wife, fellow actress Nancy Davis. This easy-to-make version of baked peaches includes granola, and it just may become one of your favorites.

Canola cooking spray

3 ripe peaches

1 teaspoon walnut or canola oil

6 tablespoons homemade or store-bought low-fat granola

2 tablespoons chopped raw almonds

1 tablespoon light brown sugar (if the granola is not too sweet)

⅛ teaspoon ground cinnamon

2 cups plain low-fat or nonfat vanilla yogurt

Preheat the oven to 350°F. Spray a 10-inch glass or ceramic casserole dish.

Cut each peach in half and take out the pits. Remove some of the pulp from the center of each peach half; you will have about 1 tablespoon of pulp. In a small bowl mix the peach pulp, oil, granola, almonds, brown sugar, and cinnamon. Top each peach half with equal amounts of the granola mixture.

Transfer to the prepared dish and bake, uncovered, for 30 minutes. Serve warm with the yogurt on the side.

Hangtown Egg White and Oyster Mushroom Fry

Serves 4

Hangtown Fry may be the first authentic California cuisine. During the Gold Rush of the 1840s, the northern California town of Hangtown (now Placerville) was an important supply center for the gold-mining camps. According to legend, when a miner had enough gold dust, he could afford the most expensive dish in a restaurant, a six-dollar meal of eggs, bacon, and oysters, which they termed "Hangtown Fry." This version is made with egg whites and oyster mushrooms, with the addition of smothered onions and peppers.

2 teaspoons olive oil

1 medium onion, cut in half and sliced into thin half-moons

1 red bell pepper, seeded and cut into thin julienne slices

1 teaspoon unsalted butter

6 ounces oyster mushrooms, cleaned and sliced in half

1 cup liquid egg whites or 8 fresh egg whites

2 large eggs

1 tablespoon soymilk creamer or half-and-half

¼ teaspoon kosher salt

⅛ teaspoon freshly ground black pepper

2 ounces chèvre-style goat cheese

2 tablespoons chopped fresh chives for garnish

Heat the oil in a 12-inch skillet and cook the onion for 5 minutes. Add the bell pepper and cook 2 minutes more. Add the butter and mushrooms and cook until the mushrooms are tender, about 5 minutes.

Whisk the egg whites, eggs, creamer, salt, and pepper in a medium bowl. Pour the eggs over the onion mixture in the pan. Cook, stirring, until set to your liking. Add the goat cheese and serve garnished with the chives.

Crustless Corn and Pepper Quiche

Serves 4

Before and after World War II, Mildred Lager, a radio-show host, columnist, health food store owner, and cooking teacher, popularized soy foods in Los Angeles. Her book *The Useful Soybean: A Plus Factor in Modern Living* (1945) is full of creative recipes using soymilk, tofu, soy grits, soy nut butter, and more. Mildred predicted many future uses for soy, and I think she would have enjoyed knowing that this recipe was served at an Oscar event during Academy Awards week, along with soy cappuccinos and soymilk-based scones.

2 teaspoons olive oil or unsalted butter, plus more for the pan

1 bunch green onions, all of the white and half of the green parts, finely chopped

½ red bell pepper, seeded and finely chopped

1 small poblano chile, roasted, peeled, seeded, and diced, or ¼ cup canned chopped green chiles

1 cup frozen corn kernels, thawed, or the kernels cut from 1 large ear

2 large eggs

3 large egg whites

1 cup plain soymilk

½ teaspoon kosher salt

¼ teaspoon freshly ground black pepper

1 cup grated soy pepper jack cheese or dairy jack cheese, tossed with 2 tablespoons of unbleached all-purpose flour

Preheat the oven to 375°F. Lightly oil a 9-inch pie pan.

Heat the oil in a 12-inch skillet over medium heat. Add the green onions and bell pepper and cook until softened, 3 to 5 minutes. Turn off the heat and add the roasted poblano and corn. Set aside to cool slightly.

★ Mildred Lager (1908–1960) ★

Mildred Lager was born in Superior, Wisconsin. While in her teens, she was told by doctors that she had incurable rheumatoid arthritis and would never walk again. She began to study nutrition, and after a five-month diet of fruit juice, eliminated most of her symptoms. She moved to Los Angeles, and in 1933 opened a natural food store and learning center called the House of Better Living. Her lectures and cooking classes were always free of charge, and her store soon became one of the most successful natural food stores and education centers on the West Coast. She preferred the term "natural food" over "health food," which she felt suggested sickness and food fads. Along with Otto Carque, who trademarked "natural foods of California," she was one of the first to promote the term "natural foods." In 1934 she started her own radio program, called *Food Facts*, which was also the title of a book she wrote in 1935. Among the books she wrote, the most important ones were about soy foods.

In a medium bowl whisk the eggs and egg whites with the soymilk, salt, and pepper. Add the vegetable mixture and the cheese. Pour into the prepared baking dish. Place on the center rack of the oven and bake until puffed, golden, and a knife inserted into the center comes out clean, about 30 minutes. Let rest for 10 minutes.

Cut into wedges and serve with warm tortillas, black beans, salsa, and guacamole, if desired.

Spanish Egg White Scramble with Yellow Grit Cakes

Makes 18 grit cakes;
serves 4 to 6

In 1915, silent film mogul Carl Laemmle bought a 230-acre chicken ranch on the outskirts of Los Angeles and dubbed his new movie studio Universal City. Laemmle invented the studio tour when he charged guests a twenty-five-cent entrance fee to watch the films being made. The fee included a boxed lunch, and on the way out Laemmle sold them eggs. Laemmle's chicken ranch is now Universal Studios, the largest film and television studio in the world. The Hollywood Bowl was also a chicken ranch in 1920, years before Frank Sinatra, the Beatles, and Judy Garland ever performed under the well-known band shell. Spanish eggs have been popular in Los Angeles for over a hundred years. The 1911 *Los Angeles Times Cookbook Number Four* included various recipes for Spanish eggs and omelets made with fresh roasted green chiles, tomato sauce, and peppers.

YELLOW GRIT CAKES

2 teaspoons olive oil, plus more for the pan

½ cup water

¾ cup plain soymilk

¼ teaspoon kosher salt

½ cup yellow grits

1 teaspoon unsalted butter

1 teaspoon minced jalapeño chile

1 tablespoon minced fresh chives

½ cup shredded goat Gouda or soy jalapeño jack cheese

¼ teaspoon freshly ground black pepper

EGG WHITE SCRAMBLE

2 teaspoons extra-virgin olive oil

½ medium onion, finely chopped

2 plum tomatoes, seeded and chopped into ½-inch dice

2 green onions, all of white and most of green parts, chopped fine

2 teaspoons minced jalapeño or serrano chile

2 cups liquid egg whites, or 16 fresh egg whites, whisked until frothy

¼ teaspoon kosher salt

⅛ teaspoon freshly ground black pepper

2 tablespoons chopped fresh cilantro

For this recipe, make the grit cakes first; while they are cooling, get all of the ingredients prepped for the egg white scramble so they will be ready at the same time.

Oil an 8 x 8-inch baking pan.

To make the grit cakes, bring the water, soymilk, and salt to a boil over medium-high heat in a 2-quart saucepan. Whisk in the grits, bring back to a boil, and then reduce to a simmer. Cook for about 4 minutes, whisking constantly. Remove from heat and add the butter, jalapeño, chives, cheese, and pepper. Stir until the cheese is melted and the grits have thickened. Spread onto the prepared pan. Let cool in the refrigerator for 30 minutes.

Preheat the oven to 250°F. When the grit cakes are cooled down and firm, cut into 3 slices vertically then horizontally, making 9 squares. Cut each square in half, making 18 triangles. Heat the oil over medium-high heat in a large nonstick skillet until very hot. Add the grit cakes and cook for 1 to 2 minutes on each side, or until golden brown. Remove the grit cakes from the pan and drain on a paper towel–lined baking sheet or plate. Keep warm in the oven while you make the egg white scramble.

To make the egg white scramble, heat the oil in a 10-inch nonstick skillet over medium-high heat. Add the onion and cook for 5 minutes, or until translucent. Add the tomatoes, green onions, and jalepeño to the onions and cook an additional 2 minutes. Add the egg whites, salt, and pepper to the onion mixture and cook, stirring constantly, until the eggs are set. Garnish with the cilantro and season with additional salt if needed. Serve with the warm grit cakes.

★ Harry Chandler (1864–1944) ★

Harry Chandler moved to Los Angeles from New Hampshire in 1882, penniless and in search of a cure for his lung problems. By 1884, Chandler's health was restored, and he had saved $3,000 by picking and selling fruit. When he returned to New Hampshire his health failed again, so he came back to California. He bought a 300-acre ranch, where he grew fruit and produced honey commercially—six tons in 1890—which he sold for 5½ cents a pound. He eventually became publisher of the *Los Angeles Times* and a powerful and influential man who was instrumental in helping to build Los Angeles. Chandler erected the first Hollywoodland sign to promote a housing development, one of his many enterprises.

In 1899, Chandler proposed to *Times* staff writer Harry Ellington Brook that they start a health section of the newspaper. "Care of the Body" ran in the Sunday magazine section and reported on health foods, diets, nature cures, and more. It was the first health section of its kind in a major American newspaper. Brook wrote the column for twenty-five years, and Dr. Philip M. Lovell took over in 1924. During Chandler's time, the *Times Mirror Press* published many health and diet books, including some by Lovell that sold nationwide.

The *Times* had many other health, diet, and food columns, including one by beauty editor Lydia Lane, who from 1934 to 1982 wrote about the natural health, weight loss, and exercise "secrets of the stars." Lydia's column ran in more than 375 newspapers nationwide, bringing celebrity beauty and health tips to the rest of America. Nancy Reagan, Shirley MacLaine, and Sophia Loren were just a few of the stars interviewed in Lydia's long-running column, which was the first column of its kind. Marilyn Monroe discussed her high-protein diet, Audrey Hepburn shared how Adelle Davis had taught her about vitamin C, and Doris Day said she only used raw sugar in her yogurt and stewed fruit, and claimed that every morning she would make a quart of fresh carrot juice for breakfast.

Curried Scrambled Tofu

Serves 3 to 4

Swingers in West Hollywood is an ultra-hip motel coffee shop packed with vintage-clothed screenwriters, young actors, and tattooed musicians. Breakfast choices range from the Easy Rider (two eggs any style, pancakes, bacon or sausage) to healthy choices like smoothies, vegan brown rice–black bean burritos, and a mushroom tofu scramble. Like Swingers, tofu scramble has become a Los Angeles institution, and can be found on restaurant menus all across the city. The latest L.A. hot spot for tofu scramble is M Café de Chaya, where chef Lee Gross (a former personal chef to Gwyneth Paltrow) serves his version with tempeh bacon served in a toasted roll. My recipe relies on lots of Indian spices and I like to serve it with chapatis or flour tortillas.

2 teaspoons clarified butter or canola oil

½ teaspoon ground turmeric

1 teaspoon black mustard seeds

½ teaspoon ground cumin

½ teaspoon ground coriander

1 teaspoon paprika

⅛ teaspoon red chile flakes (optional)

2 green onions, both white and green parts, finely chopped

1 clove garlic, minced

½ serrano chile, seeded and finely diced

1 medium-size tomato, finely chopped

12 ounces firm water-packed tofu, drained, patted dry, and crumbled into scrambled egg–size pieces

1 tablespoon Bragg Liquid Aminos

¼ teaspoon kosher salt

½ teaspoon freshly ground black pepper

1 tablespoon finely chopped fresh cilantro

Heat the clarified butter in a 10-inch nonstick skillet over medium-high heat. Add the turmeric, swirl the pan, and cook for 30 seconds, or until darkened in color. Add the mustard seeds, let sizzle for 30 to 40 seconds, then add the cumin, coriander, paprika, and chile flakes, and cook 30 seconds more, stirring constantly.

Add the green onions, garlic, chile, and tomato and cook for 2 to 3 minutes, or until the tomatoes dry up a bit. Add the crumbled tofu, liquid aminos, salt, and pepper. Cook another 2 to 3 minutes, stirring often. Garnish with the cilantro.

Chia-Sunflower Cereal

Serves 1

In the early 1970s, Hollywood ate a real "power breakfast" at the Source restaurant on Sunset Boulevard. The breakfast menu included soy waffles, whole-wheat pancakes, and a high-protein raw cereal that was hand-cranked fresh for every order. It was served with local raw milk from Alta Dena, the dairy pioneer in the natural foods industry since 1945. The cereal contained chia seeds, an energy source for Native Americans long before the Chia Pet hit the market. Paul Bragg was a fan of chia seeds and claimed they gave him an extra drive that no other food did. Chia seeds can also be added to pancake and waffle batter.

2 tablespoons whole spelt or wheat berries

2 tablespoons rolled oats

1 tablespoon raw sunflower seeds

1 tablespoon chia seeds (see Resources)

1 tablespoon flaxseed

½ cup cow's milk or plain soymilk

Sliced apples, bananas, or dates

Honey for serving

1 tablespoon almonds

In a small electric spice or coffee grinder, grind the first five ingredients separately until finely ground. Alternatively, you can use a hand-cranked grain mill. Serve with the milk, fruit, and honey to taste. Top with the almonds.

Crunchy Blueberry Granola

Makes about 7 cups

"Crunchy Granola" is so associated with the counterculture that anyone looking like a throwback to the 1960s is often described as "crunchy" in appearance. Granola was most likely the first trademarked health food product, and has come a long way since its early days. Granola today is very different from John Harvey Kellogg's original hard dry nuggets, and in true W. K. Kellogg style, the Kellogg Company put cereal-lover Jerry Seinfeld on the back of the box in 1992.

4 cups rolled oats

⅓ cup shredded unsweetened coconut

¼ cup chopped almonds

⅓ cup whole pumpkin seeds

⅓ cup chopped cashews

1 teaspoon ground cinnamon

¼ teaspoon ground cardamom

¼ cup packed light brown sugar

Finely grated zest of 1 orange

⅛ teaspoon fine sea salt

¼ cup canola oil

¼ cup sage or orange blossom honey

1½ teaspoons pure vanilla extract

2 tablespoons pure maple syrup

¾ cup dried blueberries

¼ cup ground flaxseed

★ Granola ★

Granola's popularity as the first cold breakfast cereal died down with the successful marketing of Kellogg's cereals after the turn of the twentieth century. Since Kellogg was a Seventh-Day Adventist, it is no surprise that Los Angeles author and fellow Adventist Dorothea Van Gundy Jones included the first written recipes for granola in her book *The Soybean Cookbook* (1963). Two years later, packaged granola first appeared when another Adventist, Layton Gentry, sold his homemade "crunchy granola" recipe to Sovex in Tennessee and Lassen's Foods of California. In 1972, *Time* magazine called Gentry "Johnny Granola-Seed," since he singly started the new granola revolution.

Celebrity nutritionist Adelle Davis made granola a star in 1971, when her friend Egon Reich asked Adelle to put her stamp of approval on Better Way Granola. They used the tagline "Created from an Adelle Davis Recipe" on each package and Egon soon had the granola selling in every health food store in America. That same year, *Life* interviewed Davis and included her granola recipe, called "Adelle's Homemade Cereal." Considering that *Life* was as popular as *People* is today, and Adelle Davis was a household name, she deserves much of the credit for granola's comeback into the breakfast world.

Granola almost made it to the big screen in Robert Altman's movie *HealtH* (1982), which starred Carol Burnett and Lauren Bacall, who played an Adelle Davis type of character. Sovex Granola was one of the natural food companies that participated in creating the film's health food convention scene. Although they were interviewed and filmed, Sovex Granola fell to the cutting-room floor. They did, however, get a credit at the end.

Preheat the oven to 300°F and set the oven racks toward the center of the oven.

In a large bowl toss together the oats, coconut, almonds, pumpkin seeds, cashews, cinnamon, cardamom, brown sugar, orange zest, and salt.

Combine the oil and honey in a small saucepan over medium heat and stir until the honey dissolves, about 1 minute. Add the vanilla and maple syrup to the honey mixture, then mix into the oat mixture, tossing to distribute the ingredients evenly.

Cover 2 baking sheets with parchment paper. Spread the granola equally over the 2 sheets. Bake for 10 minutes, stirring once or twice. Rotate the pans and continue to cook for another 3 to 5 minutes, checking often, until lightly browned. One sheet may bake quicker than the other depending on your oven, so check during the last 5 minutes. Remove from the oven and let cool. After the granola has cooled, add the dried blueberries and ground flaxseed. Toss well and store in a covered container.

Keeps for at least 1 week.

Walnut Griddle Cakes with Blood Orange Syrup

Makes twenty-four 3-inch pancakes, serves 6 to 8

In 1907, before the film industry came to Hollywood, the California Fruit Growers Exchange (soon to be Sunkist) and the Southern Pacific Railroad launched an advertising campaign using the slogan "Oranges for Health—California for Wealth" to lure Americans to the Golden State. Citrus recipes were often promoted by Sunkist cook booklets and in cookbooks published by the *Los Angeles Times*. This recipe was inspired from one found in the *Los Angeles Times Cook Book Number Two* (1905). The syrup is truly remarkable, and when made with blood oranges it looks exactly like maple syrup. When blood oranges are out of season, use half cranberry or pomegranate juice to give the syrup its rich color.

BLOOD ORANGE SYRUP
½ cup blood orange or Valencia orange juice
I cup sugar
Finely grated orange zest from 2 small blood or other oranges

WALNUT GRIDDLE CAKES
1¼ cups unbleached all-purpose flour
¼ cup whole-wheat flour

1½ teaspoons baking powder

½ teaspoon baking soda

½ teaspoon fine sea salt

2 tablespoons sugar

½ cup finely chopped toasted walnuts

1 large egg

1½ cups plain soymilk

2 tablespoons blood orange or Valencia orange juice

1 tablespoon walnut oil

Canola cooking spray

To make the blood orange syrup, heat the orange juice and sugar in a small saucepan over medium-high heat. Bring to a simmer, and then immediately take off the heat. Add half of the grated orange zest. Reserve the syrup while you make the pancakes.

In a medium bowl whisk together the flours, baking powder, baking soda, salt, sugar, and walnuts. In another bowl whisk together the remaining orange zest, egg, soymilk, orange juice, and oil. Pour the liquid mixture into dry in-gredients, stirring with a wooden spoon just enough to combine.

Heat a 12-inch nonstick skillet or griddle over medium-high heat and spray with cooking spray. Spoon batter onto the skillet for each pancake, tilt-ing the skillet to distribute. Cook until bubbles appear on the top of the batter, then flip and cook until the bottom is lightly browned. Repeat with the rest of the batter. Serve immediately, with the blood orange syrup.

Cinnamon French Toast with Pomegranate-Cherry Compote

Serves 6

The Zagat Survey once wrote that breakfast at Hugo's Restaurant in West Hollywood is better than *Breakfast at Tiffany's,* and regulars like Jerry Seinfeld, Julia Roberts, and Denzel Washington seem to agree. Their famous

French toast, made with thickly sliced cinnamon swirl bread, inspired this recipe. Hugo's is also famous for their specialty teas and Yogi Tea cappuccinos; owner Tom Kaplan created the first commercially processed packaged chai suitable for making latte-style drinks.

POMEGRANATE-CHERRY COMPOTE

1 cup pomegranate juice

⅓ cup dried pitted cherries

1 tablespoon unsalted butter

6 small apples (about 2¼ pounds), peeled and
   chopped into ½-inch pieces

⅓ cup pure maple syrup

CINNAMON FRENCH TOAST

3 large eggs

¾ cup eggnog-flavored or spice-flavored soymilk

2 teaspoons pure vanilla extract

¼ teaspoon ground cinnamon

⅛ teaspoon freshly grated nutmeg

Six 1-inch-thick slices cinnamon swirl or challah bread (about ½ loaf)

2 tablespoons unsalted butter

Sifted powdered sugar for topping

To make the compote, heat the pomegranate juice in a small saucepan over medium-high heat until it boils. Turn off the heat, add the cherries, and let sit for 15 minutes.

Heat a 12-inch skillet over medium-high heat. Melt the butter in the pan and add the chopped apples. Cook the apples until they begin to soften but still hold their shape, 5 to 6 minutes. Add the maple syrup to the apples along with the pomegranate juice and the cherries. Simmer until the juice reduces to a syrup, 5 to 10 minutes.

To make the French toast, preheat the oven to 200°F. In a large bowl whisk together the eggs, soymilk, vanilla, cinnamon, and nutmeg. Place the bread slices in a flat casserole dish and cover with the egg mixture. Let soak for 5 to 10 minutes.

Heat a 12-inch nonstick skillet over medium-high heat and melt 1 tablespoon of the butter in the pan. Add 3 slices of the soaked bread to the pan and cook until golden brown, about 4 minutes per side. Remove from the pan, place on a baking sheet, and keep warm in the oven. Melt the remaining tablespoon butter in the pan and cook the remaining bread slices.

Top the French toast with the compote and sprinkle with the powdered sugar before serving.

Grape-Nut and Flaxseed Waffles with Honey Strawberries

Serves 4

C. W. Post was a patient of John Harvey Kellogg's before founding his own food empire in 1897. His first product was Postum, a coffee substitute favored by Gloria Swanson and still served at Musso & Frank, Hollywood's oldest restaurant. Post wrote a book called *I Am Well!,* which eventually was condensed into a recipe booklet entitled *The Road to Wellville,* which he included in every box of Grape-Nuts, his second product. The term "the road to Wellville" was a favorite metaphor of Post's and in 1994, T. C. Boyle's book *The Road to Wellville* became a movie starring Anthony Hopkins as Dr. John Harvey Kellogg, with Mathew Broderick as his patient.

GRAPE-NUT AND FLAXSEED WAFFLES
Canola cooking spray or canola oil
¾ cup unbleached all-purpose flour
1 tablespoon packed light brown sugar
1 teaspoon baking powder
½ teaspoon baking soda
¼ teaspoon fine sea salt
2 tablespoons ground flaxseeds

2 tablespoons Grape-Nuts or Kashi Seven Whole Grains & Sesame cereal

I large egg, separated, at room temperature

¾ cup plain soymilk

½ teaspoon pure vanilla extract

I ½ teaspoons orange juice

I tablespoon canola oil

HONEY STRAWBERRIES

I cup diced strawberries

2 tablespoons orange blossom or sage honey

2 teaspoons fresh lemon juice

I teaspoon pure vanilla extract

To make the waffles, preheat oven to 200°F. Grease a waffle iron with cooking spray or brush with oil and preheat it.

In a large bowl sift together the flour, brown sugar, baking powder, baking soda, and salt. Stir in the ground flaxseeds and cereal. In a separate bowl whisk together the egg yolk, soymilk, vanilla, orange juice, and oil. Pour into the dry mixture and stir to combine. In a dry, grease-free medium bowl beat the egg white until stiff but not dry. Fold the egg white into the batter using a rubber spatula.

Place about ⅓ cup of the batter into each waffle grid and spread the batter almost to the edges. Close the lid and bake for 3 to 5 minutes, or until steam no longer comes out of the waffle iron. Transfer the waffles to a small baking sheet and keep warm in the oven while you make the rest of the waffles.

While you're cooking the waffles, make the honey strawberries by combining the strawberries, honey, lemon juice, and vanilla in a small bowl. Taste and add more honey if needed. Serve over the waffles.

Pineapple Upside-Down Bran Muffins

Makes 12 muffins

One of the first Los Angeles celebrity chefs was Chef Arthur Leslie Wyman, who, along with his wife, Maybelle, traveled through the United States teaching cooking with California foods. By 1920 he was writing a daily column for the *Los Angeles Times* and headed up the home economic department. His book, *Chef Wyman's Daily Health Menus* (1927), had sections on meat substitutes, California fruits, Spanish recipes, honey recipes, and health breads made with whole grains. Chef Wyman was known for his cooking classes, and in 1914 he gave a cooking class for Los Angeles housewives, where he demonstrated how to make bran muffins, which is the inspiration for this recipe.

Canola cooking spray

⅔ cup packed light brown sugar

2 tablespoons pure maple syrup

2 tablespoons unsalted butter, softened

1 tablespoon water

8 ounces (1 cup) fresh or canned pineapple, chopped into ½-inch pieces

1¾ cups bran flakes

1½ cups unbleached all-purpose flour

¼ teaspoon fine sea salt

2 teaspoons baking soda

1 teaspoon baking powder

⅓ cup raisins or dried cherries

¼ cup canola oil

¼ cup mild molasses

¼ cup pure maple syrup

1¼ cups plain soymilk

¼ cup orange juice

1 teaspoon pure vanilla extract

1 teaspoon finely grated orange zest

Preheat the oven to 375°F. Coat a 12-cup muffin pan with cooking spray.

In a small bowl whisk together the brown sugar, maple syrup, butter, and water. Using a pastry brush, divide the mixture equally between the 12 muffin cups. Then divide the pineapple among the muffin cups.

In a large bowl combine the bran flakes, flour, salt, baking soda, and baking powder. Mix 2 to 3 teaspoons of the dry ingredients with the raisins and set aside.

In another bowl whisk together the oil, molasses, maple syrup, soymilk, orange juice, vanilla, and orange zest. Make a well in the center of the dry ingredients and pour in the liquid mixture. Lightly fold in the raisins. Do not overmix or the muffins will be dense.

Fill the muffin cups and place on a parchment-lined baking sheet (to catch any drips from the topping). Bake for 20 minutes, checking with a toothpick at 18 minutes for doneness. Remove from the oven and immediately invert the muffin tin onto a cooling rack. If any of the pineapple topping remains in the tin, quickly replace it back on top of the muffins.

Maple-Glazed Fauxnuts

Makes 6 Fauxnuts

I have learned a lot about baking with natural sweeteners from my friend Mani Niall, author of *Covered in Honey* (2003). Mani is the founder of Mani's Bakery in Los Angeles, and when actor Danny DeVito was making *Other People's Money* (1991) the production company came to him to develop a low-fat doughnut that DeVito's character could eat throughout the movie. Mani's creation—"fauxnuts"—were baked, not fried, and overnight he became the "baker to the stars."

FAUXNUTS

Unsalted butter or canola cooking spray

1 cup unbleached all-purpose flour, plus more for the pan

1½ teaspoons baking powder

¼ teaspoon baking soda

¼ teaspoon fine sea salt

⅛ teaspoon freshly grated nutmeg

1 large egg

½ cup plain soy or low-fat yogurt

½ teaspoon pure vanilla extract

⅓ cup pure maple syrup

4 tablespoons canola oil or melted unsalted butter

MAPLE GLAZE

½ cup powdered sugar, sifted

2 tablespoons pure maple syrup

To make the fauxnuts, preheat the oven to 400°F. Butter and flour or spray a 6-section mini Bundt cake pan. Sift the flour, baking powder, baking soda, salt, and nutmeg together into a medium bowl.

In another bowl whisk the egg, yogurt, vanilla, maple syrup, and oil together. Make a small well in the center of the dry ingredients. Pour the wet ingredients into the well, then stir with a spatula or wooden spoon until the dry ingredients are moistened but still lumpy. Don't overmix the batter or your fauxnuts will be heavy. Divide the batter evenly into the prepared Bundt pan.

Bake about 20 minutes, until golden brown and a toothpick inserted into the center of a fauxnut comes out clean. Cool the fauxnuts in the pan on a rack for a few minutes, then turn out of the pan to cool completely on the rack. While the fauxnuts are baking, make the glaze by whisking the sugar and maple syrup together in a small bowl. Drizzle the cooled fauxnuts with the maple glaze.

Pear and Pistachio Scones with Fig Chutney

Makes twelve 3-inch scones and about 1½ cups chutney

One of my favorite catering clients was the late Herb Ritts, who, along with shooting covers for *Vogue, Vanity Fair,* and *Rolling Stone,* directed numerous videos and television commercials and created advertising campaigns for Giorgio Armani, Chanel, Donna Karan, Calvin Klein, and more. I catered many photo shoots for Herb, who loved clean, healthy cooking. A typical week of photo shoots with Herb was with Bette Midler, Cher, Antonio Banderas, and Richard Gere. I was normally the one back in the kitchen cooking lunch, but I had to show up when we catered for Richard Gere, who was even nicer than he is handsome. We always served scones like these for breakfast. I like to change the fruit seasonally with this scone dough, and have used mangos, peaches, plums, and apples. You can leave out the nuts and use dried cranberries, blueberries, or currants instead.

FIG CHUTNEY
¼ cup apple cider vinegar

¼ cup sugar

¾ cup orange juice

¼ cup minced white onion

½ teaspoon grated lemon zest

½ teaspoon grated orange zest

½ pound dried Black Mission figs, stems removed, chopped into 8 pieces each

1 cinnamon stick

PEAR AND PISTACHIO SCONES
1½ cups unbleached all-purpose flour

½ cup yellow cornmeal

¼ cup sugar, plus additional sugar for topping

1 tablespoon baking powder

1 teaspoon baking soda

½ teaspoon fine sea salt

1 cup buttermilk or plain soymilk mixed with 2 teaspoons lemon juice

¼ cup canola oil or melted unsalted butter

1 large pear, peeled and cut in ½-inch pieces (about 1 cup)

¼ cup chopped pistachios

To make the chutney, combine the apple cider vinegar and sugar in a medium saucepan over medium-high heat and heat to dissolve the sugar. Add the orange juice, onion, lemon zest, orange zest, figs, and cinnamon stick. Bring to a boil, then reduce to a simmer and simmer for 20 minutes, stirring occasionally. Let the chutney cool to room temperature and remove the cinnamon stick. Refrigerate before serving.

The chutney can be made up to 1 week in advance.

To make the scones, preheat oven to 375°F and line a baking sheet with parchment. In a large bowl combine the flour, cornmeal, sugar, baking powder, baking soda, and salt.

In a medium bowl whisk together the buttermilk and oil. Make a well in the dry ingredients, pour the wet mixture into the dry, and mix together with a wooden spoon or spatula, stirring to combine with as few strokes as possible. Lightly fold in the chopped pear and pistachios.

Scoop the batter onto the prepared baking sheets, forming 12 scones total. Top with about 1 teaspoon of sugar per scone. Bake for 12 to 14 minutes, or until lightly browned. Serve with the fig chutney and yogurt or crème fraîche.

3

The Fabulous Baker Boys

YEAST BREADS AND QUICK BREADS

Burt Lancaster, perhaps best known for his beach scene with Deborah Kerr in *From Here to Eternity* (1953), helped bake the bread down at the Rancho La Puerta resort in Baja California, where they originally made bread fresh daily from an ancient recipe, using water and whole wheat berries. Greta Garbo always kept some of Gayelord Hauser's breads in her freezer, and Mae West started her day with a slice of Jack LaLanne's high-protein bread. In recent years, with the popularity of all of the low-carb diets, I can't begin to tell you how many bread baskets have gone untouched at my catered events. Hollywood has always been fond of extremely healthy bread and with the new food pyramid promoting whole grains, what better way to eat them than in a delicious slice of home-baked whole-grain bread?

No history of healthful breads in Hollywood or anywhere

else is complete without giving praise to Reverend Sylvester Graham (1794–1851), an ordained Presbyterian minister who started the health food industry in America. Reverend Graham acquired a different kind of following in Boston by preaching health reform and vegetarianism. The focus of his diet was bread made from whole-wheat (Graham) flour. Graham and his followers (Grahamites) opened boarding houses in the 1830s that served vegetarian meals, and sold the first packaged "health" foods. These houses were the first vegetarian restaurants and health food stores in America. Dr. John Harvey Kellogg and many of Hollywood's early health crusaders were influenced by Dr. Graham's teachings. I suppose Graham would turn over in his grave if he saw today's graham crackers, which are typically made with white flour and white sugar. Fortunately, more healthful versions are available in natural food stores and supermarkets.

In 1933, General Mills and "Betty Crocker" teamed up with Hollywood to promote bread as an energy food. For many years, Marjorie Child Husted was the marketing genius, and often voice and persona, behind Betty Crocker. Husted was sent to Hollywood as Betty Crocker, and MGM, Paramount, and Warner Bros. all agreed to let Husted/Crocker interview their contracted actors and studio commissary chefs about Hollywood eating habits. In Betty Crocker's *Vitality Demands Energy* (1934), Oscar-winning stars like Bette Davis and Claudette Colbert promoted bread as part of a healthy diet, and in exchange, *Vitality Demands Energy* gave the actresses free publicity for their new films. Apparently, Husted kept in touch with her Hollywood contacts, since she tested the recipes and wrote the foreword to *The Brown Derby Cookbook* (1949).

Reverend Graham might not be too happy with me, either, since I don't strictly use only whole-wheat flour in my bread baking. I prefer spelt flour, which is an ancient grain related to wheat. You may find that your bread doesn't rise as high with spelt flour, but don't be alarmed by that—it will still taste great. Spelt flour can be found in natural food stores or by mail order (see Resources). Feel free to substitute unbleached white flour for any recipe calling for spelt flour.

Black Mission Fig Bread
with Orange Glaze

Makes 1 cake;
serves 12 to 16

One of the earliest American recipes for a fruit and nut bread was for German Nut Loaf, found in *Souvenir California Raisin Recipe Book* (1914), published when Sun-Maid was still called Sun-Made. Since then, dried fruits and nuts have been used in every type of quick bread imaginable. Early health pioneer Otto Carque was known for his promotion of dried California fruits, especially the Black Mission fig. In the early 1910s, he shipped his dried figs and other fruits nationwide and even into Canada. Fig cakes were popular in Los Angeles at the turn of the last century, and even the 1936 trade edition of *The Joy of Cooking* included a recipe for Fig Spice Cake, which inspired this recipe.

FIG BREAD

Canola cooking spray

¾ pound dried Black Mission figs

One ¼-inch slice fresh ginger

2 tablespoons fresh lemon juice

1-inch piece lemon zest

½ cup plain soy or dairy yogurt

2 cups unbleached all-purpose flour, plus more for the pan

1 teaspoon baking powder

½ teaspoon baking soda

½ teaspoon fine sea salt

½ teaspoon ground cinnamon

½ teaspoon ground ginger

¼ teaspoon ground cloves

¼ teaspoon ground cardamom

½ cup canola oil, plus more for the pan

1 cup sugar

½ cup egg whites (from about 4 eggs)

2 teaspoons finely grated orange zest

I teaspoon pure vanilla extract

¼ cup minced candied ginger

¾ cup chopped walnuts

ORANGE GLAZE

2 cups confectioners' sugar

I tablespoon finely grated orange zest

3 to 4 tablespoons orange juice

Preheat the oven to 350°F. Place an oven rack in the lower third of the oven. Spray and flour 9- or 10-inch Bundt pan.

Place the figs, ginger slice, lemon juice, and lemon zest strip in a 1-quart saucepan over low heat. Cover with cold water, bring to a simmer, and simmer until the fruit is soft, about 20 minutes. Drain the fruit into a bowl and measure out ½ cup of the stewing liquid. Discard the ginger and lemon zest. When the figs have cooled, remove the stems, cut the figs into ¼-inch pieces, and set aside. Add the yogurt to the liquid.

Sift the flour, baking powder, baking soda, salt, cinnamon, ground ginger, cloves, and cardamom into a medium bowl.

In another bowl, use a handheld beater to beat the oil with the sugar until light and fluffy, about 5 minutes. Add the egg whites in four parts, beating well after each addition. Add the grated orange zest and vanilla. Add the dry ingredients in three parts, alternating with the yogurt mixture in two parts, mixing just until blended. Do not overmix, or the batter will be tough. Stir in the figs, candied ginger, and walnuts. Spread the batter evenly into the prepared pan.

Bake for 40 to 45 minutes, or until the cake springs back when pressed lightly in the center and a toothpick inserted in the center comes out clean.

Cool in the pan on a rack for 15 minutes, then turn out onto the rack to cool completely.

While the cake is cooling make the glaze by whisking all the glaze ingredients together until smooth and creamy. Drizzle the glaze over the cooled bread.

Date-Nut Bread

Makes 1 loaf

Date-Nut Bread was served with Palm Springs Salad at the famed Racquet Club in Palm Springs. The Racquet Club was founded by two movie stars—Charlie Farrell and Ralph Bellamy, who wanted more places to play tennis out in the desert. Legend has it that Marilyn Monroe was discovered at the Racquet Club, where star-studded poolside love affairs and glamorous parties were known the world over. I add mashed bananas to this bread, so I can cut down on the fat.

Canola cooking spray
Flour, for the pan
1 cup chopped pecans
1 cup whole-wheat pastry flour
1 cup unbleached all-purpose flour
1 tablespoon baking powder
½ teaspoon baking soda
½ teaspoon fine sea salt
¼ cup canola oil
¾ cup light honey such as sage or acacia
2 large fresh egg whites or ¼ cup liquid egg whites
¼ cup plain soymilk
2 cups mashed bananas (about 3 to 4 large)
1½ cup dates chopped into ½-inch pieces, tossed with 1 tablespoon flour

Preheat the oven to 325°F. Lightly spray a loaf pan with canola cooking spray, then dust with flour.

Place the pecans on a small baking sheet or cake pan and toast in the oven for 15 minutes, turning once or twice. Let cool while you make the cake.

In a large bowl whisk together the flours, baking powder, baking soda, and salt. In a medium bowl whisk together the oil, honey, egg whites, soymilk, and bananas.

Make a well in the dry ingredients and add the wet ingredients. Mix lightly with a wooden spoon or spatula until the flour is moistened. Fold in the dates and ½ cup of the pecans. Carefully spoon the batter into the prepared pan and sprinkle with the remaining pecans.

Bake for 30 to 35 minutes, or until the cake springs when touched and a toothpick inserted in the center comes out clean. Cool in the pan for 10 minutes, than remove the bread and let cool on a wire rack for at least 20 minutes before slicing.

Bill Baker's Soy Bread

Makes 1 loaf

In 1925, film stars were driving up to Santa Barbara to see Dr. W. D. Sansum, who wrote the *Normal Diet* (1925) and "prescribed" breads made with soy or lima bean flour. Bill Baker, known as the "Ojai Baker," was one of the first to develop multigrain breads, and started making breads for Dr. Sansum in 1928. By 1931, Baker was adding soybean flour to his own breads, and the *Los Angeles Times* reported that he was sending huge cases of bread to President Hoover and other celebrities. Baker was also known for his elaborate cakes, especially the ones he sent to presidents Herbert Hoover and Franklin D. Roosevelt for Christmas.

¼ cup warm (105° to 115°F) water

1 package (2¼ teaspoons) active dry yeast

½ cup warm (105° to 115°F) plain soymilk

3 tablespoons canola oil, plus more for oiling the bowl

2 tablespoons honey

1 teaspoon fine sea salt

2¼ to 2½ cups unbleached all-purpose flour

¼ cup soy flour

Put the warm water in a large bowl or in the bowl of a freestanding heavy-duty electric mixer fitted with the dough hook. Sprinkle the yeast over the water. Let stand for about 10 minutes, or until the yeast dissolves and foams.

Stir in the soymilk, oil, honey, and salt. Add the all-purpose and soy flour, mixing well. The dough should be moist but not sticky. Knead by hand on a floured board for 10 minutes, or on low speed in the mixer, adding a bit more flour if needed, until the dough is smooth and elastic, about 10 minutes. You can also knead the dough in a food processor fitted with the plastic blade.

Place the dough in an oiled bowl and turn over once to cover with the oil. Cover the bowl loosely with a clean towel or plastic wrap and place in a warm, draft-free place until doubled in size, about 1½ hours.

Punch the dough down, knead briefly, and shape into an 8-inch-long loaf. Place in a greased 8½ x 4½-inch (6-cup) loaf pan, seam side down. Cover loosely with oiled plastic wrap and let rise in a warm place until doubled, about 1¼ hours.

Preheat the oven to 375°F. Bake the bread for 20 minutes, then lower the heat to 350°F and bake an additional 20 minutes. Turn out of the pan and let cool on a rack.

Olive Pizza Bread

Makes one 11x17-inch flatbread

I had thought that olive bread was first popularized in California during the early 1980s, but natural foods pioneer Otto Carque may have baked the first loaf of olive bread in Los Angeles. In 1915, he made some for Olive Day, and according to the *Los Angeles Times,* his new idea was so popular that the next day he had orders for 500 loaves. This dough is somewhere between a pizza and pizza bread; and if you'd like, top with some pizza sauce and mozzarella.

1 cup warm (105° to 115°F) water

1 teaspoon honey

1 package (2¼ teaspoons) active dry yeast

3 to 3½ cups white spelt flour or unbleached white flour

1½ teaspoons kosher salt

3 tablespoons extra-virgin olive oil, plus more for oiling the bowl and brushing the bread

1 cup kalamata olives, pitted and cut in half

2 plum tomatoes, seeds removed and chopped into ½-inch square pieces

2 teaspoons minced fresh rosemary

Combine the warm water with the honey in a large bowl or the bowl of a freestanding heavy-duty electric mixer fitted with the dough hook. Sprinkle the yeast over the water and stir with a fork or small whisk until the yeast is dissolved. Let stand until creamy and foamy, 5 to 10 minutes.

If using an electric mixer, add the flour, salt, and 1 tablespoon of the oil. Knead on medium speed until the dough is smooth and elastic. Add more flour if needed. You can also knead this bread by hand or in a food processor until smooth and elastic.

Form the dough into a ball and place in an oiled bowl, turning once to cover with the oil. Cover the bowl loosely with a clean towel or plastic wrap and place in a warm, draft-free place until doubled in size, about 45 minutes.

Punch the dough down, fold over a few times, and cover again. Return to the warm spot and let rise again for 30 minutes.

Oil an 11 x 17-inch baking sheet. Flatten the dough on the baking sheet with wet or oiled hands. Cover with a towel and let relax for 10 minutes, then pull it until it reaches the edges of the pan. Cover with a towel and let rise for 45 minutes to 1 hour. Preheat the oven to 400°F.

Just before baking, brush the dough with additional olive oil and press the olives into the dough in a symmetrical or unsymmetrical pattern. (I like mine "Jackson Pollock"–style.) Top with the tomatoes and press the rosemary into the dough. Bake for 20 to 25 minutes, or until golden brown. Immediately turn out of the pan and let cool on a rack.

Cinnamon-Raisin Bread

Makes 1 loaf

Silent film star Anita King eating Raisin Pie, 1916.
(COURTESY OF SUN-MAID GROWERS OF CALIFORNIA)

The California raisin industry was born in 1873, when a heat wave hit the San Joaquin Valley vineyards and dried the grapes on the vine. The desperate growers sold the dried grapes as "Peruvian Delicacies," and they sold out immediately. Sun-Maid referred to raisins dried in the California sun, and a pretty "maid" gathering the harvest on the box became the growers' trademark in 1915. In 1916, silent film star Anita King became the first woman to drive alone cross-country in an automobile. She claimed raisins gave her energy along the way, and was photographed in the trademark Sun-Maid sunbonnet eating raisin bread. Anita may have been the first celebrity spokesperson to promote a California product.

¼ cup warm (105° to 115°F) water

1 package (2¼ teaspoons) active dry yeast

3 tablespoons nonhydrogenated vegetable shortening or unsalted butter, melted

1 cup warm (105° to 115°F) plain soymilk

3 tablespoons sugar

1 tablespoon finely grated orange zest

1 teaspoon fine sea salt

1 large egg, at room temperature, beaten

½ cup whole-wheat flour

3½ to 4 cups unbleached all-purpose flour

¾ cup raisins

Canola oil for the bowl

1½ teaspoons unsalted butter, at room temperature

4 tablespoons sugar mixed with 2 teaspoons ground cinnamon

Put the warm water in a large bowl or in the bowl of a freestanding heavy-duty electric mixer fitted with the dough hook. Sprinkle the yeast over the water. Let stand for about 10 minutes, or until the yeast dissolves and foams.

In a small saucepan melt the vegetable shortening over low heat, then add the soymilk and sugar. Heat until lukewarm, then remove from heat and add the orange zest and salt. Add to the yeast mixture and mix in the egg. Stir in the flours, mixing well. The dough should be moist but not sticky.

Knead by hand on a floured board for 10 minutes or on low speed in the mixer, adding more flour if needed, until the dough is smooth and elastic. Fold the raisins into the dough.

Form the dough into a ball and place it in an oiled bowl, turning once to cover with the oil. Cover the bowl loosely with a clean towel or plastic wrap and place in a warm, draft-free place for about 2 hours, or until doubled in size.

Punch the dough down. On a floured marble or wooden surface, roll the dough into an 8 x 8-inch square. Spread the softened butter over the surface.

Sprinkle 3 tablespoons of the sugar-cinnamon mixture over the butter, reserving the rest for the top of the bread. Roll up the dough into a loaf as tightly as you can.

Place seamed side down into a greased 8½ x 4½-inch (6-cup) loaf pan. Cover with oiled plastic wrap and let rise for another 1½ hours.

Preheat the oven to 375°F. Sprinkle the top of the dough with the remaining sugar-cinnamon mixture and bake for 40 to 45 minutes. Turn out of the pan and let cool on a rack.

Honey-Flaxseed Bread

Makes 2 loaves

Adelle Davis may have learned about healthy bread baking while working with Gayelord Hauser in her early days. Davis's influence was widespread, and in a 1962 issue of *Life* magazine on food, Jane Fonda shared her recipe for homemade health bread that she adapted from an Adelle Davis recipe. This is my version of my mom's Adelle Davis loaf. I prefer spelt flour to regular wheat flour, and many people who have an intolerance to wheat can digest spelt.

⅓ cup warm (105° to 115°F) water

2 packages (4½ teaspoons) active dry yeast

2 cups warm (105° to 115°F) plain soymilk

3 tablespoons canola oil, plus more for greasing the bowl

2 tablespoons buckwheat or alfalfa honey

2 tablespoons molasses

2 teaspoons fine sea salt

3 cups whole-grain spelt flour

3 to 3½ cups white spelt flour

⅓ cup flaxseeds

Put the warm water in a large bowl or in the bowl of a freestanding heavy-duty electric mixer fitted with the dough hook. Sprinkle the yeast over the water. Let stand for about 10 minutes, or until the yeast dissolves and foams.

★ Adelle Davis (1904–1974) ★

Adelle Davis taught Audrey Hepburn about vitamin C and Jane Fonda about bread baking; even *Joy of Cooking* author Marion Rombauer Becker was a fan. The media touted her as "America's most celebrated nutritionist," and she was the headline opener of the big talk shows of the day, hosted by Merv Griffin, Dinah Shore, and Johnny Carson. Her big books, *Let's Eat Right to Keep Fit* (1954), *Let's Cook It Right* (1947), *Let's Get Well* (1965), and *Let's Have Healthy Children* (1951), sold more than 14 million copies. She was featured and profiled in countless magazines, including *Vogue*, *Life*, and the *New York Times Magazine*.

Her Hollywood friends included Aldous Huxley, author of *Brave New World*, *The Doors of Perception*, and the screenplays for *Jane Eyre* and *Pride and Prejudice*. Her friendship with Huxley and his wife, Laura, most likely influenced her to write *Exploring Inner Space: Personal Experiences Under LSD-25* (1961). It was the first book written by a woman about the psychedelic experience. She wrote under the pseudonym Jane Dunlap because her publisher refused to let her write under her real name. In *Exploring Inner Space* she wrote about her controlled experiences under the influence of LSD, which began as a quest for spiritual enlightenment. The profits from her signature breads and packaged granola went to the Adelle Davis Foundation, which funded nutritional studies and gave financial aid to students.

Stir in the soymilk, oil, honey, molasses, and salt. Add the whole-grain spelt flour and 3 cups of the white spelt flour, mixing well, adding additional flour if the dough is too sticky. The dough should be moist but not sticky. Knead by hand on a floured board for 10 minutes, or on low speed in the mixer, adding a bit more flour if needed, until the dough is smooth and elastic. You can also knead the dough in a food processor fitted with the plastic blade. Knead in the flaxseeds.

Form the dough into a ball and place it in an oiled bowl, turning once to cover with the oil. Cover the bowl loosely with a clean towel or plastic wrap and place in a warm, draft-free place until doubled in size, about 1½ hours.

Grease two 8½ x 4½-inch (6-cup) loaf pans. Punch the dough down, knead briefly, and form into two 8-inch-long loaves. Place in the loaf pans seam side down. Cover loosely with oiled plastic wrap and let rise in a warm place until doubled, about 1¼ hours.

Preheat the oven to 375°F. Bake for 40 to 45 minutes. Turn out of the pans and let cool on racks.

Whole-Wheat Popovers

Makes 8 popovers

Prudence Penny was a part-time actress, dietitian, food editor, and cookbook author. She starred in *Penny Wisdom,* the Oscar winner for Best Short Film in 1937. In the film, Penny plays herself, the culinary columnist for the *Los Angeles Examiner* who saves the day for a housewife whose cook walks out just moments before her husband's boss comes home for dinner. Penny wrote about popovers in *Coupon Cookery* (1943), her wartime answer to thrifty cooking during food rationing. Under "Prudent Tips and Penny Savers," she suggested popovers as a delicious and economical patty shell. You can use a regular muffin pan to make these but I highly recommend purchasing a special popover pan, which is available at most kitchen supply stores.

3 large eggs
1 cup plain soymilk or low-fat milk
2 tablespoons unsalted butter, melted
½ cup unbleached white flour
6 tablespoons whole-wheat flour
¼ teaspoon fine sea salt
1 to 2 tablespoons unsalted butter, melted

Preheat the oven to 450°F.

Whisk the eggs, soymilk, and melted butter in a medium bowl. In a larger bowl mix together the unbleached flour, whole-wheat flour, and salt. Make a well in the middle of the dry ingredients, add the egg mixture, and whisk to combine. Let the batter sit for ten minutes.

While the batter is resting, place the popover or muffin tin in the oven for five minutes. Remove and brush eight of the wells with melted butter. Divide the batter into the eight wells, filling each about two-thirds of the way. Without peeking, bake for 15 minutes at 450°F, then reduce the heat to 350°F and bake for an additional 20 minutes. The popovers should be browned, puffed, and golden. Serve immediately.

Stuffin' Muffins

Makes 6 muffins

Sophie and Harry Cubbison started the first whole-wheat bread bakery in Los Angeles in 1916, and in 1925 they went into the Melba toast business. Melba toast was named after Nellie Melba, an actress fond of "dry, thin toast." By 1929, Melba toast had became a hit when, according to Sophie, the Mayo Clinic had prescribed it as part of the Hollywood Diet for actress Ethel Barrymore. When the diet was publicized in newspapers and fan magazines, the national demand was so great, they needed three factories to fill the orders. When television gained popularity in the 1950s, Sophie used to appear on children's shows like *Romper Room* and *Bozo the Clown,* telling food stories. Sophie's name lives on today with Mrs. Cubbison's Stuffing mix, which she first developed using Melba toast crumbs. Stuffin' Muffins was one of her signature recipes.

Canola cooking spray

5½ cups whole-grain or rustic bread, cut into ½-inch cubes

2 tablespoons unsalted butter

1 medium onion, finely chopped

2 ribs celery, finely chopped

1 tablespoon minced fresh sage

1½ teaspoons poultry seasoning

1½ cup vegetable stock

½ cup chopped dried cherries

2 tablespoons chopped fresh parsley

½ teaspoon kosher salt

¼ teaspoon freshly ground black pepper

Preheat the oven to 250°F. Coat six holes of a 12-cup muffin pan with cooking spray, or spray six 4-ounce ramekins.

Place the bread cubes on a baking sheet and toast for 20 minutes, or until the bread is crisp and lightly brown. Increase oven temperature to 350°F.

In a 12-inch nonstick skillet, heat the butter over medium heat. Add the onion and cook for 5 minutes. Add the celery, sage, and poultry seasoning; cook for 2 minutes. Add the vegetable stock and heat until almost boiling. Turn off heat.

Scrape the onion and celery mixture into a large bowl. Add the bread cubes, dried cherries, parsley, salt, and pepper. Mix well. Using an ice cream scoop, fill six of the muffin tins or six individual ramekins. Divide equally into the prepared muffin tin. Bake at 350°F for 30 minutes. Let cool for 10 minutes. Serve immediately.

"Good Stuff" Cashew Cornbread

Serves 8 to 10

The inspiration for this recipe came from Alice Irvine, who was married to Clark Irvine, the original publisher of *California Health News* and *Let's Live* magazine. I absolutely fell in love with Alice, who told me that she has been cooking with healthy ingredients for over fifty years, and she always puts some ground cashews into her cornbread and other nuts ("the good stuff") into just about everything else she bakes. It's the best cornbread I have ever tasted.

1 tablespoon canola oil or unsalted butter

1 cup yellow cornmeal

½ cup unbleached all-purpose flour

1 cup raw cashews, ground

★ Clark Irvine, 1892–1975 ★

Clark Irvine, founder of California Health News *and* Let's Live *magazine.* (COURTESY OF *LET'S LIVE* MAGAZINE)

Clark Irvine was born in Salem, Oregon, and moved with his family to Santa Monica when he was about eight years old. Clark was in the film industry in its early years, writing screenplays and playing small parts on film and stage; he also worked as MGM's and Charlie Chaplin's first publicity director. He wrote a syndicated column called "Studioland" and published a weekly newspaper called *The Screamer.* His friends included Will Rogers, John Barrymore, Douglas Fairbanks, Mary Pickford, and Charlie Chaplin, whom he played tennis with at Hearst Castle. He helped his friend Fatty Arbuckle get into the movie business by introducing him to Mack Sennett, director of the legendary Keystone Kops, and put the first "grease paint" on his good friend actress Myrna Loy. He eventually quit the movie business and traveled the world as a roving reporter for the United Press wire service.

In 1933 he launched *California Health News,* one of the first California natural food industry periodicals. Irvine often reported on his travels in the magazine. The magazine sold in health food shops nationwide, and Irvine often traveled to other cities to report on the health happenings in other towns. *California Health News* became *Let's Live* in 1942, and Irvine often reported on the eating habits of Hollywood, or as he would call it, "Cinema City" or "Movieland." A typical cover might feature a young Gayelord Hauser serving vegetable cocktails to actress Jean Harlow.

Irvine also wrote a little book called *Health! With Remedies and Recipes,* which sold very well. In 1946 Irvine married Alice Marks, who helped him write and publish the magazine and was a frequent recipe contributor. They lived in Hollywood near a peach orchard, where they started the first business of renting trailers to film stars. Irvine loved fruit, especially watermelon, and never drank, except for the occasional champagne when they went out dancing in Hollywood with Paul Bragg and his girlfriends. In 1949 he sold *Let's Live* and left Hollywood for the small town of Alpine, near San Diego, where he published the *Alpine Sun,* known as "America's Tiniest Newspaper." At sixty-five he learned to fly a plane and made two radio broadcasts a week called "Early Days in Hollywood," which is also the title of his still-unpublished manuscript. Almost seventy-five years later his magazine *Let's Live* still features celebrities on the cover and is still going strong.

1 teaspoon baking soda

1 teaspoon baking powder

½ teaspoon fine sea salt

¼ cup canola oil

2 tablespoons sage honey

1½ cups plain soymilk or low-fat buttermilk

1 teaspoon lemon juice (if using soymilk)

2 small jalapeño chiles, seeded and minced

Preheat the oven to 375°F. Put the oil into a 9-inch cast-iron skillet. Place the skillet in the oven while it preheats.

In a medium bowl combine the cornmeal, flour, ground cashews, baking soda, baking powder, and salt. Whisk to blend, making sure you break up any lumps in the baking soda or baking powder.

In a separate bowl whisk together the oil and honey. Whisk in the soymilk, lemon juice, and jalapeños.

Make a well in the center of the dry ingredients. Pour in the wet ingredients and, using a rubber spatula, stir together lightly until just blended—don't overmix.

Wearing an oven mitt, remove the hot skillet from the oven. Using a pastry brush, distribute the oil all over the skillet. Scrape the batter into the skillet and place back in the oven. Bake about 30 minutes, or until golden brown on top. Let cool for 10 minutes before serving.

4

Love at First Bite

APPETIZERS AND LITTLE BITES

*M*ost early-twentieth-century cookbooks, both mainstream and health-oriented ones, did not include large chapters on hors d'oeuvres. In his introduction to *Hors d'Oeuvre & Canapés,* James Beard wrote that the first sign of these little treats probably appeared in some pioneer bar on the California coast, where free snacks were served with five-cent beer. This concept of "free lunch" became a national institution. When Prohibition began in 1920, the free snack or lunch concept, along with drinking, was taken out of the bar and brought into the home. An immediate need for some food to serve with drinks became both necessary and popular. Prohibition ended in 1933, but most culinary historians agree that it wasn't until 1940, when James Beard wrote *Hors d'Oeuvre & Canapés,* that Americans started paying attention to serious cocktail food. Beard was an actor who started a catering company during the Great Depression, when jobs were scarce. His specialty was cocktail parties featuring his imaginative appetizers. Six years later, in 1946, his acting skills came in handy when he hosted *Elsie Presents James Beard in I Love to Eat,* the first nationally televised cooking show.

Most of the health-oriented cookbooks written during the first two-thirds of the twentieth century did not have sections on cocktail food because hors d'oeuvres were typically served with alcohol at parties, and moderate drinking and abstinence were part of healthful teachings. Gayelord Hauser, a fabulous party giver, did offer healthy choices for cocktail food, and told his readers to eat and drink in moderation. He coined the terms "beauty and sunshine cocktails" and gave recipes for nondrinkers made with fresh juices, fruits, vegetables, and yogurt. In *Be Happier, Be Healthier* (1955), Hauser gave his formula for a mental cocktail: a meditation and visualization of happy, peaceful thoughts to promote rest and sleep. Hauser also recommended serving platters of raw vegetables, called finger salad, with low-calorie yogurt dip. *Paul Bragg's Health Cookbook* (1947) includes a chapter on canapés.

Parties and events are big productions in Los Angeles, and the movie crowd has been keeping caterers busy since the beginning of the film business. And like New York, charity and promotional events happen nightly in Hollywood, with celebrities coming out for causes of all kinds. Chefs step out for causes, too, especially the Environmental Media Awards, where Ben Ford (Harrison's son) and Alan Jackson of Jackson's Somerset Catering have joined me to prepare an organic dinner for 1,000 guests. I will never forget the amazing dinner that Ben prepared at LOHAS (Lifestyles of Health & Sustainability), where Hollywood convenes with the health and wellness industry to discuss the environment, social justice, personal development, and sustainable living. When Hollywood needs a caterer for star-studded dinners at the Museum of Television & Radio or for the Screen Actors Guild Awards, they call on Alan of Jackson's Somerset Catering.

Whenever I cater parties that include a large buffet or sit-down dinner, I try to keep the appetizers light and bite-sized. Sometimes I create an entire meal out of appetizers, passed on trays or served buffet-style. I also make appetizers out of larger dishes, like mini versions of the Swinger (page 122), shot glasses of Curried Cauliflower Puree (page 86), or shredded "Banjo" Duck (page 157) on Sesame-Flaxseed Wonton Chips (page 64).

White Truffle Hummus with Spiced Flatbread Crisps

Makes about 2 cups

When I first started catering parties, my cooking bibles were Anna Thomas's *Vegetarian Epicure,* I and II. While writing those books, Anna was a graduate film student at UCLA; she financed her master's thesis film, *The Haunting of M,* with the advance money from *The Vegetarian Epicure II.* Her film credits include the Academy Award–nominated *El Norte, My Family (Mi Familia), Selena,* starring Jennifer Lopez, and *Frida,* starring Salma Hayek. The first time I made hummus was using a recipe for hummus bi Tahini from *Vegetarian Epicure II.* I use these flatbread crisps a lot when catering parties. Sometimes I top them with gorgonzola, Fig Chutney (page 32), and prosciutto. They are just as good with grilled chicken, pesto, and chopped tomatoes.

HUMMUS

1 tablespoon extra-virgin olive oil

1 clove garlic

1 red bell pepper, roasted, peeled, seeded, and cut into ¼-inch dice (about ⅓ cup)

1 (15-ounce) can cannellini beans, rinsed and drained

½ teaspoon kosher salt

¼ teaspoon freshly ground white pepper

1 teaspoon white truffle oil, plus more for serving

1 to 2 tablespoons chopped flat-leaf parsley, to taste

SPICED FLATBREAD CRISPS

1 pound lavosh-style whole-wheat or white thin flatbread

2 tablespoons extra-virgin olive oil

1 tablespoon butter, melted

1 teaspoon minced fresh thyme

1 teaspoon minced fresh rosemary

¾ teaspoon coarse sea salt or kosher salt

½ teaspoon freshly ground black pepper

¼ to ½ teaspoon crushed red chile flakes (optional)

To make the hummus, heat the olive oil in a 10-inch skillet over medium-high heat. Add the garlic and bell pepper and cook for 1 minute, or until the garlic begins to soften.

Puree the beans, salt, pepper, and truffle oil in a food processor until smooth. Transfer to a medium bowl and fold in the sautéed peppers. Garnish with the parsley and drizzle with additional truffle oil just before serving.

To prepare the flatbread crisps, preheat the oven to 350°F. Lay the flatbread out on 2 or 3 baking sheets. In a small bowl combine the oil and butter, and brush equally over the flatbread. Sprinkle with the thyme, rosemary, salt, pepper, and chile flakes, if using.

Bake for 6 to 7 minutes, checking every minute after 5 minutes, as they can burn easily. Remove from oven, and when cool, break into irregular-shaped pieces. Leftovers can be stored in an airtight container for up to 3 days.

Warm Artichoke Dip with Spinach and Goat Cheese

Serves 6 to 8
as an appetizer

The golden anniversary of the Academy of Motion Picture Arts and Sciences was celebrated in 1978. Oscar winners that year included Woody Allen's *Annie Hall* for best picture and Diane Keaton for best actress. Five-inch miniature Oscars were brought to each table on top of two-tiered anniversary cakes, while Fred Astaire, Bette Davis, and John Travolta sang "Happy Birthday, Dear Oscar." The elaborate menu included Artichoke Hearts Florentine. This recipe is much simpler than the one served that night, but the combination is always a classic. Serve with baguettes or Spiced Flat-bread Crisps (page 53).

Canola cooking spray or olive oil

1 bag (5 ounces) baby spinach

2 green onions, both white and green parts, sliced ⅛ inch thick

¼ teaspoon kosher salt

1 can water-packed baby artichoke hearts, drained and coarsely chopped

8 ounces soft goat cheese

2 tablespoons light mayonnaise

⅛ teaspoon freshly ground black pepper

⅓ cup grated Parmigiano-Reggiano or Pecorino Romano cheese

Preheat the oven to 325°F. Coat a 6½-inch-wide casserole dish with canola cooking spray or olive oil.

Bring a large pot of salted water to a boil. Plunge the spinach into the boiling water just to blanch it, about 30 seconds. Drain well, pressing the water out of the spinach, and set aside to cool.

Chop the spinach and mix in a medium bowl with the green onions, salt, and artichokes. Puree the goat cheese, mayonnaise, and pepper in a food processor until smooth.

Place the spinach-artichoke mixture on the bottom of the prepared casserole dish. Top with the goat cheese mixture. Sprinkle with the Parmigiano-Reggiano and bake for 25 minutes, or until lightly browned on top and bubbling. Serve with crackers or Spiced Flatbread Crisps (page 53).

Pimento Cheese Bites with Cream of Tomato Dip

*Makes 12 pimento
cheese bites;
serves 6
as an appetizer*

When I catered Billy Bob Thornton's Christmas party one year, he whipped up some of his special soy-based pimento cheese sandwiches for all of us cooking in the kitchen. The following summer, when I catered Billy's birthday, I made the sandwiches as an appetizer and served them with a cream of tomato dip—an idea that my friend Sergio Gomez gave me. When Emeril Lagasse made pimento cheese on his show, he told the audience that when you're in the South as a guest in someone's home and they bring out the pimento cheese, it's a special thing, so I was really honored when Billy made this dish for me.

NOTE: Any leftover dip can be thinned out a bit with more soymilk and served as soup. When I cater parties, I place the dip in small shot glasses, cut the sandwiches into long strips, and serve them on top of the glasses.

CREAM OF TOMATO DIP

1 tablespoon extra-virgin olive oil

½ cup diced onion

1 large shallot, minced

1 teaspoon kosher salt

1 (28-ounce) can whole tomatoes in juice, chopped (retain juice)

1 tablespoon tomato paste

1 cup vegetable broth

1 bay leaf

¼ cup chopped fresh basil

½ teaspoon dried thyme leaves or 1 teaspoon fresh

2 tablespoons white rice flour

1 cup plain soymilk

¼ cup soy milk creamer

1 teaspoon sugar, optional

Freshly ground black pepper to taste

PIMENTO CHEESE BITES

1 cup grated soy cheddar cheese, or cheese of your choice

2 tablespoons vegan or light mayonnaise

2 tablespoons chopped green onion

¼ cup diced pimentos, drained

1 tablespoon chopped green olives

⅛ teaspoon kosher salt

⅛ teaspoon freshly ground black pepper

¼ teaspoon hot red pepper sauce

6 slices spelt, whole-wheat, or sliced sourdough bread

Canola cooking spray, olive oil, or 1 tablespoon nonhydrogenated soy spread

To make the dip, heat the olive oil over medium-low heat in a 4-quart soup pot. Add the onions and shallots and sauté until softened and clear, about 8 minutes. Add the salt, tomatoes, tomato juice, tomato paste, vegetable broth, bay leaf, basil, and thyme. Bring to a boil, lower to a simmer, and cook for 30 minutes.

Mix the rice flour with the soymilk and the soy creamer. Whisk into the tomato mixture and simmer 5 minutes more. Remove the bay leaf.

Puree the dip in 2 batches in a blender until smooth and creamy. At this point, taste the soup. If you think it needs to be sweeter, add the sugar, then season to taste with freshly ground pepper.

To make the Pimento Cheese Bites, mix the cheese, mayonnaise, green onion, pimento, olives, salt, pepper, and red pepper sauce in a small bowl. Divide equally among 3 slices of the bread and top with the remaining bread slices. Heat a 10- or 12-inch nonstick sauté pan over medium heat. Spray with the cooking spray. If you're not watching your fat grams, add a tablespoon of the nonhydrogenated soy spread to the pan. Cook the sandwiches on each side until browned and cheese has melted. Add more spray or soy spread as you go along. Cut into quarters and serve with the dip.

Walnut-Quinoa Cakes with Tomato Chutney

Makes 28 small appetizers, about 4 cups of chutney

Walnuts have been an important ingredient in meatless recipes dating back to the turn of the century, and California-based Diamond Walnuts has been operating as a cooperative of growers since 1912. A walnut roast was served at the first dinner put on by the California Vegetarian Society in 1912. Kellogg spokesperson and actress Loretta Young gave a recipe for Walnut Roast in *What Actors Eat When They Eat* (1939), claiming that a nonmeat diet a few days a week would do wonders for anyone. This recipe has been adapted from one of Diamond Walnuts' promotional booklets published in the 1930s, entitled *Win Fame with Walnuts.* You can also serve these with store-bought chutney, but making your own is worth the trouble.

Note: Covered and refrigerated, leftover chutney lasts for about a month.

TOMATO CHUTNEY

2 teaspoons canola oil

1 tablespoon black mustard seeds

1 large jalapeño chile, minced, with seeds

2 cloves garlic, chopped

½ teaspoon fennel seeds

½ teaspoon fenugreek seeds

½ teaspoon paprika

⅛ teaspoon cayenne pepper

1¾ cups white wine vinegar

1½ pounds firm tomatoes, scored with an X on the end

1½ cups sugar

½ pound apples, peeled, cored, and chopped into ½-inch pieces

1 teaspoon kosher salt

1 bay leaf

¼ cup raisins

WALNUT-QUINOA CAKES

¾ cup raw walnuts, finely chopped by hand or in a food processor

¼ cup dry whole-wheat or spelt bread crumbs

¾ cup cooked red quinoa

¼ cup minced white onion

1 large egg, beaten

¼ teaspoon kosher salt

1 teaspoon poultry seasoning

⅛ teaspoon granulated garlic

½ teaspoon paprika

⅛ teaspoon crushed red chile flakes

¼ teaspoon celery seeds

½ teaspoon minced fresh rosemary

⅛ teaspoon freshly ground black pepper

2 to 3 teaspoons olive oil

To make the chutney, heat the oil in a 12-inch skillet over medium-high heat. Add the mustard seeds and cook for 30 seconds, or until they sizzle. Add the jalapeños, garlic, fennel seeds, fenugreek seeds, paprika, and cayenne. Cook for 2 to 3 minutes. Set aside.

Bring the vinegar to a boil over medium-high heat in a 2-quart stockpot. Add the tomatoes to the pot, turn off the heat, and let cool. Remove the tomatoes with a slotted spoon, then peel, seed, and chop into 1-inch cubes. Add them back to the vinegar, along with the sugar, apples, salt and bay leaf. Bring back to a boil, then reduce the heat to a simmer. Add the spices to the tomato mixture and simmer for about 40 minutes. Add the raisins and cook an additional 25 to 30 minutes, or until the chutney has thickened to the consistency of thin preserves or jam. Let cool.

To make the walnut cakes, combine the walnuts, bread crumbs, cooked quinoa, onion, egg, salt, poultry seasoning, garlic, paprika, chile flakes, celery seeds, rosemary, and pepper in a medium bowl. Using a small scoop or your hands, form the mixture into 28 small patties.

Heat the oil in a 12-inch nonstick skillet over medium-high heat. Cook the patties, in batches, about 1 minute on each side, or until golden brown. Add more oil to the pan as needed. The patties may be held in a warm oven for 30 minutes, or cooled and reheated at serving time. Serve warm with the tomato chutney or a good-quality store-bought chutney.

Black Bean Pupusas with Tomato Salsa and Spicy Coleslaw

Makes 12 pupusas

This recipe always makes me think of Linda McCartney, since I made these for the party I catered to launch her book *Linda McCartney's Sixties: Portrait of an Era* (1993). I adored Linda and always had huge respect for her promotion of vegetarianism with her cookbooks and frozen-food line. Pupusas are great on a buffet, served with bowls of the coleslaw and salsa on the side. You can also make bigger pupusas and serve them for breakfast or brunch with poached eggs or scrambled tofu.

SPICY COLESLAW
1 cup white wine vinegar
1 teaspoon crushed red chile flakes
1 teaspoon chopped fresh oregano
1 teaspoon sea salt
½ head green cabbage, finely shredded
1 carrot, grated

TOMATO SALSA
1 (14.5-ounce) can fire-roasted crushed tomatoes
¼ cup minced white onion

¼ teaspoon finely ground black pepper

1 clove garlic, minced

1 medium tomato, peeled, seeded, and chopped

Pinch of crushed red chile flakes

BLACK BEAN PUPUSAS

2 cups masa harina

½ teaspoon fine sea salt

2 tablespoons nonhydrogenated vegetable shortening

1¾ to 2 cups warm (105° to 115°F) water

1 (15-ounce) can black beans, rinsed and drained

2 green onions, both white and green parts, finely chopped

1 tablespoon chopped fresh oregano

1 tablespoon chopped fresh cilantro

¼ teaspoon freshly ground black pepper

1½ cups grated Monterey jack, mild sheep, or soy jack cheese

To make the coleslaw, combine the vinegar, chile flakes, oregano, and salt in a medium bowl. Add the cabbage and carrots. Set aside to marinate for 1 hour.

To make the salsa, combine the canned tomatoes, onion, pepper, garlic, tomato, and chile flakes in a food processor or blender. Pulse until mixed but still chunky. Transfer to a bowl and set aside.

To make the pupusa dough, place the masa harina and salt in a large bowl. Cut in the shortening with a fork. Slowly add enough of the warm water, stirring, until a soft dough forms. Divide the dough evenly into 12 balls about 1½ inches in diameter. Place on a tray and cover with plastic film to prevent drying out. Let dough balls rest at least 30 minutes before cooking the pupusas.

To make the filling, mash the beans with a potato masher in a medium bowl. Mix in the green onions, oregano, cilantro, pepper, and cheese.

To assemble the pupusas, wet your hands and slightly flatten a ball of dough in the palm of your hand. Turn up the edges to form a little cup. Place a small amount of filling in the center, then fold the edges over and pinch together. Pat again to smooth and flatten into a thick pancake.

Heat a nonstick griddle or cast-iron skillet over medium heat. Cook the pupusas, turning a few times, until they are lightly browned and crisp. Serve with the tomato salsa and the coleslaw on the side.

Shiitake Pot Stickers with Mirin Dipping Sauce

Makes 24 pot stickers; serves 8 to 12

My very first job as a private chef in Los Angeles was for Bob and Gail Levine, owners of Bob Gail—The Main Event, a large event planning company in Beverly Hills. Bob and Gail were extremely health conscious—no white flour, white sugar, or junk food of any kind for them or their four kids. When MTV gave me ten days' notice to produce an elaborate event under a tent with wild animals, two bands, and six ethnic food stations, Bob and Gail's company helped me put it together. At the Asian station, we served these pot stickers, which are easy to prepare and can also be made in advance and frozen until you are ready to use them.

MIRIN DIPPING SAUCE

¼ cup rice vinegar

¼ cup mirin

1 tablespoon fresh ginger juice (squeezed from finely grated fresh ginger)

3 tablespoons light brown sugar

2 tablespoons tamari

⅛ teaspoon crushed red chile flakes

3 cloves garlic, thinly sliced

POT STICKERS

1 ounce dried shiitake mushrooms, soaked in hot water for 30 minutes

1 tablespoon toasted sesame oil

2 tablespoons minced fresh ginger

1 leek, white part only, finely chopped

6 green onions, white part only, minced

5 whole canned water chestnuts, minced

2 tablespoons tamari

1 tablespoon mirin (Japanese cooking wine)

3 ounces extra-firm tofu

Kosher salt and freshly ground black pepper

Cornstarch for dusting

24 round pot-sticker/wonton wrappers

Canola cooking spray

Peanut or canola oil for cooking

Chopped chives or green onions for garnish

Black sesame seeds for garnish

To make the dipping sauce, combine the vinegar, mirin, ginger juice, brown sugar, tamari, chile flakes, and garlic in a small saucepan. Bring to a boil over medium heat and simmer for 3 minutes. Remove to a bowl, let cool, and refrigerate until ready to serve.

To make the pot stickers, drain the soaked shiitakes and discard the soaking liquid. Remove and discard the stem from each mushroom and mince the caps. Set aside.

Heat the sesame oil in a 12-inch skillet over medium heat. Cook the ginger for about 30 seconds, add the mushrooms, and cook for 2 to 3 minutes, stirring constantly. Add the leek, green onions, water chestnuts, tamari, and mirin. Cook for 30 seconds, stirring constantly.

Mince the tofu in a food processor and add to the mushroom mixture. Allow the filling to cool, then season with salt and pepper to taste.

Line a baking sheet with parchment paper and dust with cornstarch. Fill a small bowl with water. Place a pot sticker wrapper on a wooden or marble board. (Keep unused wrappers covered with plastic wrap so they won't dry out.) Put 1 tablespoon of filling in the center of the wrapper. Moisten the edges of the wrapper with water and fold the wrapper in half over the filling and pinch shut at the top center of the pot sticker. Starting on the right side of the sealed edge, and working toward midpoint, pinch small pleats around the wrapper edges. Repeat on the left side.

Put the stuffed pot sticker on the parchment, dust with cornstarch, and cover with plastic wrap to prevent drying. Repeat with the remaining ingredients, until all the wrappers are filled. At this point the pot stickers can be wrapped in plastic wrap and refrigerated for a few hours, or flash-frozen on the tray until hard and kept frozen in zip-top bags for several weeks. (I make them ahead and freeze them for catered parties.) Partially thaw frozen pot stickers before cooking, or cook refrigerated pot stickers straight from the refrigerator.

To cook the pot stickers, coat a large nonstick or cast-iron skillet with cooking spray and place over medium-high heat. Add 1 tablespoon peanut oil to the skillet. Arrange 8 pot stickers, pleat side up, in the skillet. Cook the pot stickers 1 to 2 minutes on each side, or until golden brown and crisp. Wipe out pan with a dry cloth between batches. Add more peanut oil as needed for each batch.

Garnish with chopped chives or green onions (green part only) and toasted sesame seeds. Serve immediately with the dipping sauce or keep warm in a 200°F oven until ready to serve.

Polynesian Seviche with Sesame-Flaxseed Wonton Chips

Serves 6 to 12, depending on how many other appetizers you are serving

Stemming from the popularity of Don the Beachcomber, the Luau opened in Beverly Hills in 1954. The restaurant was designed with lavish Polynesian decor and the lacquered ship-catch-covered tables were filled with celebrity patrons such as Marlon Brando, Hugh Hefner, and Fred Astaire.

One of the earliest American recipes for Polynesian-style seviche (Possin Cru) appears in *Paul C. Bragg's Personal Health Food Cookbook* (1935). Bragg had been visiting Polynesia since the early 1930s and he includes in his book a recipe called South Sea Raw Fish, which he describes as "one of the delicacies of the natives of the Isles of Eden."

POLYNESIAN SEVICHE

6 ounces firm-fleshed fish such as halibut or snapper, skin removed, boned, and
    cut into ½-inch pieces

3 tablespoons fresh lime juice

¼ teaspoon finely grated lime zest

4 tablespoons coconut milk

2 tablespoons minced raw onion

2 green onions, white and most of green parts, minced

1 small mango, peeled and chopped into ¼-inch squares

1 serrano chile, seeded and minced

½ teaspoon kosher salt

⅛ teaspoon freshly ground white pepper

SESAME-FLAXSEED WONTON CHIPS

Canola cooking spray or canola oil

12 wonton wrappers, cut into 4 triangles each

1 egg white

¼ teaspoon kosher salt

2 teaspoons tan sesame seeds

2 teaspoons black sesame seeds

2 teaspoons flaxseed

To make the seviche, combine the fish, lime juice, lime zest, coconut milk, onion, green onions, mango, chile, salt, and pepper in a medium bowl. Cover and marinate in the refrigerator at least 1 hour and up to 8 hours, stirring occasionally.

To make the wonton chips, preheat the oven to 350°F. Line a baking sheet with parchment paper and spray with cooking spray or brush with oil. Place the wonton triangles on the tray. Using a pastry brush, brush each triangle with some egg white. Sprinkle with the salt, sesame seeds, and flaxseed. Bake for 7 to 9 minutes, watching carefully the last couple of minutes because these burn easily. When I am catering large parties I usually wind up burning one or two trays even if I set the timer—it just happens.

Wild Salmon Tartare on Daikon Rounds

Makes 36 bite-size appetizers

When I catered a hospitality suite for the MTV Video Awards at the Tribeca Grand Hotel in New York, we served this dish with a garnish of fresh chopped watermelon. Rock and roll's favorite chef Kate Paul (Janet Jackson, Tina Turner, and Ozzy Osbourne) helped me cook while my daughter, Amrit, came along to greet Lindsay Lohan and MTV nominees Simple Plan and the Black-Eyed Peas. This recipe also works well with sushi-grade tuna or albacore, and although daikon rounds are much healthier, homemade or good-quality potato chips taste great.

2 teaspoons fresh lime juice

1 green onion, white and most of the green parts, finely chopped

1½ teaspoons vegan or light mayonnaise

⅛ teaspoon wasabi powder

4 ounces skinned sashimi-grade wild salmon (from the belly),
    cut into ¼-inch cubes

½ small avocado, peeled, pitted, and diced into ¼-inch cubes

Kosher salt and freshly ground pepper

1 daikon radish, peeled and sliced into thirty-six ¼-inch rounds
    (save any remaining daikon for grating into salad)

Fresh cilantro leaves for garnish

To make the tartare, in a medium bowl mix together the lime juice, green onion, mayonnaise, and wasabi. Add the chopped fish and avocado. Season with salt and pepper to taste.

Mound the tartare on the daikon slices and garnish with fresh cilantro leaves. Serve immediately.

Grilled Mahi-Mahi and Mango Satay with Mai-Tai Dipping Sauce

Makes 2 dozen skewers

In 1937, Cora Irene Sund and Ernest Raymond Beaumont-Gantt opened Don the Beachcomber, which had been Ernest's nickname when he owned a tacky tropical bar in a Hollywood hotel. Don the Beachcomber was a hard-to-find hideaway frequented by the Marx Brothers, Clark Gable, Bing Crosby, and Marlene Dietrich. "Don" is the acknowledged founding father of tiki chic; cocktail historians give him credit for starting the tropical drink craze in America. Irene hired Chinese chefs to create a South Seas fusion cuisine made with then-uncommon ingredients like water chestnuts, lychee nuts, and oyster sauce. We served these skewers when I catered Pierce Brosnan's Polynesian-themed birthday.

MAI-TAI DIPPING SAUCE

1 cup pineapple juice

½ cup dark rum

2 tablespoons orange curaçao

2 tablespoons soy sauce or tamari

2 tablespoons Hawaiian white honey

1 tablespoon fresh lime juice

2 teaspoons grated fresh ginger

1 teaspoon toasted sesame oil

Pinch of crushed red chile flakes

MAHI-MAHI AND MANGO SATAY

1 pound fresh Mahi-Mahi, skin removed, cut into 1-inch pieces

½ teaspoon kosher salt

¼ teaspoon freshly ground black pepper

1 large or 2 small unripe mangos, peeled and cut into 1-inch pieces

Canola oil or canola cooking spray for the grill

To make the dipping sauce, combine the pineapple juice, rum, curaçao, soy sauce, honey, lime juice, ginger, sesame oil, and chiles in a 1-quart saucepan over medium-high heat. Bring to a boil, reduce the heat to low, and simmer for 10 to 12 minutes. Divide the dipping sauce in half and let cool.

To make the satay, soak twenty-four 6-inch bamboo skewers in cold water for at least 30 minutes. Season the fish with salt and pepper. Arrange the fish on the skewers with the mango pieces, using 1 piece fish and 1 piece mango per skewer. Place the skewers in a shallow casserole dish and cover with half of the dipping sauce. Cover with plastic wrap and refrigerate for at least 30 minutes and up to 4 hours.

Heat a large grill pan over medium-high heat, prepare an outdoor grill, or plug in an electric indoor grill. Brush with oil or coat with cooking spray. Remove the skewers from the marinade and grill 1 minute on each side. Serve with the reserved dipping sauce.

Chickpea Pancakes with Pineapple-Mint Relish

Makes 24 small pancakes

Credit must be given to the Beatles, especially George Harrison, for helping to popularize Indian music, culture, and spiritual philosophy. The Beatles first infused Indian music with their own in *Help!,* their second feature film, in 1965. From then on, George's interest in Indian philosophy grew, and after he read Yogananda's *Autobiography of a Yogi,* images of saints and yogis appeared on the cover of *Sergeant Pepper's Lonely Hearts Club Band.* One of the defining moments of the counterculture during the late 1960s was when the world watched the Beatles, Mike Love of the Beach Boys, Mia Farrow, and Donovan embrace Transcendental Meditation with Maharishi Mahesh Yogi in Rishikesh, India. They may have eaten pancakes similar to these, since besan, or chickpea, flour is used in Northern India for all kinds of fritters and snacks. You can also top these pancakes with the Tandoori Shrimp Salad (page 128). I like to slice the cooked shrimp in half.

PINEAPPLE-MINT RELISH

1 cup fresh pineapple chopped into ¼-inch dice

¼ cup finely chopped white onion

¼ cup finely minced red bell pepper

1 small green chile, such as serrano, minced

⅛ teaspoon kosher salt

1 teaspoon sugar

1 tablespoon fresh lime juice

2 tablespoons finely chopped fresh mint

CHICKPEA PANCAKES

¾ cups besan flour (also known as chickpea or garbanzo flour)

⅛ teaspoon freshly ground black pepper

½ teaspoon dried basil

¾ teaspoon fennel seeds

½ teaspoon caraway seeds

⅛ teaspoon crushed red chile flakes

½ teaspoon ground turmeric

1 teaspoon fine sea salt

⅛ teaspoon baking soda

¾ cup warm (105° to 115°F) water

1 small onion, minced

1 shallot, minced

1 clove garlic, minced

2 teaspoons finely grated fresh ginger

1 small green chile such as serrano, minced

2 tablespoons finely chopped fresh cilantro

3 to 4 tablespoons clarified butter or canola oil

To make the relish, combine all of the ingredients in a small bowl and chill at least 1 hour or up to 4 hours before serving.

To make the pancakes, combine the besan flour, pepper, basil, fennel seeds, caraway seeds, chile flakes, turmeric, salt, and baking soda in a medium bowl.

In a separate bowl combine the warm water, onion, shallot, garlic, ginger, green chile, and cilantro. Whisk the wet ingredients into the dry ones and stir with a wooden spoon to combine—don't overmix.

Heat a heavy cast-iron or nonstick skillet over medium-high heat. Brush the pan with about 1 tablespoon of the clarified butter. Drop the batter by 2 teaspoonfuls into the pan, making about 8 pancakes at a time. Cook until the bottom starts to brown and bubbles begin to appear on the top, about 45 seconds. Flip and cook until golden on the other side and cooked through, about 30 seconds. Repeat with the remaining batter, adding more clarified butter as needed. Serve warm with the relish.

Blue Corn Nachos with Radiant Radish Guacamole and Chipotle Salsa

Serves 2 to 3

Beach Boy Brian Wilson's Radiant Radish health food store, Los Angeles, 1969. (COURTESY OF EDDIE J. CARAEFF PHOTO ARCHIVES)

The original health crusaders— Gypsy Boots, songwriter eden ahbez, and Paul Bragg—all influenced the California surf culture of the late 1960s. The Beach Boys used to eat at H.E.L.P. restaurant, where Janice Joplin dined on vegetable burgers and salads. Brian Wilson wrote a song entitled "H.E.L.P.," claiming that the restaurant had the best food in town. The lyrics also mention the Radiant Radish, Wilson's West Hollywood health food store. California surf culture had a huge influence on healthful eating all over America and helped to promote juice fasting, smoothies, raw foods, and a vegetarian diet.

Note: When I cater parties, I assemble these on round blue corn chips as mini-nachos and pass them in baskets lined with banana leaves.

CHIPOTLE SALSA

1 (14.5-ounce) can fire-roasted tomatoes, drained

1 whole canned chipotle chile, with 1 tablespoon adobo sauce from the can

2 teaspoons chopped fresh cilantro

1 tablespoon fresh lime juice

½ teaspoon kosher salt

REFRIED BEANS

2 teaspoons canola oil

¼ cup finely chopped onion

1 clove garlic, minced

½ teaspoon ground coriander

½ teaspoon paprika

½ teaspoon ground cumin

⅛ teaspoon kosher salt

⅛ teaspoon freshly ground black pepper

1 (15-ounce) can pinto beans, rinsed, drained, and mashed

¼ cup vegetable stock or water

RADISH GUACAMOLE

1 large avocado, peeled and pitted

2 large radishes, finely chopped

2 green onions, both white and green parts, finely chopped

2 tablespoons finely chopped cilantro

Juice of ½ lime

½ teaspoon kosher salt

BLUE CORN NACHOS

1 (4.5-ounce) bag blue corn tortilla chips

2 green onions, both white and green parts, sliced

¼ cup ripe black California olives, sliced

3 cups shredded Monterey jack, goat jack, or soy jack cheese

Chopped fresh cilantro for garnish

To make the salsa, place the tomatoes, chipotle chile and adobo sauce, cilantro, lime juice, and salt in a blender and puree until smooth.

To make the beans, heat the oil in a 10-inch skillet over medium-high heat. Add the onion and cook until lightly browned, about 4 minutes. Add the garlic and continue to cook, stirring, until lightly browned, about 1 minute longer. Add the coriander, paprika, cumin, salt, and pepper, and cook until fragrant, about 1 minute more. Add the beans and vegetable broth and cook an additional 3 to 4 minutes.

To make the guacamole, mash the avocado with the radishes, green onions, cilantro, lime juice, and salt in a small bowl.

To assemble the nachos, preheat the broiler. Spread the tortilla chips over a baking sheet. Drizzle with ⅓ cup of the salsa, the green onions, olives, and cheese. Top with ¼ cup more salsa, then place under broiler for 1 to 2 minutes, or until the cheese melts. Garnish with cilantro and serve with the refried beans and guacamole.

Wild Mushroom and Sweet Potato Quesadillas with Cranberry Salsa

Serves 4

Jack LaLanne is the only health guru to have the honor of a star on the Hollywood Walk of Fame. In his book *Foods for Glamour* (1961), LaLanne wrote about celebrities like Gloria Swanson whom he believed embodied the true definition of Hollywood glamour—beauty on the inside and out. He included the sweet potato as one of his top "glamour foods," since it contains large amounts of vitamins A and C. I came up with this recipe utilizing seasonal ingredients including sweet potatoes and cranberries for a last-minute party I catered for Winona Ryder.

Note: When I cater parties, I use spinach- or cilantro-flavored tortillas for the natural green color. I also cut the tortillas into bite-sized 2-inch rounds and assemble them individually.

CRANBERRY SALSA

1 (12-ounce) bag fresh cranberries

1 teaspoon finely grated orange zest

½ cup sugar

1 small jalapeño chile, seeded and minced

¼ cup chopped fresh cilantro

⅛ teaspoon kosher salt

WILD MUSHROOM AND SWEET POTATO QUESADILLAS

1 medium sweet potato, quartered lengthwise and cut into ¼-inch slices

Olive oil

Kosher salt

Freshly ground black pepper

1 medium red onion, sliced into ¼-inch moons

4 ounces any variety wild mushrooms, wiped clean and thinly sliced

4 ounces button mushrooms, wiped clean and thinly sliced

¼ teaspoon dried thyme

2 tablespoons finely chopped fresh sage, plus whole leaves for garnish

4 green onions, all of white part and 2 inches of green, finely chopped

6 ounces Manchego, Monterey jack, or mild cheddar cheese, shredded

4 (8-inch) flour tortillas, preferably spinach- or cilantro-flavored

Canola oil or vegetable cooking spray for cooking the quesadillas

To make the salsa, pulse the cranberries with the orange zest, sugar, and jalapeño in a food processor until finely chopped. Transfer to a bowl and mix with the cilantro and salt. The salsa can be kept, refrigerated, for up to 3 days.

To make the quesadillas, preheat the oven to 400°F. Line a baking sheet with parchment paper. Brush the sweet potato slices with the olive oil and sprinkle with salt and pepper. Roast, turning once, until crisp on the outside but still soft on the inside, 15 to 20 minutes. Set aside to cool.

Heat the oil in a 12-inch nonstick skillet over medium-high heat and cook the red onions for 5 minutes. Add the mushrooms, thyme, and sage and cook an additional 5 minutes, or until the mushrooms are tender. Add the green onions and set aside.

To assemble each quesadilla, sprinkle an eighth of the cheese over one side of a tortilla. Cover with a quarter of the sweet potatoes, a quarter of the mushrooms, and another eighth of the cheese. Fold the tortilla in half. Repeat with the remaining tortillas. The quesadillas can be made a few hours in advance and refrigerated, covered with plastic wrap to keep them from drying out.

Heat a 12-inch cast-iron or nonstick skillet over medium-high heat, and brush with oil or coat with cooking spray. Cook the quesadillas one at a time, flipping them every minute, until the tortillas are crisp and the cheese melts. Cut into quarters and serve immediately with the salsa.

Pan-Seared Samosas with Tamarind-Date Dipping Sauce

Makes about 36 samosas and about 2 cups of dipping sauce

The first "yoga teacher to the stars" was Russian-born Indra Devi (1899–2001), whose students included Gloria Swanson, Ramón Novarro, and Marilyn Monroe. Born to nobility as Eugenie Peterson, Indra was an actress in her early life, which included a career in India as a "Bollywood" film star. She was often seen lunching at vegetarian restaurants in Los Angeles with her student and friend Greta Garbo. As a vegetarian, she was known to go into restaurants and order a chef salad, hold the ham, cheese, and dressing, and then tell the waiter to just bring a head of organically grown lettuce. Since then, Hollywood, and much of the world, has been fascinated with all things Indian, including yoga, fashion, and classic Indian snacks like samosas. The Tamarind-Date Dipping Sauce lasts for at least a month, covered and refrigerated, and is also good with chicken or pappadams, the Indian lentil wafers.

TAMARIND-DATE DIPPING SAUCE

1 cup hot water

2 tablespoons seedless tamarind paste

1 cup chopped dates

¼ cup sage or orange blossom honey

Pinch of cayenne pepper

SAMOSAS

1¼ pounds russet or Yukon Gold potatoes

1 tablespoon clarified butter or canola oil, plus more for
   cooking the samosas

2 teaspoons black mustard seeds

2 teaspoons ground coriander

1 small onion, finely minced

1 tablespoon minced fresh ginger

1 clove garlic, minced

½ teaspoon amchoor (dried mango powder)

½ teaspoon garam masala

1 small green chile such as serrano, finely minced

½ teaspoon kosher salt

2 tablespoons finely chopped cilantro

Freshly ground black pepper

Cornstarch for dusting

36 to 40 round pot sticker (gyoza) wrappers

To make the tamarind-date sauce, combine the hot water, tamarind paste, dates, honey, and cayenne in a small saucepan over medium heat. Bring to a simmer and cook for 5 minutes. Transfer the mixture to a food processor and puree until smooth. The sauce can be made up to 2 weeks in advance.

To make the samosas, place the potatoes in a medium saucepan, cover with cold water, and bring to a boil. Reduce the heat to medium and cook until tender, about 20 to 25 minutes. Drain and let cool slightly. Peel and cut the potatoes into ¼-inch dice.

Heat the clarified butter in a 12-inch nonstick skillet over medium-high heat. Add the mustard seeds and cook for a few seconds, until they sizzle and pop. Add the coriander, onion, ginger, and garlic and cook until the onion is softened, 5 to 7 minutes.

Add the amchoor, garam masala, chile, salt, and potatoes. Cook an additional 2 to 3 minutes, mashing the potatoes slightly as you stir. Remove from the heat, add the cilantro and pepper, and let cool.

Line a baking sheet with parchment or wax paper and dust with cornstarch. Working with 3 wrappers at a time and keeping the rest covered with plastic wrap, brush the edges with water. Spoon 2 teaspoons of filling into the center of each wrapper. Fold the wrappers in half over the filling, pressing out any air bubbles and sealing the edges. Gently press the samosas so they stand upright with the seam on top, and then transfer them to the prepared baking sheet. Repeat with the remaining ingredients until all the wrappers are filled.

At this point the samosas can be covered in plastic wrap and refrigerated for a few hours, or flash-frozen on the tray until hard and then kept frozen in plastic bags for several weeks. (I make them ahead and freeze them for catered parties, thawing just slightly before cooking.)

To cook the samosas, heat the clarified butter in a large nonstick skillet over medium-high heat. Add 8 samosas and cook 1 to 2 minutes on each side, or until golden brown and crisp. Continue to cook the samosas in batches, adding clarified butter as needed for each batch.

Serve immediately, or keep warm in a 200°F oven until ready to serve. Serve with the dipping sauce.

Caramelized Maui Onion Tart

Serves 6

In his book *Rational Diet* (1923) Otto Carque wrote about the purifying properties of onions, and how the Egyptians spent nine tons of gold buying them for the workmen during the building of the pyramids. Many people called Carque the father of the natural food industry, and Paul Bragg said he was one of the kindest and most generous people he had ever known. I, too, believe in the healing power of onions, as well as their delicious taste, especially when caramelized. I once served this tart at a dinner party and the guests included screen legends Gregory Peck and Elizabeth Taylor. Mr. Peck loved the Maui Onion Tart so much that I sent one with him as a parting gift. I will never forget meeting him, especially his fabulous voice, which completely floored me when he thanked me for dinner.

CRUST

1¼ cups unbleached all-purpose flour

½ teaspoon fine sea salt

2 tablespoons unsalted butter, chilled

4 tablespoons nonhydrogenated vegetable shortening, chilled

2 to 4 tablespoons ice water, as needed

ONION FILLING

1 tablespoon unsalted butter or extra-virgin olive oil

2½ pounds Maui or other sweet onions (about 3 large), cut in half, root to stem, and sliced into ¼-inch-thick half moons

2 shallots, minced

½ teaspoon kosher salt

1 teaspoon fresh thyme leaves

¼ teaspoon freshly ground black pepper

6 tablespoons grated Parmigiano-Reggiano cheese

2 red bell peppers, roasted, peeled, seeded, cut in half lengthwise and sliced ½-inch thick

20 small black olives such as niçoise, pitted

To make the crust, line a 10-inch removable-bottom tart pan or a 11 x 7 x 2-inch baking pan with parchment paper. Combine the flour and salt in a medium bowl. Cut in the butter and shortening using a pastry cutter and work into the flour until the mixture is crumbly and resembles coarse meal. Add the ice water, 1 tablespoon at a time, until the dough begins to stay together and

★ Otto Carque, 1867–1935 ★

Otto Carque, second from right, and his health wagon, around 1912. (COURTESY OF *LET'S LIVE* MAGAZINE ARCHIVES)

There might never have been a "Healthy Hollywood" without Otto Carque, who preceded all of the early health entrepreneurs. Carque was born in Germany and came to California for the first time in 1889. He lived in New York for a few years, finally settling in Los Angeles in 1905. His mission was to market and sell the dried fruits and natural products of California, especially the Black Mission fig. By 1912 he was selling natural foods out of his "health wagon," a mobile truck that carried the banner "Carque's Pure Food." He eventually trademarked the name "Natural Foods of California" and was the first company to use the term "natural foods," as well as the first to speak out against the use of preservatives.

His trademark was a black leather doctor's bag filled with dried fruits and nuts, along with literature about health. One of his friends referred to Carque's little "black bag" as the symbol of the future doctor, since he treated patients with food, not drugs. After years of selling wholesale, Carque opened his first health food shop in 1922. He sold olives, olive oil, fruit juices, nut butters, freshly milled flours, grains, unsulphured dried fruits, and a variety of other products. By 1926, there were three Carque shops, including one in the heart of Hollywood, a block away from the famed Pantages and Warner Pacific Theater, originally built as the flagship palace for Warner Bros. Studios.

Carque was the first to package and sell an all-natural "health bar" called Carque's California Fruit Bar, which he made with carob, nuts, and dried fruit. The bar sold for five cents in 1927, and eventually was distributed all over the country. Recipes for his "fruit and nut confections" appeared in his books, *Natural Food, The Safeway to Health* (1925) and *Facts About Food* (1933). Carque was an avid hiker, and he claimed that his dried fruit confections would produce "muscular energy and endurance for the traveler, long distance walker, and mountain climber." This was over seventy years ago, many fig seasons away from the "energy bar" craze of today.

forms a ball. Transfer the dough to parchment or wax paper and flatten into a 6-inch disk. Wrap with plastic and refrigerate for 1 hour before rolling it out.

Meanwhile, make the filling: Heat the butter in a 12-inch skillet over medium-low heat. Add the onions, shallots, and salt and cook, covered, stirring occasionally, until the onions are golden brown and caramelized, 20 to 30 minutes. Add the thyme and pepper near the end of cooking time. Remove the mixture from the pan and let cool.

Preheat the oven to 375°F. Roll out dough to fit the tart pan or baking sheet. Sprinkle with the Parmigiano-Reggiano and spread the onion mixture over the prepared crust. Decorate the top with the pepper slices and olives. Bake for 40 to 45 minutes, or until both the crust and onions are golden.

Endive Petals with Curried Chicken Salad

Makes about 3 dozen

Orson Welles wrote, produced, directed, and starred in *Citizen Kane* (1941), a film believed by many critics to be the best movie ever made. Welles was a loyal patron of Ma Maison and ate there almost every day for lunch and dinner the seven years before he died. Ma Maison was the hip Hollywood haunt of the 1970s and the place where chef Wolfgang Puck got his start in Hollywood. Ma Maison was known for fresh, light cuisine, especially the low-calorie chicken salad, a recipe developed by the owner, Patrick Terrail. I use plenty of low-carb appetizers on my catering menus, like this Ma Maison–inspired chicken salad, which I serve over endive petals. If any of the salad is left over, it makes a great lunch the next day.

Two 8-ounce boneless, skinless chicken breasts
Two ¼-inch slices fresh ginger
1 bay leaf
½ cup finely chopped celery
2 green onions, both white and green parts, finely chopped

½ cup finely chopped red bell pepper

1 small mango, peeled and chopped into ½-inch pieces

½ cup light mayonnaise

2 tablespoons mango chutney or sweet Thai chile sauce

2 teaspoons fresh lime juice

½ teaspoon curry powder

¼ teaspoon freshly ground black pepper

Kosher salt

4 or 5 firm heads Belgian endive

Chopped toasted cashews or almonds for garnish

Fresh cilantro leaves for garnish

Place the chicken in a 2-quart saucepan and add water to cover by 2 inches. Add the ginger and bay leaf. Bring to a boil, then reduce to a simmer and cook, uncovered, for about 20 minutes. Remove the chicken from the pan and place on a plate to cool. When cooled, shred the meat into small pieces as you would for tacos or enchiladas.

In a medium bowl place the chicken, celery, green onions, bell pepper, and mango. In a small bowl combine the mayonnaise, chutney, lime juice, curry powder, and pepper and stir until creamy. Add to the chicken mixture, taste, and add salt if needed. Refrigerate while you prepare the endive petals.

Cut ½ inch off the bottom end of each endive head. Separate the leaves and trim each leaf to measure about 4 inches in length. You can keep the leaves in ice-cold water with a squeeze of lemon until you use them, or layered in the refrigerator with wet paper towels. (Pat dry thoroughly with paper towels before filling.)

Fill each endive petal with about 1 tablespoon of the chicken salad. Garnish with the chopped cashews and 1 or 2 cilantro leaves.

Filet Mignon Japanese

*Makes about 20
to 24 appetizers*

I always say, if I could have my own chef it would be my friend Donna Prizgintas—I am that crazy about her food and the energy she puts into it. I first experienced Donna's cuisine when she catered an event for the Organic Farming Research Foundation. Donna is a devotee of everything organic, and uses only organic meats for her A-list clients, who include Michelle Pfeiffer and David E. Kelley. When Donna was the chef for mega-producer Norman Lear, she first became involved in the Environmental Media Awards, which honors media that promote positive environmental messages. It was Donna's brainstorm to create an all-organic dinner for the awards, since she always says, "Eating is an environmental activity." Because of Donna, the food is donated from Whole Foods Market and chefs like Jar's Suzanne Tracht, "Border Girls" Mary Sue Milliken and Susan Feniger, Table Eight's Govind Armstrong, Campanile's Mark Peel, and Wilshire's Christopher Blobaum participate each year. This recipe is one of Donna's clients' favorites, and she says they like to snack on it cold if there is any left over. I like to serve it as an appetizer, either sliced and skewered or in a Bibb lettuce "cup" garnished with slivers of carrots and sliced green onions. Donna uses all organic ingredients in this recipe.

½ cup low-sodium tamari

½ cup seasoned rice wine vinegar

1 pound organic, grass-fed filet mignon beef, sliced into 2 or 3 steaks

20 to 24 lettuce leaves

Green onions, finely sliced, for garnish

1 carrot, slivered

Freshly ground black pepper (optional)

Combine the tamari and the vinegar in a small bowl. Divide in half and reserve half of the marinade for later. Place the remaining marinade in flat-bottomed glass dish. Place the steaks in the marinade, refrigerate, and marinate for one hour, turning once.

Preheat a stovetop or outdoor grill. Grill the steaks for about 3 to 4 minutes on each side for medium-rare doneness. Return the cooked filets to the remaining tamari mix and let rest for several minutes. To serve, cut the meat into twenty to twenty-four portions and place into twenty to twenty-four lettuce "cups." Spoon the reserved marinade over the meat and garnish with the green onions and carrot. Season to taste with pepper.

5

Some Like It Hot

SOUPS AND STEWS

In 1897, Joseph Campbell introduced America to canned soup. By the twentieth century, everyone was canned-soup crazy, not just for eating, but also to use in casseroles and sauces.

Homemade soups from old country recipes still prevailed in the homes of immigrants and followers of Gayelord Hauser using his recipe for Hauser Broth to make a pot of the Duchess of Windsor's favorite Black Bean Puree. Health-conscious eaters in Los Angeles could find freshly made soups at vegetarian restaurants, Jewish delis, and Italian or Chinese restaurants.

While the rest of America was opening a can of cream of celery soup, Dr. Henry Bieler's patients, like Greta Garbo and Hedda Hopper, were probably sipping his famous Dr. Bieler's Broth (page 88).

Cold soups were en vogue after Chef Louis Diat of New York invented vichyssoise in 1917. In *The American Century Cookbook*

(1997), Jean Anderson recalls the first time she tasted cold avocado soup, and described it as "stellar." She was sent to Los Angeles by *Ladies' Home Journal* to interview actress Joan Fontaine, who served her a cold curried avocado soup. Jean traced pureed avocado soup to a 1943 issue of *Sunset*; I found one in L.A. raw food queen Vera Richter's *Cook-Less Book* (1925), in the section called "Soups for the Toothless."

Hauser Broth

Makes about 2 quarts; serves 6 to 8

Hauser Broth was an important part of Gayelord Hauser's 7-Day Elimination Diet, which he created in 1922 when he opened his first food clinic in Chicago. He wrote about it in his books and *Diet Digest* magazine, a quarterly published in the 1940s and '50s. The small magazine included information on Hauser's adventures, diet recommendations, health problems, natural remedies, foods, recipes, and vitamins. Sometimes they contained photos of Hauser and film stars reading his books, hanging out on the set, or lunching at the Brown Derby. This is my version of Hauser's famous broth. Feel free to add any leftover vegetable trimmings you have saved.

1 cup finely chopped or shredded carrots
1 cup finely chopped or shredded parsnips
2 cups finely chopped or shredded celery, including leaves
1 large onion, chopped
1 leek, white and pale green parts only, sliced
1 cup chopped spinach
2 tablespoons chopped fresh parsley
2 shallots, chopped
1 clove garlic, chopped
1 bay leaf
1 teaspoon black peppercorns
Seasoned vegetable salt

★ Gayelord Hauser (1895–1984) ★

The most influential health guru to come to Hollywood from Germany was Gayelord Hauser, the original "nutritionist to the stars." When Hedda Hopper reported on the famous lunch Gayelord Hauser made in Paris for the Duchess of Windsor and other socialites, she said that Hauser made "spinach fashionable on three continents."

Hauser was the man who glamorized health food and inspired people all over the world to change their eating habits. He coined the term "food for beauty," and inspired Helena Rubenstein to open a "food for beauty" restaurant. It was Hauser's teachings that Ann Delafield used when she directed Elizabeth Arden's Maine Chance Farms, the first luxury health resort on the East Coast and a known get-

Gayelord Hauser and actress Jean Harlow drinking vegetable cocktails, 1933.
(COURTESY OF *LET'S LIVE* MAGAZINE ARCHIVES)

away for film stars and socialites. Even the legendary Maxim's in Paris once held a private party for Hauser, complete with a "Hauser Bar," stocked with vegetable and fruit juices. When President Perón (husband to Eva) was inspired to bring him to Argentina because he felt his people were eating too much meat, the street markets were sold out of fruits and vegetables the next day.

As with many of the early pioneers, Hauser had a health crisis at an early age. Given up to die by conventional doctors, he went to Europe for a "nature cure." In Switzerland a family friend told him, "If you keep on eating dead foods, you will certainly die. Only living foods can make a living body." He took the advice and discovered what diet could do. He traveled through Europe, studying with top experts such as Dr. Bircher-Benner in Zurich. Once cured, Hauser set out to share his miracle with the rest of the world.

Hauser came to Hollywood in 1927, and he met Greta Garbo through conductor Leopold Stokowski. He changed her diet while she made her classic movie *Ninotchka* (1939). Garbo and Hauser nearly married at one point, and their sightings and goings-on were written about in all of the gossip columns.

Hollywood embraced Hauser following the success of *Ninotchka,* and he was given the job of keeping twelve beautiful showgirls energized during the filming of *The All-American Co-Ed* (1941). He created the first beauty bar in Hollywood, and gave the actresses energy drinks made with fresh fruit and vegetable juices. Cameras were known to stop filming so everyone could take a "Hauser Break" and drink fresh juices.

His company, Modern Products, still exists today and his products are sold all over the world.

Place 2 quarts of water, carrots, parsnips, celery, onion, leek, spinach, parsley, shallots, garlic, bay leaf, and peppercorns, in a 4-quart stockpot. Bring to a boil over high heat, then reduce to a simmer and cook, covered, for 30 to 40 minutes. Turn off the heat. Season to taste with vegetable salt. Strain. Use as a base for soups, or drink as is between meals.

Curried Cauliflower Puree

Makes 2 quarts;
serves 6 to 8

Like many of the early health pioneers, Bernard Jensen overcame his early physical problems with natural methods. Jensen studied with many of the world's top naturopathic doctors, including Dr. John Harvey Kellogg of Battle Creek. In 1939, Jensen opened Nature's Retreat in Altadena, fourteen miles outside of Los Angeles. Nature's Retreat was a sanitarium where the patients were treated like personal guests in the doctor's home. Special diets were prescribed and chiropractic and spa treatments were available. Jensen wrote many books, including *Foods That Heal* (1988), in which he claimed that the greatest amount of calcium in cauliflower is found in the greens around the head.

1½ quarts Hauser Broth (page 84) or vegetable stock
2 tablespoons finely grated or minced fresh ginger
2 large onions, chopped
½ cup sliced shallots

3 cloves garlic, minced

1 leek, white and pale green parts only, cleaned and finely chopped

1 large head cauliflower, broken into florets, greens and stems finely chopped

1 teaspoon ground turmeric

1 teaspoon ground coriander

¼ teaspoon ground cumin

½ teaspoon Jensen's Vegetable Salt or sea salt

2 tablespoons white miso paste

In a large, heavy stockpot combine the Hauser Broth, ginger, onions, shallots, garlic, leek, cauliflower, turmeric, coriander, cumin, and salt over medium-high heat. Bring to a boil, then reduce the heat to a simmer, cover, and cook until the vegetables are soft, about 30 minutes.

Remove from the heat, add the miso, and puree in a blender or food processor, in batches, until smooth and creamy.

White Corn Chowder

Serves 6

When Clark Gable and Carol Lombard drove home from the studio, it was to one of the small farms that still existed in the San Fernando Valley before World War II. Back on the farm, he called her Ma and she called him Pa. Studio publicists photographed Clark driving a tractor or mending a fence and sometimes milking the cows or gathering eggs with Carol. The Gable-Lombard Acres sent their grapes to the hospital, the Farmers Association sold their citrus, the MGM commissary bought their fowl, and the Brown Derby restaurant bought their corn. Today's equivalent of the star-filled Brown Derby is the Ivy, where Hollywood hangs for upscale American fare, old-fashioned desserts, and a very popular corn chowder.

1 tablespoon olive oil or unsalted butter

1 large leek, white and pale green parts only, cleaned and diced

1 rib celery, finely diced

2 shallots, minced

1 clove garlic, minced

3 cups Hauser Broth (page 84) or vegetable stock

2 cups plain soymilk

2 cups fresh or frozen (and thawed) corn kernels

2 medium potatoes, peeled and finely diced

1 bay leaf

½ teaspoon fresh thyme

1 teaspoon kosher salt

½ red bell pepper, seeded and finely diced

Freshly ground black pepper

1 to 2 tablespoons chopped chives or fresh tarragon for garnish

Heat the oil in a heavy stockpot or Dutch oven over medium heat. Add the leek, celery, shallots, and garlic and cook over medium heat for 3 to 4 minutes. Add the Hauser Broth, soymilk, corn kernels, potatoes, bay leaf, thyme, and salt. Bring to a boil and simmer for 5 to 7 minutes, or until the potatoes are tender.

Remove 1 cup of the vegetables and ½ cup of the broth. Puree in a food processor or blender until smooth and return to the pot. Add the bell pepper and simmer another 2 minutes. Season with pepper to taste and garnish with the chopped chives.

Dr. Bieler's Broth

Makes 2 quarts;
serves 6

The works of prolific food writer M. F. K. Fisher have taught many the art and love of eating. The early 1940s were known as Fisher's "Hollywood years," which she spent writing screenplays at Paramount and finishing her masterpiece, *The Gastronomical Me* (1943). She socialized with directors Billy Wilder and Frank Capra and shared meals at the Garden of Allah with her friend Gloria Stuart (*Titanic*, 1997). Fisher was a patient of Gloria Swanson's favorite physician, Dr. Henry Bieler, whose signature cure-all was known as Bieler's Broth. Fisher joined Hedda Hopper and Greta Garbo in praising Dr. Bieler on the jacket of his bestselling book *Food Is Your Best Medicine* (1966) and she thanked him for his "knowledge" in her translation of Brillat-Savarin's *The Physiology of Taste* (1949). She dedicated *An Alphabet for Gourmets* (1949) to Hal Bieler, "who has taught me more than he meant to about the pleasures of the table."

NOTE: Dr. Bieler used no salt in his recipe—I usually cheat and add a tablespoon of miso.

1½ quarts Hauser Broth (page 84), vegetable stock, or water

¾ pound thin green beans, ends trimmed and cut into 2-inch pieces

5 zucchinis, stem ends removed, cut into 1-inch slices

1 leek, white part only, cleaned and chopped

2 inner ribs celery, coarsely chopped

½ cup flat-leaf parsley sprigs

1 tablespoon white miso paste (optional)

1 tablespoon unsalted butter or extra-virgin olive oil (optional)

In a large, heavy stockpot, combine the Hauser Broth, green beans, zucchini, leek, celery, and parsley. Bring to a boil over medium-high heat. Reduce the heat to a simmer, cover, and cook until the vegetables are soft, about 30 minutes.

Add the miso and butter and puree the soup in a blender or food processor, in batches, until smooth and creamy.

Lima Bean Chowder

Serves 8

At the turn of the century, Beverly Hills was a vast field of lima beans, an important California crop 100 years ago. All the beans were gone in 1907 when the housing development of Beverly Hills was created. In 1919 Douglas Fairbanks bought a hunting lodge in Beverly Hills and remodeled it as a gift to his new bride, Mary Pickford. In the 1920s and '30s they were the reigning King and Queen of Hollywood and their home, Pickfair, was the royal palace. Soon other film folk followed them into Beverly Hills and movie stars replaced lima beans as the town's most important commodity.

1 tablespoon olive oil

1 medium onion, finely chopped

2 large shallots, finely chopped

1 cup finely chopped celery (about 4 ribs)

1 large leek, white and pale green parts only, cleaned and finely chopped

2 carrots, chopped into ¼-inch pieces

1 large parsnip, chopped into ¼-inch pieces

1½ quarts Hauser Broth (page 84) or vegetable stock

½ teaspoon ground turmeric

1 bay leaf

1 teaspoon fresh thyme leaves

1 teaspoon kosher salt

½ teaspoon freshly ground black pepper

1 teaspoon smoked or regular paprika

2 (15-ounce) cans baby lima beans

⅓ cup red miso paste

3 tablespoons chopped flat-leaf parsley

Heat the oil in a large, heavy stockpot over medium heat. Add the onion, shallots, celery, leek, carrots, and parsnip and cook until tender and aromatic, about 10 minutes. Add the Hauser Broth, turmeric, bay leaf, thyme, salt, pepper, and paprika. Raise the heat, bring to a boil, then reduce the heat to low and simmer for 15 minutes, or until the vegetables are tender. Add lima beans and cook an additional 10 minutes.

In a small bowl, whisk the miso with ½ cup of the soup broth, then add it back into the soup. Stir in the chopped parsley, remove the bay leaf, and serve immediately.

Kabocha Squash Soup with Spiced Pumpkin Seeds

Serves 6

L.A.'s best-known vegan restaurant is Real Food Daily, which was founded by my friend Ann Gentry, a former off-Broadway actress who discovered macrobiotic foods while living in New York and eating at the famed Angelica's Kitchen. Ann was once Danny DeVito's private chef, and her vegan restaurants are one of Hollywood's healthy hangouts. One of my favorite Real Food Daily soups is made from kabocha squash, a firm, starchy squash that can be found at natural food stores and in Asian groceries. Any other squash, such as butternut, will work perfectly in this recipe.

KABOCHA SQUASH SOUP

One 2- to 3-pound kabocha squash, peeled and chopped (about 3 cups)

2 medium parsnips or carrots, chopped

1 medium onion, chopped

1 clove garlic, minced

2 tablespoons finely minced fresh ginger

1 teaspoon kosher salt

1 quart Hauser Broth (page 84) or vegetable stock

1½ cups plain soymilk

2 tablespoons tamari or soy sauce

⅛ teaspoon freshly grated nutmeg

Freshly ground white or black pepper

SPICED PUMPKIN SEEDS

⅔ cup raw pumpkin seeds

¼ teaspoon curry powder

1 teaspoon tamari or soy sauce

Freshly ground black pepper

In a large stockpot combine the squash, parsnips, onion, garlic, ginger, salt, and Hauser Broth. Bring the stock to a boil over medium-high heat. Reduce to a simmer, cover, and cook until the vegetables are soft, about 30 minutes.

While the soup is cooking, place the pumpkin seeds in a medium, heavy nonstick skillet over medium-high heat. Cook, stirring constantly, for about 5 minutes, or until they begin to brown and pop. Add the curry powder, turn off heat, and add the tamari. Stir evenly to coat, and season with pepper to taste.

Add the soymilk and tamari to the soup. Puree in a blender, in three separate batches, until smooth and creamy. Add the nutmeg and pepper to taste. Garnish with the pumpkin seeds.

Red Lentil Bisque

Serves 6 to 8

Many of the swamis and yogis who taught in Los Angeles not only influenced their students to study and practice yoga but introduced them to vegetarian diets and Indian cuisine. Peter Max, whose art became the symbol of a generation, dedicated *The Peter Max New Age Organic Vegetarian Cook Book* (1971) to Integral Yoga head Sri Swami Satchidananda, whom Max helped bring to America in 1966. Max's beautifully illustrated book includes a recipe for sambar, a traditional Southern Indian dal, made with red lentils. My recipe is milder than a traditional sambar, which can be very spicy.

2 cups red lentils, rinsed and picked over for stones

1 teaspoon ground turmeric

2 quarts Hauser Broth (page 84) or vegetable stock

2 bay leaves

1 teaspoon dried thyme

1 large white onion, minced

2 large leeks, white and pale green parts only, cleaned and finely chopped

2 ribs celery, minced

1 (14.5-ounce) can diced tomatoes

2 teaspoons clarified butter or unsalted butter

1 teaspoon black mustard seeds

2 teaspoons kosher salt

1 teaspoon freshly ground black pepper

2 tablespoons white miso paste

In a large stockpot combine the lentils, turmeric, Hauser Broth, bay leaves, thyme, onion, leeks, celery, and tomatoes. Bring to a boil over medium-high heat, then lower the heat and simmer, uncovered, for 50 to 60 minutes, or until the vegetables are thoroughly cooked and the lentils are completely softened.

Meanwhile, heat the clarified butter in a small skillet over medium heat, add the mustard seeds, and cook, stirring, for 1 minute, or until they pop.

Add the mustard seeds to soup, along with the salt and pepper. Add the miso and puree the soup in a blender or food processor, in batches, until smooth and creamy.

Holy Basil Matzo Ball Soup

Serves 6; makes 12 matzo balls

Movie mogul Louis B. Mayer (1882–1957) was once the most powerful producer in Hollywood and was one of the original founders of MGM Studios back in 1924. Mayer was responsible for classics like *The Wizard of Oz* (1939), *Gone With the Wind* (1939), and *The Philadelphia Story* (1940), as well as the *Thin Man, Lassie,* and the *Andy Hardy* series starring Mickey Rooney. Growing up poor, Mayer vowed that if he ever became a rich man, he would have chicken soup every day of his life. He put his mother's recipe on the menu at the MGM commissary, where it cost 30 cents a bowl back in 1934. During lunchtime at the studio, he used to go from table to table, praising the merits of chicken soup. My recipe uses holy basil, ginger, and lemongrass, which make this chicken soup a real healer. If you can't find holy basil, use Thai basil, which can be found (along with lemongrass) at most Asian markets.

2 quarts homemade vegetable or chicken stock

1 stalk lemongrass, cut into 2-inch pieces

One 2-inch piece fresh ginger, thinly sliced

¼ teaspoon ground turmeric

2 teaspoons sesame oil

1 leek, green parts only, cleaned and coarsely chopped

1 leek, white part only, cleaned and cut into thin matchsticks

1 carrot, cut into thin matchsticks

1 parsnip, cut into thin matchsticks

2 eggs

2 tablespoons canola oil

1 jalapeño chile, minced

½ teaspoon fine sea salt

⅛ teaspoon freshly ground black pepper

2 tablespoons fresh holy basil, Thai basil, or cilantro, finely chopped

½ cup matzo meal

2 tablespoons seltzer water

In a large stockpot combine the broth, lemongrass, ginger, and turmeric and simmer for 30 minutes. Drain, then return to the pot.

Heat the oil in a 12-inch skillet over medium heat. Add the leek and cook for 2 to 3 minutes, or until softened. Add the leek, carrot, and parsnip to the broth and simmer for 10 minutes, then turn off the heat.

Meanwhile, in a medium bowl whisk together the eggs, oil, jalapeño, salt, pepper, and basil. Fold in the matzo meal and seltzer water. Cover and refrigerate for 30 minutes.

Bring a large stockpot of salted water to a boil. Wet your hands with cold water and form the batter into 12 small balls. Drop the matzo balls into the boiling water. Reduce the heat to a simmer, cover, and cook for 30 minutes—don't open the lid. The matzo balls will sink and come back to the top as they cook. Remove the matzo balls with a slotted spoon and add to the soup immediately, or set them in a pot of cold water to cool and refrigerate until ready to use. They may be reheated either in the broth or in a pot of boiling water.

Shiitake Mushroom Barley Soup

Serves 6 to 8

John Gower came to Los Angeles from Hawaii in 1869 and bought a 160-acre parcel of land in an area that today is Hollywood. Gower initially planted wheat and barley on the land, but eventually the intersection of Sunset and Gower became the center of the film industry. The first Hollywood stage set was built on Sunset and Gower, and movie extras used to hang in that area hoping for a day's work. Movies in those days were short (only about eighteen minutes), and were shot in two to three days. The barley is long gone, but mushroom barley soup is still a star.

2 cups water

2 ounces dried porcini or other wild mushroom

1 tablespoon unsalted butter or olive oil

1 large onion, finely chopped

1 large or 2 small shallots, finely chopped

½ teaspoon kosher salt

2 leeks, white and pale green parts only, cleaned
    and finely chopped

8 ounces shiitake mushrooms, stems wiped clean,
    trimmed, and sliced

2 quarts Hauser Broth (page 84) or vegetable stock

2 ribs celery, finely chopped

1 large carrot, diced

1 large parsnip, diced

½ cup whole barley

1 bay leaf

1 teaspoon fresh thyme leaves

Freshly ground black pepper

Chopped flat-leaf parsley for garnish

Bring the water to a boil in a 1-quart saucepan. Add the porcini mushrooms, turn off the heat, and cover. Let sit for 20 minutes, or until the mushrooms have softened. Drain, reserving the liquid, and finely chop the mushrooms.

Heat the butter in a large stockpot, over medium-high heat. Add the onion, shallots, and a pinch of salt. Cook for about 5 minutes, or until the onions are translucent and fragrant. Lower the heat to medium, add the leeks, and cook for another 3 minutes. Add the shiitakes and soaked porcini mushrooms and cook another 5 to 8 minutes, stirring often, until the mushrooms are softened.

Add the Hauser Broth, celery, carrot, parsnip, barley, bay leaf, and thyme. Bring to a boil, then reduce to a simmer. Cook for 1 hour, or until the barley is tender. Season with salt and pepper to taste. Garnish with the chopped parsley.

Hauser Black Bean Soup

Serves 6 to 8

Only Gayelord Hauser could glamorize the humble black bean soup by serving it to the Duchess of Windsor, one of his friends and followers. In *The Gayelord Hauser Cookbook* (1946), he includes Duchess of Windsor Bean Soup, a recipe that was one of her favorites. The recipe calls for his famous Hauser Broth, which was part of all his diet plans and fasting regimes. The footnote to the recipe claimed that "even your most blasé relatives will like this soup."

NOTE: Spike is Hauser's signature vegetable salt, and gives this soup a great flavor.

1 tablespoon olive oil

1 small onion, diced

3 ribs celery, diced

1 cup dried black beans, soaked overnight and drained

8 cups Hauser Broth (page 84)

1 bay leaf

Dash of paprika

½ teaspoon Spike or other seasoned vegetable salt

Juice of 1 lemon
Kosher salt and freshly ground black pepper
1 tablespoon sherry
1 lemon, sliced paper-thin
3 to 4 hard-boiled eggs, finely grated, for garnish (optional)
Chopped chives for garnish

Heat the oil in a large, heavy stockpot over medium heat. Add the onion and celery and cook until tender, 5 to 10 minutes. Add the beans, Hauser Broth, and bay leaf. Bring to a boil, then reduce to a simmer and cook until the beans are tender, 1½ to 2 hours, adding more broth or water if needed. Remove the bay leaf.

Add the paprika, Spike, lemon juice, and salt and pepper to taste. Puree the soup in a blender or food processor, in batches, until smooth and creamy. Strain through a fine sieve to remove any remaining bean skin, pressing through to strain.

Reheat the soup, stir in the sherry, and serve piping hot with a thin slice of lemon, some finely grated hard-boiled egg, and chives for each bowl. Season with salt and pepper to taste.

Cold Avocado Soup with White Corn Salsa

Serves 4

The California avocado industry began in the late 1920s with the development of the Hass avocado. It was named after Rudolf Hass, a postman who grafted the tree in his backyard in La Habra, California. I found an early recipe for avocado soup in Vera Richter's *Mrs. Richter's Cook-Less Book,* first published in 1925. The following recipe is based on Vera's version, which was made with tomato juice, avocados, and pine nuts; the only difference was that Vera didn't have a blender. This is a great soup to make in the summer when tomatoes and white corn are in season. I like to serve it at dinner parties in small demitasse cups with small spoons as an amuse-bouche or a passed appetizer.

AVOCADO SOUP
3 cups chopped ripe tomatoes
¼ cup fresh lime juice
2 ripe Hass avocados (about 1 pound)
¼ cup chopped green onions
¼ cup raw pine nuts
1½ teaspoon salt
¼ teaspoon freshly ground white pepper
Pinch of cayenne pepper (optional)
1 cup ice water

WHITE CORN SALSA
1 small red onion, diced
Kernels from 1 ear of white corn
1 large tomato, seeded and finely diced
2 green onions, all of white and 2 inches of green parts, finely chopped
1 tablespoon fresh lime juice
2 tablespoons chopped fresh cilantro
1 small jalapeño chile, seeds removed, finely chopped
¼ teaspoon kosher salt

To make the soup, blend the tomatoes and lime juice in a blender on high. Strain through a fine-mesh strainer and return to the blender.

Cut open the avocados and scoop out the flesh. Add the avocado to the tomatoes, along with the green onions, pine nuts, salt, pepper, cayenne, and water. Blend until smooth and creamy.

Thin with additional water if needed.

To make the salsa, in a small bowl combine the onion, corn, tomato, green onions, lime juice, cilantro, jalapeño, and salt. Mix together and serve. The salsa can be made ahead and refrigerated until ready to use.

Serve the soup, garnished with the salsa.

Punjabi Four-Bean Dal

Serves 6 to 8

My friend Richard Lasser (*Great Vegetables from the Great Chefs*, 1990) is currently writing screenplays instead of writing about food, but he still enjoys cooking. We both loved eating at the original Spago in Hollywood and were once brave enough to invite Wolfgang Puck over for dinner. We cooked a full Indian feast, and Richard made his specialty—an Indian ice cream called *kulfi*. I made this dal, which I first tasted at an Indian temple while on a rock and roll tour in Australia. Don't worry if it's soupy; that's how it's supposed to be. Serve with Oven-Roasted Curried Cauliflower (page 221), Tomato Chutney (page 58), and steamed basmati rice.

5¼ cup dried red lentils

½ cup dried yellow split peas

½ cup dried white gram beans (urad dal)

⅓ cup dried kidney beans

2½ quarts cold water

½ teaspoon ground turmeric

1 bay leaf

2 tablespoons clarified butter or canola oil

1 large onion, finely chopped

2 tablespoons minced fresh ginger

2 cloves garlic, sliced

1 teaspoon cumin seeds

½ teaspoon freshly ground black pepper

1 teaspoon ground coriander

¼ teaspoon crushed red chile flakes

1 teaspoon garam masala

2 teaspoons kosher salt

3 tablespoons minced fresh cilantro

Pick through the beans for any stones and rinse them well. Place the lentils, split peas, and beans in a stockpot with the cold water, turmeric, and bay leaf. Bring to a boil over high heat, then lower the heat, cover, and simmer for about 40 minutes, or until the lentils and beans are very soft.

While the dal is cooking, heat the clarified butter in a 12-inch skillet over medium heat. Add the onion, ginger, and garlic and cook until the onions are completely softened, about 15 minutes. Add the cumin seeds, black pepper, coriander, and chile flakes and cook another 5 minutes.

Add the onion-ginger mixture to the dal and cook an additional 40 minutes, stirring occasionally to prevent sticking. Add the garam masala and salt. Garnish with the cilantro and serve with chapatis.

Red Bean Chili with Millet-Cornmeal Dumplings

Serves 6

Vincent Price will always be known for his sinister laugh (perhaps best remembered in the narrative on Michael Jackson's *Thriller*), and for films like *House of Wax* (1953), the first major studio release in 3-D. Price was just as much a chef as an actor, and his first cookbook, *A Treasury of Great Recipes* (1965), included recipes from fine restaurants all over the world. He also wrote *Come into the Kitchen Cook Book* (1969) and *A National Treasury of Cookery* (1967). He hosted a popular British television show called *Cooking Price-Wise,* and in the late 1970s released a series of audiotapes on cooking called *Push-Button Cookery,* which was marketed as "an exciting new concept in cuisine." Price also worked as a culinary spokesperson for the American Dairy Association, and lent his image to print ads promoting "real" cheese and a recipe for vegetarian chili with cornbread. Price's chili was made with red kidney beans and canned tomatoes—both rich in antioxidants.

RED BEAN CHILI

1 tablespoon olive oil

1 large onion, finely chopped

2 ribs celery, chopped

2 cloves garlic, chopped

1 (15-ounce) can red beans or red kidney beans

1 quart Hauser Broth (page 84) or vegetable stock

1 bay leaf

2 sprigs fresh thyme

1 teaspoon dried oregano

2 teaspoons chili powder

1 (14.5-ounce) can diced fire-roasted tomatoes

2 medium zucchinis, chopped into ½-inch pieces

Kernels from 1 ear of corn

¼ teaspoon kosher salt

⅛ teaspoon freshly ground black pepper

Chopped cilantro, for garnish

MILLET-CORNMEAL DUMPLINGS

⅓ cup cornmeal

¼ cup millet flour

½ cup unbleached all-purpose flour

1½ teaspoons baking powder

½ teaspoon fine sea salt

½ cup plain soymilk or low-fat cow's milk

2 teaspoons olive oil

2 green onions, white and most of green parts, minced

1 serrano chile, seeded and finely chopped

2 tablespoons minced fresh cilantro

To make the chili, heat the oil in a heavy stockpot over medium-high heat. Add the onion, celery, and garlic and cook for 5 minutes. Add the beans,

Hauser broth, bay leaf, thyme, oregano, chili powder, tomatoes, zucchini, and corn and bring to a boil. Reduce the heat and simmer for 20 minutes.

Meanwhile, prepare the dumpling batter: whisk together the cornmeal, millet flour, all-purpose flour, baking powder, and salt in a medium bowl. In a separate bowl whisk together the soymilk, oil, green onions, chile, and cilantro. Add the wet ingredients to the dry, folding lightly until the ingredients are just mixed.

Add the salt and pepper to the chile, then drop the dumpling batter by tablespoons into the simmering chili. You should have 12 dumplings total. Cover the pot with a tight-fitting lid and cook for 12 minutes. Don't peek. Serve garnished with the chopped cilantro.

Mung Bean and Basmati Risotto

Serves 4 to 6

When I first became a private chef, one of Yogi Bhajan's students, a holistic doctor in Beverly Hills, used to "prescribe" this dish to his celebrity patients and send me to make it for them. Originally called Mung Beans and Rice, this dish is filled with all things good for you, and I think of it as Punjabi comfort food. My favorite mung-bean client is the beautiful and lovely actress Linda Gray, star of the long-running series *Dallas*. For some reason, this dish loses its creamy consistency when frozen, so don't freeze it, or you'll be disappointed. I also like to season it with dried red chile flakes if I am not serving it to children. You can also serve it with low-fat yogurt on the side.

½ cup green mung beans

1 teaspoon ground turmeric

½ teaspoon celery seeds

1 fresh or dried bay leaf

1 large onion, sliced into half-moons

2 ribs celery, diced

¼ cup minced fresh ginger

2 cloves garlic, minced

6 cups water or Hauser Broth (page 84)

½ cup basmati rice, rinsed

1 large carrot, chopped

1 large parsnip, chopped

2 small zucchinis, chopped

1 teaspoon garam masala

Freshly ground black pepper

Clarified butter (optional) for serving

In a large stockpot combine the mung beans, turmeric, celery seeds, bay leaf, onion, celery, ginger, garlic, and water over high heat. Bring to a boil, then lower the heat to a simmer. Simmer, partially covered, until the mung beans are split and softened, about 40 minutes.

Add the rice, carrots, and parsnip and continue to simmer, stirring often, until the vegetables are cooked and the rice softens and begins to blend with the rest of the ingredients, about 30 minutes. Add the zucchini and garam masala and continue to cook, stirring, until the zucchini is cooked, and the mixture is quite thick and a stew-like consistency. You will need to stir frequently at this point, and if needed, add more water to prevent scorching. The mung beans should be completely split open and softened. Remove the bay leaf before serving, and drizzle each serving with a little clarified butter for flavor, if desired.

White Bean and Swiss Chard Soup

Serves 4 to 6

Victor Lindlahr lectured on health and nutrition on his nationwide radio show. His dieting book sold over a half-million copies, and he conducted "reducing parties" on his broadcast. His book *You Are What You Eat* (1940) was a kitchen handbook on good-for-you fruits and vegetables. Swiss chard, which he considered to be an excellent vegetable that deserved to be more popular, made the list. He wrote that even those who don't like it as a vegetable will like it in soup.

1 tablespoon olive oil
1 large onion, finely chopped
1 leek, white part only, cleaned and chopped
2 large carrots, cut into ¼-inch dice
2 ribs celery, minced
2 cloves garlic, minced
4 chopped fresh sage leaves
2 (15-ounce) cans cannellini beans
2 quarts Hauser Broth (page 84) or vegetable broth
1 bay leaf
2 sprigs fresh thyme
2 bunches red or green Swiss chard, trimmed and chopped
½ teaspoon kosher salt
¼ teaspoon freshly ground black pepper

Heat the oil in a large, heavy stockpot over medium heat. Add the onion, leek, carrots, and celery and cook until the vegetables are tender and aromatic, about 15 minutes. Add the garlic and sage and cook for 2 minutes more. Add the beans, Hauser Broth, bay leaf, and thyme. Bring to a boil, then reduce the heat to low and simmer for an additional 10 minutes.

Remove the bay leaf, add the chopped chard, salt, and pepper and cook until the chard wilts, 5 to 8 minutes.

6

High Noon

SANDWICHES AND WRAPS

What's lunch without the popular sandwich? Back in the 1920s and '30s, Hollywood lunched at the Montmartre, where Joan Crawford did the Charleston and lunched with Hedda Hopper. At the Montmartre, the "Charlie Chaplin" Camembert on rye sold for sixty cents and the "Gloria Swanson" corn omelet on toast was forty cents. Reuben's Restaurant in New York was also known for naming sandwiches after celebrities, and other delis have followed suit. Contrary to popular belief, Hollywood doesn't live on sprouts and avocados alone, and we have our own well-known delis, just like New York. Since 1943, Nate n' Al's has been a Beverly Hills hang-out for actors, comedians, and their agents, serving New York–style deli sandwiches. The always popular Canter's Deli, located near CBS studios and in Vegas, has been a California landmark since 1931. Everyone from Elvis to Marilyn has been to Canter's, which is famous for chicken soup as well as deli sandwiches.

Gossip columns were mentioning avocado and nut burgers back in 1939, and by the 1950s, it was the Mushroom Burger, served at Yogananda's SFR India Café, that made the veggie burger popular in Hollywood. Since Yogananda had many students all over the world, it was at his restaurant that many Americans experienced their first meatless burger. Adding alfalfa sprouts to sandwiches is definitely a California tradition; one of the first recipes for a sprout sandwich appeared in *El Molino Best Recipes* (1953). El Molino was one of the original stone ground mills in Los Angeles and sold freshly ground grains and flours to health food shops nationwide. When *Seventeen* magazine wrote about "The New Food Freaks" in 1972, they of course mentioned The Source Special, an avocado, sprout, and cheese sandwich, first discovered by the film crowd in 1969. Back to Eden in Los Angeles, an organic food store, had a Garden Burger made with wheat, mushrooms, onions, nuts, and soybeans, and served on a sprouted wheat bun. Nearly ten years later Paul Wenner, the creator of the Gardenburger, launched his Gardenburger empire at his Gardenhouse restaurant in Portland, Oregon. In Wenner's book *Garden Cuisine* (1997), he credits Hollywood health crusader Paul Bragg's book *The Miracle of Fasting* as being the catalyst to changing his health and life. Bragg had all kinds of healthy sandwiches in his cookbooks, including a version of the Elvis standby, peanut butter and banana.

The hip place to hang for healthy sandwiches, both vegetarian and not, is the Newsroom Café in West Hollywood, where my friend chef Eddie J. Caraeff is manning the stoves. Eddie is a Rock and Roll Hall of Fame photographer who decided to become a chef, proving that if you're creative in one field, you can be just as good in another. Eddie's archives are filled with one-of-a-kind shots of Elton John, The Doors, and Jimi Hendrix, and his recipe box is every bit as exciting. In the film *Sunset Strip* (2000), one of the characters is based on Eddie's life as a teenage photographer hanging out on the Sunset Strip in the early 1970s. Thirty-five years later, he's still making the scene.

The Dagwood

*Makes 2
large sandwiches*

The *Blondie* comic strip was created by Murat Bernard "Chic" Young (1901–1973) in 1930. Columbia Pictures made twenty-eight *Blondie* films starring Arthur Lake and Penny Singleton, who also was the voice of Jane Jetson on the long-running animated *Jetsons* show. The only thing that the lovable, bumbling Dagwood was capable of making in the kitchen was a towering stack of leftovers, wedged between two slices of bread. This sandwich became branded as a "Dagwood," and eventually made its way into the *Webster's New World Dictionary*. This version can be made vegetarian with deli-style soy meat.

4 slices corn rye or whole-grain bread

Whole-grain mustard or Dijon mustard

Light mayonnaise

Handful of arugula leaves or watercress

1 large ripe beefsteak or 2 Roma tomatoes, sliced

4 paper-thin slices red onion

1 tablespoon red wine vinegar

¼ teaspoon dried oregano

Kosher salt and freshly ground black pepper

2 ounces each nitrate-free turkey, ham, and salami
    (or deli-style soy meat)

2 large white mushrooms, wiped clean, sliced paper-thin

2 ounces sliced mozzarella, goat cheddar, or soy cheese

½ ripe avocado, peeled, pitted, and sliced

2 red leaf lettuce leaves

2 large black California olives

2 pickle slices

Spread the mustard on 2 of the bread slices and the mayonnaise on the other 2. Cover 2 of the bread slices with arugula. Top each with a layer of the tomatoes and onions, drizzle with vinegar, and sprinkle with the oregano, salt, and pepper.

Create another layer with the meats, mushrooms, cheese, and avocado. Finish the sandwich with the red lettuce leaves, and season with a little more salt and pepper. Lay the remaining bread slices on top. Secure with a long toothpick that has been speared with the olives and pickle slices. Slice in half, if you dare.

In the true Dagwood style, feel free to vary the cheese and meats according to what you have on hand.

Curried Egg Salad Tea Sandwiches

Makes 2 dozen open-faced sandwiches

One of the prettiest parties I ever catered was for an event honoring Jane Goodall, hosted by Pierce and Keely Brosnan. The party was held in Malibu at an estate owned by Dick Clark, overlooking the Pacific Ocean. We re-created a high tea on the grass, complete with organic tea brewed to order, artisanal cheese, vanilla-infused grilled pineapple skewers, freshly baked scones, organic jam, and clotted cream. The sandwiches and other snacks featured African flavors. Jane Goodall was a total inspiration; it was truly an honor to meet her.

4 large hard-cooked eggs, peeled and grated
2 to 3 tablespoons light mayonnaise
¾ teaspoon curry powder
¼ cup minced green onion, both white and green parts
Kosher salt and freshly ground black pepper to taste
Twelve ¼-inch slices of artisan-style raisin-walnut bread
1 bunch watercress
Edible flowers like borage or pansies, for garnish (optional)

Cut bread into twenty-four 2-inch rounds, or trim crusts and cut into triangles. In a small bowl, add the grated eggs, mayonnaise, curry powder, and green onion. Mix gently. Season with salt and pepper to taste.

Top the bread slices with little spoonfuls of the egg salad. Garnish with watercress leaves and edible flowers.

Open-Face Grilled Tempeh Reuben

Makes 4
open-face
sandwiches

Tempeh makes a great sandwich. It's good enough to stand on its own merits, not trying to be anything else, and it really works on a Reuben. It seems everyone has a great story about the origin of the Reuben sandwich. The Reuben was actually created in Omaha, Nebraska, by Reuben Kulakosfky, but the Hollywood story is much more fun. According to Patricia B. Taylor, daughter of Arnold Reuben, who founded Reuben's Restaurant and Delicatessen in New York, her father made the first Reuben sandwich in 1914 for one of Charlie Chaplin's leading ladies, Annette Seelos. Annette tried to convince Reuben to name the sandwich after her but he decided to call it the Reuben Special. Broadway stars like Judy Garland, Ginger Rogers, and Jackie Gleason all ate at Reuben's, which had numerous sandwiches named after its famous customers. I like this sandwich with coleslaw, so I included a recipe for it.

RUSSIAN DRESSING
½ cup light or vegan mayonnaise
⅓ cup ketchup
1 tablespoon prepared horseradish (optional)
1 teaspoon vegetarian Worcestershire sauce
1 tablespoon minced shallot

TEMPEH REUBEN
3 tablespoons tamari or soy sauce

2 tablespoons horseradish mustard

1 tablespoon extra-virgin olive oil

1 teaspoon light brown sugar or honey

¼ teaspoon freshly ground black pepper

⅛ to ¼ teaspoon crushed red chile flakes (optional)

One 8-ounce block of tempeh

Additional olive oil or olive oil cooking spray

4 slices deli-style rye bread

¼ pound sauerkraut, well drained

4 ounces grated Swiss cheese or mild sheep cheese such as Petit Basque

COLESLAW

¼ cup white wine vinegar

2 tablespoons sugar

2 tablespoons light or vegan mayonnaise

¼ teaspoon freshly ground black pepper

¼ teaspoon celery salt

½ head green cabbage, finely shredded

2 large carrots, peeled and finely shredded

To make the dressing, in a small bowl whisk together the mayonnaise, ketchup, horseradish, Worcestershire sauce, and shallot.

To make the Reubens, in a small bowl whisk together the tamari, mustard, oil, brown sugar, pepper, and chile flakes. Slice the tempeh block in half vertically to make 2 rectangles. Slice each rectangle in half to make 4 equal rectangles. Place the tempeh slices in a shallow rectangular dish and add the marinade, turning each slice to coat on both sides. Let marinate for at least 30 minutes or up to 2 hours.

While the tempeh is marinating, make the coleslaw: mix together the vinegar, sugar, mayonnaise, pepper, and celery salt in a small bowl. In a large bowl mix together the cabbage and grated carrot. Add the vinegar mixture and toss. Serve as soon as the sandwiches are ready, or make ahead of time and refrigerate until ready to serve.

Heat an electric grill or stovetop grill pan over medium-high heat and brush with oil or coat with cooking spray. Add the tempeh and grill until browned, about 3 minutes each side, basting with extra marinade as you turn the slices.

Lightly toast or grill the bread. Spread each slice with some of the Russian dressing. Layer each slice with the sauerkraut and 1 tempeh slice and top with cheese. Broil until the cheese melts, about 1 minute. Serve with coleslaw on the side.

Grilled Bruschetta with White Bean Hummus and Escarole

Makes 8 open-face sandwiches

In 1929, Charlie Chaplin built a beautiful building on La Brea Avenue in the middle of Los Angeles for his private offices. Before the building was completed, Chaplin lost the property in a divorce settlement to his first wife, Lita Grey. The building is now home to Campanile and La Brea Bakery, which every Thursday night creates a special menu for what has become known as Grilled Cheese Night. Grilled cheese devotees include *Friends* star David Schwimmer and TV's favorite duo, Sean Hayes and Megan Mullally of *Will & Grace.* This recipe was inspired by one of the sandwiches. Feel free to garnish with pieces of crisp cooked applewood-smoked bacon, as they do at Campanile.

2 tablespoons extra-virgin olive oil

2 small shallots, finely chopped

1 head escarole, chopped into bite-size pieces

⅛ teaspoon kosher salt

⅛ teaspoon freshly ground black pepper

½ teaspoon smoked paprika

8 slices rustic bread such as ciabatta

1 clove garlic, peeled and ends cut off

1 recipe White Truffle Hummus (page 53)

2 ounces Parmigiano-Reggiano or Pecorino Romano cheese, thinly shaved with
　a vegetable peeler

Preheat the oven to 400°F or prepare an outdoor grill, or heat an electric grill.

Heat 1 tablespoon of the oil in a 12-inch skillet over medium-high heat. Add the shallots and cook for 2 minutes, or until fragrant. Add the escarole, salt, pepper, and paprika and cook, stirring constantly, until wilted, about 3 minutes.

Brush each bread slice with the remaining tablespoon of oil and bake or grill until crusty, about 1 minute a side on a grill or 5 minutes in the oven. While still hot, rub with the garlic. Top each bread slice with the hummus, escarole, and shaved cheese. Top with bacon if desired.

Beluga Lentil and Tempeh Burgers

*Makes four
4-inch burgers*

The best tempeh in Los Angeles can be found at Native Foods, where Chef Tanya Petrovna makes her own. She has been promising to give me a tempeh-making lesson for years, but I am beginning to think she doesn't want to give away her secrets. Tanya's first two Native Foods restaurants were opened in Palm Springs and the Palm Desert area, the old stomping grounds for the "Nature Boys." They would have loved her creative vegan food—no wonder PETA always calls on Tanya for their celebrity events. She is no doubt the queen of vegan cuisine. I like these tempeh burgers with alfalfa sprouts, mayonnaise, ketchup, grilled onion, and lots of pickles.

Vegetable spray or olive oil

½ cup Beluga lentils, cleaned and rinsed

1 bay leaf

1 large shallot, minced

1 clove garlic, minced

4 cups water

1 tablespoon unsalted butter or olive oil

¼ cup minced onion

¼ cup minced celery

1 teaspoon kosher salt

½ teaspoon celery salt

¼ teaspoon freshly ground black pepper

½ teaspoon paprika

⅛ teaspoon dried thyme

4 ounces tempeh, grated

¼ cup ground sunflower seeds (ground in a food processor)

¼ cup spelt or whole-wheat bread crumbs

¼ cup liquid egg whites or 2 fresh egg whites

2 green onions, all of white and 2 inches of green parts, minced

Buns, tomato slices, sprouts, onion slices, pickle slices, ketchup, mayonnaise, and
  tomato chutney for serving

Line a baking sheet with parchment paper and spray or brush with oil.

Place the lentils, bay leaf, shallot, garlic, and water in a soup pot, cover, and
bring to a boil. Reduce the heat to low and simmer for 30 to 40 minutes, or until the lentils are just tender. Drain well.

Meanwhile, heat the butter in a 12-inch skillet over medium heat. Add the
onion, celery, salt, celery salt, pepper, paprika, and thyme. Cook for 3 to 4 minutes, or until the onions are translucent. Preheat the oven to 350°F.

In a large bowl, combine the tempeh, lentils, sunflower seeds, bread
crumbs, egg whites, green onions, and sautéed onions and celery. Shape the
mixture into four 4-inch patties and place on the prepared baking sheet. Bake
until browned on both sides, turning once, 25 to 30 minutes total.

Fix up your burgers on the buns, using any combination of tomatoes,
sprouts, onions, pickles, ketchup, and mayonnaise you like.

★ Nature Boy ★

In Gordon Kennedy's book *Children of the Sun* (1998), he tells the story of Bill Pester, who was born in Germany in 1886 and left in 1906 to escape military service. *Naturmenschen* from Germany like Bill Pester came to Southern California in the early 1900s, bringing the philosophy of vegetarianism, nudism, natural medicine, and abstinence from alcohol. Pester lived on an organic ranch near Indio Hills growing grapefruit, figs, oranges, and dates. He made a living selling sandals and walking sticks, once entertaining Rudolph Valentino with his slide guitar. He was a mentor to Gypsy Boots and eden ahbez, who wrote the song "Nature Boy."

Eden ahbez wrote "Nature Boy" while living in a cave near Palm Springs. Ahbez, who always spelled his name with small letters because he believed that only God and Infinity should be capitalized, was born in Brooklyn in 1908 and claimed he had walked across America eight times by 1935. He slept in a sleeping bag in Griffith Park, lived as a vegetarian on three dollars a week, and lectured on mysticism on Hollywood Boulevard. When Nat King Cole made "Nature Boy" a number-one hit in 1948, ahbez became a celebrity. The song was partly autobiographical but was also a tribute to his mentor, Bill Pester, who influenced him to adopt the German *Naturmensch* and *Lebensreform* image and philosophy of wearing his hair and beard long and eating vegetarian. This was decades before the Beatles and the counterculture influenced America. Ahbez and his nature buddies influenced celebrity restaurateur Jim Baker when he met them in Topanga Canyon in the late 1950s, and they influenced a whole new generation when they met the flower children of the late 1960s. Ahbez married Anna Jacobson, sister of Al Jacobson, health food pioneer and founder of Garden of Eatin' organic chips—the first packaged blue corn chips, now owned by Hain-Celestial (page 283). Ahbez made a couple more recordings after "Nature Boy" and was said to have been in the studio with Beach Boy Brian Wilson sometime in the days before the legendary *Pet Sounds* and *Smile* albums were recorded. Besides Nat King Cole, "Nature Boy" has been recorded by Frank Sinatra and Celine Dion, and was sung by David Bowie in *Moulin Rouge* (2001).

"The greatest thing you'll ever learn is just to love and be loved in return."

—eden ahbez, "Nature Boy"

Grilled Thai Tofu BBQ Wrap
with Curried Honey Mustard

Makes 4 wraps

A wrap is a creative take-off on the burrito, which first sold in Los Angeles at the El Cholo Restaurant, a Hollywood haunt since the 1930s. The first nonburrito wrap sandwiches appeared at I Love Juicy, a vegan café and juice bar that first opened in the early 1980s. I Love Juicy founder Michael Mandel was once described as an "Einstein" by *Vanity Fair,* and Mandel swears that Madonna once ate there forty days in a row. Rumor has it that Madonna has been to El Cholo as well.

1 jalapeño chile, finely chopped

2 cloves garlic, minced

1 tablespoon chopped fresh cilantro

1 tablespoon sesame oil

½ cup coconut milk, regular or light

2 tablespoons Bragg Liquid Aminos

2 teaspoons sugar

2 teaspoons ground turmeric

2 teaspoons paprika

1 teaspoon ground cumin

1 teaspoon ground coriander

1 teaspoon freshly ground black pepper

16 ounces extra-firm tofu, drained, patted dry, and cut into ½-inch slices

1 red onion, cut into ½-inch slices

Canola cooking spray

4 large flour tortillas

2 ounces alfalfa or sunflower sprouts

4 ounces cucumber, cut into julienne

1 carrot, cut into julienne or grated

CURRIED HONEY MUSTARD

2 tablespoons reserved marinade from the tofu

1 tablespoon Dijon mustard

1 tablespoon white or yellow miso paste

2 teaspoons acacia or orange blossom honey

Blend the jalapeño, garlic, cilantro, oil, coconut milk, liquid aminos, sugar, turmeric, paprika, cumin, coriander, and pepper in a blender or food processor. Reserve 2 tablespoons of the marinade for the sauce. Place the tofu and onion in a shallow pan, pour the marinade over the tofu slices, and turn to coat both sides. Let marinate for 1 to 4 hours before grilling.

While the tofu is marinating, make the mustard: whisk the marinade, mustard, miso, and honey together in a small bowl until smooth.

Heat a nonstick stovetop or electric grill pan over medium-high heat and lightly coat with vegetable cooking spray. Grill the tofu and onion, basting occasionally, and cooking until the tofu is browned on both sides.

Using tongs, flip each tortilla over an open flame until softened. Spread a tablespoon of the mustard over each tortilla and layer with the sprouts, cucumber, carrot, onions, and tofu. Roll up tightly, folding in the outer edges of the tortilla as you go. Cut in half and serve with remaining marinade as a dipping sauce.

Tequila-Lime Chicken Caesar Wrap

Makes 2 wraps

During prohibition, Los Angelinos used to drive down to Tijuana for gambling, legal alcohol, and the Caesar salad made by Caesar Cardini, an Italian immigrant who owned a small hotel in Tijuana. Clark Gable, Jean Harlow, and W. C. Fields were regulars, and as a teenager Julia Child used to drive down for the salad while living in Pasadena. In *What Cooks in Hollywood* (1949), film stars lent their favorite recipes, signatures, and photos to create a cookbook whose proceeds went to disabled American veterans from

World War II. Bob Hope contributed a recipe for Caesar Salad, and the editors claimed it was hard to tell what was more popular in Hollywood, Bob Hope or Caesar salads.

¼ cup tequila

¼ cup fresh lime juice

1 tablespoon sugar

1 tablespoon tamari or soy sauce

1 teaspoon extra-virgin olive oil

1 clove garlic, minced

One 8-ounce boneless, skinless chicken breast

Kosher salt and freshly ground black pepper

Olive oil or olive oil cooking spray

1 heart of romaine, torn into bite-size pieces

2 large flour tortillas

POBLANO CAESAR DRESSING

1 poblano chile, roasted, peeled, and seeded

2 tablespoons white miso paste

1 to 2 cloves garlic, to taste

2 tablespoons fresh lime juice

⅓ cup plain soymilk

¼ cup extra-virgin olive oil

1 teaspoon Worcestershire sauce

⅓ cup grated Parmigiano-Reggiano cheese

Whisk together the tequila, lime juice, sugar, tamari, olive oil, and garlic in a medium bowl. Place the chicken breast in a shallow dish and season each side with salt and pepper. Add the tequila mixture and marinate in the refrigerator for 30 to 60 minutes.

While the chicken is marinating, make the dressing: combine the chile, miso, garlic, lime juice, soymilk, olive oil, and Worcestershire sauce in a blender. Puree until smooth and creamy.

Heat a nonstick stovetop or electric grill pan over medium-high heat and lightly oil or coat with cooking spray. Grill the chicken breast for 10 to 15 minutes, turning 2 to 3 times, until the chicken is browned and reaches an internal temperature of 165°F when tested with an instant-read thermometer.

Remove from the pan and slice the chicken breast on the diagonal. Toss the lettuce with some of the dressing. Using tongs, pass the tortillas over an open flame or on the grill to soften them a bit. Place them on a work surface and top with the tossed romaine and chicken. Roll up burrito-style and serve with additional dressing on the side.

Fried Green Tomato BLT

Makes 2 sandwiches

In the summer, I pick up green tomatoes at the Hollywood Farmers Market, which is just down the street from the Hollywood Roosevelt Hotel, one of the few remaining landmarks that represent Hollywood's golden years. Sid Grauman of Grauman's Chinese Theater was one of the founders back in 1927, when the hotel was built to house East Coast moviemakers and Broadway actors working in Los Angeles. The first Academy Awards ceremony was held in the hotel, and Shirley Temple took her first tap lesson from Bill "Bojangles" Robinson on the hotel's stairway. If you want to experience a bit of old Hollywood's glamorous past, and feel the ghosts of Marilyn Monroe and Montgomery Clift, the Roosevelt is a must. If you want to experience new Hollywood, the Roosevelt is still the place. Since its multimillion-dollar facelift, this historic Hollywood landmark has made a comeback. Lindsay Lohan and Kirsten Dunst have been spotted at the poolside Tropicana Bar and L.A. food critic Irene Virbila says, "The people-watching is so enticing, it's worth the price of a drink."

1 tablespoon olive oil

4 slices turkey bacon

4 slices sourdough or whole-wheat bread

2 romaine lettuce leaves, cut in half

1 recipe Oven-Fried Green Tomatoes (page 214)

SPICY MAYONNAISE

¼ cup low-fat or vegan mayonnaise

2 tablespoons ketchup

¼ to ½ teaspoon hot red pepper sauce, to taste

1 teaspoon chopped fresh chives

Freshly ground black and white pepper to taste

Heat the oil in a 12-inch skillet over medium heat. Add the bacon and cook until browned on both sides, 3 to 4 minutes total. Drain on paper towels.

To make the mayonnaise, in a small bowl whisk the mayonnaise, ketchup, red pepper sauce, and chives together. Season with black and white pepper, to taste.

To assemble the sandwiches, spread some of the mayonnaise on 1 slice of bread and arrange 1 lettuce half on top. Top with the Oven-Fried Green Tomatoes and arrange the bacon over the tomatoes. Top with another lettuce piece, a little more mayo, and the remaining slice of bread. Cut in half and serve immediately.

Grilled Portobello Tacos with Pomegranate Guacamole and Salsa

Serves 4

The first English-language cookbook to include a guacamole recipe was *Fashions in Food in Beverly Hills,* published by the Beverly Hills Woman's Club in 1931. There was one recipe for guacamole and one for "wakimole," contributed by actress Helen Twelvetrees. Will Rodgers wrote the foreword to *Fashions in Food in Beverly Hills* and the many famous recipe contributors included Carole Lombard, Joan Crawford, and Fannie Brice. The guacamole recipe notes that pomegranates were the original fruit used in guacamole.

SALSA

1 pound mixed red and yellow tomatoes, or heirloom tomatoes
when in season

½ cup finely chopped white onion

1 to 2 serrano or jalapeño chiles, to taste, seeded and finely chopped

¼ teaspoon kosher salt

1 tablespoon fresh lime juice

3 tablespoons minced fresh cilantro

POMEGRANATE GUACAMOLE

2 medium avocados, peeled and pitted

2 to 3 teaspoons fresh lime juice, to taste

½ teaspoon kosher salt, or to taste

1 tablespoon chopped fresh cilantro

Seeds from 1 whole pomegranate (or substitute ¼ cup finely
chopped jicama when pomegranates are not in season)

PORTOBELLO TACOS

2 tablespoons olive oil

3 tablespoons fresh lime juice

1 teaspoon paprika

½ teaspoon ground cumin

½ teaspoon dried oregano

1 teaspoon kosher salt

½ teaspoon freshly ground black pepper

1 pound portobello mushrooms, cleaned and stems removed

1 large red bell pepper, seeded and thinly sliced

1 large red onion, halved and cut into ⅓-inch slices

8 corn tortillas

1 romaine lettuce heart, finely shredded

2 ounces cojita cheese or goat's milk farmer cheese, grated

To make the salsa, quarter and seed the tomatoes. Dice the tomatoes and place them in a bowl. Add the onion, chile, salt, lime juice, and cilantro. Taste and add more salt if needed. Refrigerate until ready to use.

To make the guacamole, place the avocados, lime juice, salt, and cilantro in a medium bowl. Mash with a potato masher until well mixed. Adjust the seasonings if necessary. Add half of the pomegranate seeds (use the rest as a garnishing, or to snack on). Refrigerate until ready to use.

To make the tacos, whisk together the oil, lime juice, paprika, cumin, oregano, salt, and pepper in a large bowl. Brush the mushroom caps, bell pepper, and onion with the marinade. Place them in a deep casserole and let marinate for 20 to 30 minutes.

★ The Ashram ★

The food at the Ashram is all vegetarian and organic, and I hear that the taco plate is very popular. *Travel and Leisure* calls the Ashram "asceticism for Hollywood legends and starlets," while *Vogue* calls it the "boot camp for movie stars." Oprah Winfrey, Cindy Crawford, and Julia Roberts have all made it through the Ashram, and rumor has it that this is where Renée Zellweger came to slim down from her role as Bridget Jones. There is no stricter spa regime than the Ashram in Calabasas, which is located about thirty-five minutes outside of Hollywood.

Ashram founder Anne-Marie Bennstrom was a medical student in Sweden before coming to California in 1955 to finish her studies. She told the *Los Angeles Times* in 1969 that when she first arrived in California, she met some "health nuts" who taught her about fruits and nuts, greens, and water. Off she went to live in the jungle of Mexico for six months to "live off nature."

Bennstrom then appeared at the Golden Door, where she was the exercise director back in the late 1950s and early 1960s. In 1965 she opened the Sanctuary in Hollywood, where Mia Farrow, Peggy Lipton, and Lucille Ball came for yoga and exercise classes. In 1974 she opened the Ashram, which thirty years later is still the toughest spa regime going. Besides shaping up most of Hollywood, Bennstrom was the brains behind the ThighMaster and the Original Body Ball, which she developed from all her years of training and fitness.

Heat an outdoor grill, electric grill, or stovetop grill pan. Cook the vegetables on the grill until tender and slightly charred on the outside, turning once, and brushing with any remaining marinade. Cool the mushroom caps slightly and cut on the diagonal into ½-inch-wide slices.

Using tongs, warm the tortillas on the grill or over a flame on the stovetop. Fill with the grilled vegetables, shredded lettuce, and cheese. Top with the guacamole and salsa.

The Swinger

Serves 6

Restaurateur Jim Baker was hanging out in Topanga Canyon with Gypsy Boots and the Nature Boys in the 1950s. Their food philosophy must have influenced Jim, who in 1957 opened the Aware Inn, whose first customer was Greta Garbo. In *My Dinner of Herbs* (2003), Efrem Zimbalist Jr. reminisces about his life and his long and incredible career, which included the Broadway stage, many classic films, and two much-loved long-running television series, *77 Sunset Strip* and *The FBI*. He also includes a story about the Aware Inn, where he once spotted the reclusive Greta Garbo. He told me about the delicious food prepared at the restaurant and said it was much better than most "health food" in those days. One of the dishes was The Swinger, a ground beef patty enhanced with peppers, onions, and cheese. My version uses ground turkey and adds pickled jalapeños. I like to use goat cheddar, but feel free to use any cheese of your liking.

I pound ground turkey

⅔ cup minced onion

⅔ cup diced red or yellow bell pepper

I (15-ounce) can peeled tomatoes, drained and finely chopped

2 tablespoons pitted green olives, chopped

I to 2 tablespoons chopped pickled jalapeño (optional)

I cup grated cheddar cheese—goat, dairy, or soy

¾ teaspoon kosher salt

½ teaspoon freshly ground black pepper

6 whole-grain hamburger buns

In a medium bowl mix the ground turkey, onion, bell pepper, tomato, olives, jalapeño, cheese, salt, and pepper. Shape into six equal patties. Broil for about 4 to 5 minutes on each side, or until internal temperature is 170°F. Serve immediately on toasted buns with sliced tomatoes, onion, lettuce, alfalfa sprouts, pickles, ketchup, and mustard.

7

The Secret Garden

SALADS AND DRESSINGS

For more than a hundred years, Southern California has been the culinary center of the salad world, with its abundance of fresh vegetables to create them with. Film stars in the 1920s and '30s played an important role in discovering and popularizing legends like Caesar Cardini, since stars such as Clark Gable and Jean Harlow drove down to Tijuana just to have one of his famous Caesar salads. Since the 1920s, gossip columnists have reported on what the stars were eating, noting that Joan Crawford, Marlene Dietrich, and even W. C. Fields had green salads for lunch. Fields ate his with a glass of milk and a couple of graham crackers. Studio commissaries went as far as to name salads after their stars, and then took those titles away when the stars left the studios. In 1956, producer, writer, and director Nunnally Johnson (*How to Marry a Millionaire, The Dirty Dozen,* and *The Three Faces of Eve*) told Art Buchwald that the highest honor a movie star at Fox could receive was to have a salad or plate of eggs named after him. Studio publicity departments gave out stars' favorite salad recipes to national magazines and newspapers, which brought the healthy eating habits of Hollywood to the American public.

Hollywood gave rise to more salads than just the Caesar and Cobb. The 1960s produced the Chinese Chicken Salad, which was made popular at Madame Wu's in Santa Monica. When Michael McCarty opened Michael's in 1979, Los Angeles had its first taste of Chez Panisse–style organic greens with warm goat cheese. When Wolfgang Puck put the warm goat-cheese salad on the menu at the celebrity-filled Spago in Hollywood, it became a standard like the Caesar and the Cobb, and today is seen on restaurant menus all over the country.

Grapefruit, Orange, Avocado, and Sunflower Sprout Salad

Serves 3 to 4

In 1929, the Hollywood Diet, or 18-Day Diet, was the popular reducing regimen of the day. Lunch and dinner included a half a grapefruit, a small serving of protein, and an occasional slice of Melba toast or tomato. Socialites and actresses all over Hollywood were on the diet, and *Motion Picture* magazine showed a photo of a miserable-looking Joe Cobb (who starred in the long-running *Our Gang* series) eating grapefruit, lettuce, and a single egg. Grapefruit is much better in salads like this one, which is also great with lobster, which you got to eat for lunch on day twelve of the Hollywood Diet.

VINAIGRETTE

2 tablespoons golden balsamic vinegar

¼ cup avocado or orange blossom honey

¼ teaspoon kosher salt

⅛ teaspoon freshly ground white pepper

1 tablespoon poppy seeds

1 teaspoon dry mustard

1 shallot, minced

★ The Hollywood Diet ★

18-Day Diet

Reducing Hollywood Pounds And To Hysteria

HOLLYWOOD has only one topic of conversation these days. It is not the latest scandal or the Equity situation or the talkies or the newcomers from Broadway. Obesity has taken the place of infidelity as a subject for gossip, money, that theme of absorbing interest in the movie colony, has dropped from table talk and pounds have taken the place of pence on the lips of the stars. The eighteen-day diet is the nine days' wonder of Hollywood.

Just where it came from seems uncertain. Just who it was started the stars to counting their calories no one knows. The story goes, however, that a certain stage actress paid fifteen hundred dollars to the scientist at the head of a famous sanitarium for this marvelous diet, guaranteed to rid faithful followers of a pound a day. On her return to Broadway, svelte and slim, she gave the diet to a friend, and the friend came to Hollywood to work in a talkie, and passed it on. Now half of the stars are eating celery and grapefruit, with the devout expression of one performing a sacred ceremonial.

The eighteen-day diet has spread over the entire movie colony. Eddie Brandstatter, host of the Montmartre, has printed it on

Josephine Dunn, at the right, wonders if she can eat that egg, two pieces of toast and four slices of cucumber. And, Julia Faye, below, wears the smile of the twelfth day, when she gets a chop

International

Russell Ball

It doesn't look as if Olive Borden, above, would need to extend her diet over the entire span of eighteen days. But Joe Cobb, at the left, is likely to be in for a year or so if he wants to be the sylph of "Our Gang"

the back of his menu cards, and his waiters need no prompting when a patron orders "The seventh day lunch, please" or "The tenth day dinner." Tourists, lingering in spots where the great congregate, are amazed to see two screen sheiks, meeting, wrap their coats about their middles and thrust two fists under their bagging vests like some mystic sign, while the lovely film sirens with them chant the Ritual of the Reducing. "Seven and a half pounds in six days","I've only been on it three and I've lost five."

C. S. Bull

Hollywood hostesses, finding their caviar, creamed lobster and parfaits untouched by half of their guests, are serving hard-boiled eggs and spinach as formal fare, and the table talk has become simplified to a comparison of ounces and diets. If one's dinner partner isn't on a diet, he will be the next day. The cattiest remark overheard in Hollywood nowadays is, "She says she's lost fourteen pounds, but my dear, she doesn't show it." The murkiest scandal deals with gustatory sins, "Molly may say she's sticking to the diet, but last night Tony and I went into the Brown Derby and she was eating a chocolate sundae in a corner by herself. Can you imagine!" The tenderest love-making—one supposes—runs like this, "Darling, how slender you are! I would diet for you." Hollywood has always been a hotbed of freak diets. Here the lamb-chop-and-pine-
(Continued on page 107)

Stars following the Hollywood Diet,
Motion Picture *magazine, 1929.*

The first best-selling diet book in America, *Diet and Health with a Key to the Calories,* was written by Los Angeles–based Dr. Lulu Hunt Peters in 1918, and sold over two million copies. The book introduced the concept of counting calories, and Dr. Peters claimed she lost fifty pounds counting calories (1,200 a day), along with a daily workout of two women's suffrage rallies.

But it was the 18-Day Diet, or Hollywood Diet, that Hollywood claimed as its own. Sometimes known as the Grapefruit Diet, the Hollywood Diet made the cover of the fan magazine *Motion Picture* in 1929. The cover read "The Stars and the Hollywood Diet," and "It's Reducing Hollywood to Pounds and Hysteria." The story claimed the diet had spread all over the movie colony and was the only topic of conversation. Eddie Brandstatter, host of Montmarte (the celebrity hangout of the day), had the diet printed on the back of the menu, so when patrons ordered "seventh-day lunch," or "tenth-day dinner," the waiter knew what they wanted. Hollywood hostesses were serving the diet as formal fare instead of "caviar and creamed lobster," and dinner conversation was all about dieting. The writer of the article told the readers that if they were tempted to stray from the diet, just whisper the magic words, "What the stars can do, I can do."

The crash of 1929 most likely quieted down the 18-Day Diet revolution, but Hollywood and the rest of America continued to have a passion for dieting. Judy Mazel devised the Beverly Hills Diet when she was diagnosed with a thyroid problem and incurably fat. Her own experimentation led her to create the diet, which was #1 on the *New York Times* bestseller list for eighteen weeks. Judy's living room was her office, and it became like the red carpet on Oscar night, as her clients included big Hollywood names such as Jack Nicholson, Liza Minnelli, and Jodie Foster. *The New Beverly Hills Diet* broke every record in publishing history by selling more copies in a shorter period of time than any book published before.

Weight Watchers, Sugar Busters, the Fat Flush Plan, Eat Right for Your Type, Atkins, the Zone, the South Beach Diet, and Nikki Haskell's Star Diet all have their famous fans, and the basic principles of most of these diets can be traced back to the teachings of the original health pioneers.

1 tablespoon flaxseed oil
2 tablespoons sesame oil (not toasted)

SALAD
6 ounces (about 3 cups) sunflower sprouts
2 ounces (about 1 cup) radish or alfalfa sprouts
2 small grapefruits, peeled, sectioned, and seeds removed
1 orange, peeled, sectioned, and seeds removed
1 large or 2 small avocados, peeled, pitted, and sliced lengthwise
¼ cup toasted sunflower seeds

To make the dressing, whisk together the vinegar, honey, salt, pepper, poppy seeds, dry mustard, and shallot in a small bowl. Slowly whisk in the flaxseed and sesame oils until emulsified.

Arrange the sunflower and alfalfa sprouts on individual serving plates. Top with the grapefruit, orange, and avocado slices. Drizzle the dressing over each salad and sprinkle with the sunflower seeds.

Tandoori Shrimp Salad with Baby Spinach, Red Onions, and Chutney Dressing

Serves 4

*L*oretta Young, Paul Newman, and Natalie Wood were all fans of Alan Hooker's Ranch House restaurant in Ojai, about ninety minutes north of Los Angeles. Hooker was known for his annual Indian curry weekends, and in the late 1960s, he would bring spices from London and grind his own blends. His numerous cookbooks, starting with *Alan Hooker's New Approach to Cooking* (1966), all included Indian dishes. Fortunately, we don't have to travel to London to purchase Indian spices—they can be found at Indian grocery stores or bought online (see Resources).

Paul Newman once said, "Cuisine is cuisine, but the Ranch House is original."

TANDOORI SHRIMP SALAD

2 teaspoons chat masala

1 teaspoon fenugreek powder

½ teaspoon ground coriander

1 teaspoon mango powder

1 teaspoon kosher salt

½ teaspoon crushed red chile flakes

½ teaspoon freshly ground black pepper

2 cloves garlic, minced

2 shallots, minced (about ¼ cup)

2 tablespoons minced fresh ginger

¼ cup fresh lime juice

3 tablespoons sesame oil (not toasted)

1 pound raw shrimp (16 to 20), peeled and deveined

Canola oil spray or canola oil

5 ounces prewashed baby spinach

2 large tomatoes, cut into eighths

1 hothouse cucumber, peeled and cut into thin rounds

½ sweet red onion, halved stem to root and sliced paper-thin

2 teaspoons chopped fresh cilantro

½ cup toasted, salted pistachios

YOGURT-CHUTNEY DRESSING

1 cup plain goat's, soy, or cow's yogurt

¼ cup light mayonnaise

2 tablespoons fresh lime juice

¼ teaspoon ground cumin

1 teaspoon black mustard seeds

1 teaspoon mild honey such as clover

2 tablespoons mango chutney or tomato chutney, either homemade (page 58),
 or store-bought

In a medium bowl combine the chat masala, fenugreek powder, coriander, mango powder, salt, chile flakes, pepper, garlic, shallots, ginger, lime juice,

★ Alan Hooker (1902–1993) ★

It has been said that if Alice Waters is the mother of California cuisine, Alan Hooker is the grandfather. Hooker came to Ojai, California, in the early 1950s to be near his teacher, J. Krishnamurti. Before opening Ranch House restaurant in 1956, Alan had been a vaudeville performer, a jazz pianist, and a pie baker. Alan planted a kitchen garden at the restaurant, and was the first to serve what we now call California cuisine in a restaurant setting. The Ranch House had its share of celebrity diners, but the real star was Hooker's homemade breads, fusion-style dishes, and fresh garden salads, sometimes tossed with a dressing made from five different geranium leaves. Rumor has it that before Wolfgang Puck opened Spago, he used to drive up to Ojai to eat at the Ranch House and chat with Alan about food and cooking.

and sesame oil. Add the shrimp and marinate in the refrigerator for at least 30 minutes or up to 2 hours.

While the shrimp is marinating, make the dressing: blend the yogurt, mayonnaise, lime juice, cumin, mustard seeds, honey, and chutney in a blender until smooth and creamy.

Heat a grill pan or electric grill and lightly coat it with cooking spray or oil. Grill the shrimp for 2 minutes on each side, or until pink and just firm—don't overcook.

In a large bowl, toss the spinach with some of the dressing and arrange on plates. Top with the tomatoes, cucumber, and onion, followed by the shrimp. Garnish with the cilantro and pistachios and serve with additional dressing.

Asparagus and Tofu Salad with Daikon and White Miso Dressing

Serves about 4

T. A. Van Gundy was the first Westerner to introduce soy foods on the Pacific Coast after learning about them at the Oriental Exhibit of the 1915 World's Fair in San Francisco. He was the first to make and can tofu, one of the original ways to purchase it before mass production of tofu began in the late 1950s. Originally, fresh tofu was available only in Asian markets, where it was kept in tin boxes on the floor and packed into leaky individual trays when purchased. These days, I prefer to use prebaked tofu cubes or slices, usually found in the refrigerated section of the grocery or natural foods store. If you want to bake and season plain tofu for this recipe, you can use the recipe for Grilled Thai Tofu BBQ Wrap (page 115).

ASPARAGUS AND TOFU SALAD

Vegetable cooking spray

1 tablespoon peanut or sesame oil

2 tablespoons grated fresh ginger

1 clove garlic, minced

8 ounces fresh shiitake mushrooms, stems removed and wiped clean, cut into
    ½-inch slices

8 ounces prebaked seasoned tofu, cut into bite-size pieces

1 bunch asparagus, tough ends trimmed, sliced on the diagonal

1 bunch green onions, white and most of green parts, sliced on the diagonal

Freshly ground black pepper

1 tablespoon tamari

1 small head napa cabbage, shredded

4-inch piece daikon radish, peeled and cut into thin matchsticks

2 medium carrots, cut into thin matchsticks

½ cup roasted cashews

DRESSING

1 tablespoon finely grated fresh ginger

3 tablespoons white miso paste

¼ cup unseasoned rice vinegar

2 tablespoons mild honey

½ cup plain soymilk

½ cup canola or sesame oil (not toasted)

1 tablespoon toasted sesame oil

Spray a wok or skillet with cooking spray, add the peanut oil, and heat over medium-high heat. Add the ginger and garlic and stir-fry for 2 to 3 minutes. Add the mushrooms and cook until tender and browned. Add the tofu and cook for 2 minutes more. Add the asparagus and green onions and cook for about 40 seconds. Season with pepper to taste and add tamari.

To make the dressing, combine the ginger, miso, rice vinegar, honey, soymilk, oil, and sesame oil in a blender and puree until smooth and creamy.

In a large bowl toss the cabbage, daikon, and carrots together with some of the dressing and place on individual plates or on 1 large platter. Arrange the tofu mixture on top of the salad. Garnish with the cashews and serve with additional dressing.

Chopped Salad with Avocado Green Goddess

Makes 4 servings

Green Goddess Dressing was named after the play *The Green Goddess,* featuring British actor George Arliss, who starred in the 1930 film version of the play. The play was such a hit during its run in San Francisco in the 1920s that the Palace Hotel named a dressing after it. If Hollywood had a "green" goddess, it would have to be actress Gloria Swanson, who was a promoter of natural and organic foods way back in the early days of Hollywood. Gloria was known for carrying avocados in her handbag so she would have something to eat at social and business functions.

SALAD

1 (13.75-ounce) can artichoke hearts, rinsed, drained, and chopped

Kernels from 1 ear of corn

4 ounces thin green beans, cut in ¼-inch pieces (about ½ cup)

4 ounces peeled baby carrots (about ½ cup), diced

2 medium tomatoes, diced (about ½ cup)

1 small head radicchio, finely chopped

1 heart of romaine, outer leaves removed, finely chopped

8 ounces turkey salami, preferably nitrate-free

¾ cup chopped Manchego cheese

AVOCADO GREEN GODDESS DRESSING

1 cup light mayonnaise

1 ripe Hass avocado, peeled, pitted, and flesh scooped out

3 tablespoons tarragon or white balsamic vinegar

1 tablespoon fresh lemon juice

⅓ cup loosely packed flat-leaf parsley

Gloria Swanson—Hollywood's Green Goddess

Gloria Swanson was the highest paid and most popular, influential star of the 1920s. She starred in countless films, but is best known for her role as Norma Desmond in *Sunset Boulevard* (1950), a film she made near the end of her career.

She was also a sculptor, had her own clothing company, and at one point created an all-natural line of cosmetics called Essence of Nature. Along with being a successful businesswoman, she was an activist for the health food movement. She was known to say that most of her groceries went on her face, not in her mouth.

She lobbied for organic foods in Washington, D.C., and in 1952 was the guest speaker at the Congressional Wives Club. Although the ladies were expecting some "Hollywood dish," Swanson lectured on the hormones being injected into chickens and the pesticides being sprayed on crops all over the country. She asked the wives to go home and tell their husbands to encourage the government to stop the use of

Gloria Swanson, on the cover of a 1961 book by J. I. Rodale.
(COURTESY OF RODALE PRESS)

pesticides and ban the use of cyclamates. We can also thank her every time we buy organic brown rice at the supermarket, since she lobbied for more farmland to be allocated for growing organic rice.

In *Swanson on Swanson* (1980), she recalls her career, many marriages, and her well-known affair with Joseph Kennedy. She talks about her lifelong interest in nutrition and natural foods, telling of her first visit in 1927 to see Dr. Henry Bieler, who taught her that your body is a direct result of what you eat and what you don't eat. Even when she dined with Kennedy, she would have her Bieler meal of steamed green vegetables, rice, and dark bread.

Gloria's last husband was William Dufty, author of *Lady Sings the Blues* (1973), *You Are All Sanpaku* (1965), and *Sugar Blues* (1975), a bestseller that Dufty and Swanson promoted worldwide. So the next time you curl up to watch that screen classic *Sunset Boulevard,* honor Gloria with a meal of Dr. Bieler's Broth (page 88), steamed vegetables, and brown rice.

1 shallot, minced

2 green onions, both white and green parts, chopped

1 tablespoon capers

1 teaspoon chopped fresh tarragon

⅛ teaspoon freshly ground black pepper

In a large salad bowl combine the artichoke hearts, corn, green beans, baby carrots, tomatoes, radicchio, romaine, turkey salami, and cheese.

To make the dressing, combine the mayonnaise, avocado, vinegar, lemon juice, parsley, shallot, green onions, capers, tarragon, and pepper in a food processor or a blender. Blend until smooth and creamy.

Toss the salad with the dressing and serve.

Aware Inn Salad with Lemon-Herb Dressing

Serves 4 to 6

Jim Baker learned about healthful living from Paul Bragg and Jack LaLanne, and his quest for health and a movie audition led him to Hollywood in 1950. In 1957 he opened his first restaurant, called the Aware Inn, a restaurant where people would be "aware" of what they put into their bodies. Actor Steve McQueen used to have daily meals flown to him on location from the Inn, and customers included actors Warren Beatty, Paul Newman, and Rock Hudson. This salad was also served at Jim's later restaurant, the Source, which was originally going to be called the Salad Bowl.

AWARE INN SALAD

1 head romaine lettuce, outer leaves removed, torn into bite-size pieces

1 cup finely grated carrots

1 cup finely grated beets

1 hothouse cucumber, thinly sliced

2 ribs celery, finely chopped

★ Jim Baker (1922–1975) ★

Jim Baker was born on July 4th, 1922, in Cincinnati, Ohio. When he was fourteen, he had a health crisis that led him to the teachings of Paul Bragg, which led him to open the Baker Studio of Body Culture, called Baker's Gym before World War II. In 1957, Baker opened perhaps the first all-organic fine dining restaurant in America, called the Aware Inn. Everything was made from his recipes, and the salad dressings were created by Rosa Cardini, the daughter of Caesar Cardini, inventor of the Caesar Salad. Jim pioneered the use of organic fruits and vegetables and used only Shelton Farms free-range poultry. The restaurant critic of the *Los Angeles Times* frequently praised the Aware Inn, and the gossip columns reported on the goings-on at the restaurant, such as Oscar parties where all-organic food was served. (And I thought I was the first.)

When Baker opened the Source in 1969, he drew in the rock crowd as well as the movie people. It wasn't unusual to see Bob Dylan, Joni Mitchell, Donovan, or Warren Beatty having lunch on the patio. Everyone who has eaten there says that there has been nothing like it since. It wasn't just the food—Baker was a celebrity himself, and he had a flair for creating an environment as captivating and enticing as the Hollywood scene.

Baker met Kundalini yoga master Yogi Bhajan through Bhajan's student Gabrielle Barrett, who helped him open the Source. Once Jim started embracing yoga and meditation, the Source became part ashram and part yoga studio, and Jim became a spiritual teacher. Jim taught yoga on the patio every Sunday and eventually acquired his own following. It was the role he was always meant to play, a part much bigger than the Tarzan part he had auditioned for when he first came to Los Angeles. The Source was immortalized in Woody Allen's Academy Award–winning film *Annie Hall* (1977). In the film, Allen makes fun of California health food when the character Alvy meets Annie at a natural food café, filmed on the restaurant's patio. He tells the white-robed waitress, "I'm going to have the alfalfa sprouts and, uh, a plate of mashed yeast."

Jim was always ahead of his time, and sold the Source in 1974, moving with his family of followers to Hawaii, where he died hang gliding one year later. Damian Paul, who managed the Source in the early 1970s, carries on the Source legend at Hawaii's first certified organic foods store, also called the Source, located on the island of Oahu. The Source will always be remembered for its good food and even better vibes.

1 cup finely shredded red cabbage

2 plum tomatoes, cut into quarters

1 ounce alfalfa sprouts

¼ cup raw sunflower seeds

¼ cup raw pine nuts

1 avocado, peeled, pitted, sliced, and sprinkled with fresh lemon juice

LEMON-HERB DRESSING

3 tablespoons fresh lemon juice

1 tablespoon red wine vinegar

½ teaspoon dry mustard

¾ teaspoon lemon-pepper seasoning

¼ teaspoon dry Italian herbs

⅛ teaspoon granulated garlic

1 teaspoon Dijon mustard

¼ cup plus 2 tablespoons extra-virgin olive oil

In a large bowl, or on individual plates, layer the salad ingredients, starting with the romaine.

To make the dressing, in a small bowl combine the lemon juice, vinegar, mustard, lemon-pepper seasoning, herbs, garlic, and mustard. Slowly whisk in the oil until emulsified. Drizzle the salad with the dressing.

Turmeric-Seared Pears with Mâche, Goat Blue, and Spiced Almonds

Serves 4

In 1975, Richard Simmons opened the Anatomy Asylum, located in a warehouse section in Beverly Hills. In those days legendary celebrity trainer Kim Lee ran the gym while Richard taught the beginners classes and ran the adjoining health food cafeteria called Ruffage. Ruffage served fresh juices, protein drinks, quiches, and a full salad bar—the first ever in a gym.

Ruffage salad fans included Cher, Diana Ross, Paul Newman, and Barbra Streisand. I had so much fun catering parties for Richard, whose sincere mission to help others get in shape inspires me to this day. Richard still teaches classes at his studio, Slimmons, in Beverly Hills, and his books, diet plans, and videos have helped thousands lose weight and stay in shape. One day, I will go take a class from Richard, but until then I will eat salads like this one, which are full of Ruffage.

SALAD

2 teaspoons canola oil

½ cup almonds

¼ teaspoon cayenne pepper

¼ teaspoon ground coriander

¼ teaspoon ground cumin

¼ teaspoon plus a pinch of kosher salt

1 tablespoon unsalted butter

1 teaspoon ground turmeric

2 teaspoons wildflower honey

2 small to medium Bosc pears, peeled, cored, and cut into ½-inch wedges

4 ounces mâche or other salad greens

4 ounces goat blue or other blue cheese, crumbled

Freshly ground black pepper

VINAIGRETTE

¼ cup golden balsamic vinegar

2 teaspoons wildflower honey

¼ teaspoon kosher salt

½ cup extra-virgin olive oil

Freshly ground black pepper

Heat the oil in a 12-inch skillet over medium-high heat. Cook the almonds, stirring frequently, until golden brown. Remove from the pan to a small bowl and toss with the cayenne, coriander, cumin, and salt. Spread the nuts out on a plate and let cool.

Heat the butter in a large nonstick skillet over medium-high heat. When the butter is melted and sizzling, add the turmeric, swirl the pan, and let sizzle for 5 to 10 seconds, until darkened, then add the honey.

Add the pear slices in a single layer, season with a pinch of salt, and cook, turning once, until lightly browned, about 3 minutes. Transfer the pears to a plate.

To make the vinaigrette, combine the vinegar, honey, and salt. Slowly whisk in the oil until emulsified, and season with pepper to taste.

Toss the mâche with some of the goat cheese and some of the vinaigrette. Season with salt and pepper to taste. Top with the pears, almonds, and remaining cheese.

★ California Cuisine ★

In 1971, Alice Waters opened Chez Panisse and gave birth to California cuisine. It wasn't just brown rice and sprouts; it was a conscious cuisine, based on using organic and artisanal ingredients from local sources. In Los Angeles, Michael McCarty followed suit with Michael's in 1979, and Wolfgang Puck and Barbara Lazaroff opened Spago in 1982. Along with warm goat cheese salad, Spago popularized designer pizza, topped with everything from wild mushrooms to smoked salmon. Even before they opened the restaurant, critics were writing about Spago. On opening night the parking lot was filled with Rolls Royces and there was an immediate two-week waiting list. Every night at Spago was a Hollywood party, and even the vegetarian plate was a work of art, filled with creatively cooked organic vegetables from the Chino's family Vegetable Shop in Rancho Sante Fe. I was so inspired by the food at Spago that I completely changed the menu at the Golden Temple, where I was the chef. The opening of Spago changed the cooking and dining of Los Angeles forever. Since then, the Farmers Market of Los Angeles has been filled with restaurant chefs, private chefs, and home cooks buying the very best organic produce available.

Cucumber Pasta with Cashew Truffle Cream and Tomato Tartar

Serves 4

In the 1920s, thousands of Los Angelinos flocked to the church of evangelist Aimee Semple McPherson, who was a featured performer on various radio stations. Her story was so legendary that a movie was made about her life, *The Disappearance of Aimee* (1976), with Bette Davis and Faye Dunaway. Rumor had it that her private mountain retreat was located in Topanga Canyon, now the site of the Inn of the Seventh Ray, one of the remaining New Age–style restaurants in Los Angeles. Angja Aditi, once the raw chef at the Inn of the Seventh Ray, now runs the Nite Moon Cafe at Golden Bridge Yoga Center in Hollywood. The inspiration for this salad came from a memorable meal prepared by Angja.

¼ cup raw cashew butter

1 tablespoon fresh lemon juice

1 teaspoon white truffle oil

4 tablespoons water

½ teaspoon kosher salt

Pinch of freshly ground white pepper

2 heirloom or other tomatoes, peeled, seeded and finely chopped

Pinch of freshly ground black pepper

1 teaspoon extra-virgin olive oil

2 tablespoons finely chopped fresh basil

One 12-inch-long hothouse cucumber, peeled, cut lengthwise, and seeded

In a small bowl whisk together the cashew butter, lemon juice, truffle oil, water, ¼ teaspoon of the salt, and white pepper until smooth and creamy.

In a small bowl toss the tomatoes, remaining salt, black pepper, olive oil, and basil.

Cut the cucumber into strips two inches long and ¼ inch wide to make the "pasta."

In a medium bowl toss the cucumber "pasta" with the cashew sauce. Place on a serving plate and garnish with the tomato mixture. You can serve family-style or divide among 4 plates.

★ Raw, Raw, Raw ★

Raw food guru Arnold Erhet came from Germany to Los Angeles in 1914 to search for new fruits. His books *Rational Fasting* and the *Mucusless Diet* have been in print for sixty-five years and his teachings revamped the raw food movement in the surf and countercultures of the late 1960s and '70s. Erhet's teachings are still part of the raw food movement that is so popular today.

Raw food dining arrived in Los Angeles in 1917 when Vera and John Richter came to town and opened Eutropheon, the first raw food restaurant in America. The Richters pioneered solar baking, dehydrated vegetable seasoning, and the making of raw cakes, pies, and candies. The Eutropheon cafeterias were open for over twenty-five years, and by the 1940s the dining room sat 350. John gave lectures at the restaurant, and from those talks compiled a book called *Nature—The Healer* (1936). Vera eventually compiled her recipes and self-published a small booklet called *Mrs. Richter's Cook-less Book, with Scientific Food Chart* (1925). It was the first raw food cookbook published of its kind, and recipes for Bean Sprout Salad (was she the first to serve sprouts in salads?), Spanish Relish (cucumber, bell pepper, tomato, onion, and nasturtium leaves), and Beauty Salad were just a few of the innovative recipes in this little book. In 1941, *California Health News* magazine reported that visitors to the restaurant included tourists from many states and that Leopold Stokowski (*Fantasia* conductor) and Greta Garbo "rejoiced in the vital foods there." Vera went on to say, "Artists and other professionals have made up a large proportion of our clientele." The restaurant and raw foods were so popular that in 1932, the *Los Angeles Times* reported that a raw food club was formed called The Trophers. The Trophers had thousands of members, who maintained clubrooms and weekly meetings, published a weekly paper, and spent every weekend together hiking, swimming, or sunbathing.

Actor Woody Harrelson, whose now-defunct raw food restaurant and oxygen bar O2 revived the Los Angeles raw food scene in the 1990s, inspired Roxanne Klein to try a raw diet. Roxanne, who became the Charlie Trotter of live foods, took vegetables, fruits, and nuts to an entirely new level at her now-defunct restaurant, Roxanne's, in northern California. In Hollywood, raw food delivery and packaged foods is the latest trend and a huge variety can be found at Erewhon, a natural food market in West Hollywood, where you might rub shopping carts with Brad Pitt, Madonna, or Gwyneth Paltrow.

Grilled Figs with Arugula, Humboldt Fog Goat Cheese, and Pine Nuts with Pomegranate Dressing

Serves 4

Built in the middle of a fig orchard in 1887, Hollywood has had a close connection with the fruit. Hollywood health gurus have advocated the eating of fresh and dried figs, and fig recipes are found in early Los Angeles cookbooks dating back to 1881. The fig orchard is long gone, but perfectly ripe figs can be found at the Hollywood Farmers Market from mid-June to September. I served this salad at a photo shoot by Karl Lagerfeld, one of the most exciting people I have ever met.

SALAD

⅓ cup pine nuts

2 teaspoons extra-virgin olive oil

6 fresh Black Mission figs, cut in half

1 tablespoon balsamic vinegar mixed with 2 teaspoons honey

4 ounces arugula leaves

4 ounces Humboldt Fog goat cheese, crumbled

POMEGRANATE DRESSING

¾ cup pomegranate juice

¼ cup balsamic vinegar

2 tablespoons fresh lemon juice

¼ cup extra-virgin olive oil

1 tablespoon Dijon mustard

Kosher salt and freshly ground black pepper

Heat a cast-iron skillet over medium-high heat and dry-roast the pine nuts until lightly browned and fragrant. Remove from skillet and cool.

Heat the oil in the same skillet or a grill pan over medium-high heat. Grill the figs cut side down, 2 to 3 minutes each side. Add the vinegar-honey mixture and cook another 30 to 40 seconds, just until the figs and vinegar caramelize.

To make the dressing, boil the pomegranate juice and vinegar in a 1-quart saucepan for 5 to 7 minutes, or until thickened and reduced by a third.

In a small bowl whisk the pomegranate reduction with lemon juice, oil, and mustard. Season with salt and pepper to taste.

In a salad bowl toss the arugula with some of the pomegranate dressing and place on individual plates. Place the cheese and the figs on top of the salad plates, scatter with the pine nuts, and drizzle with additional dressing.

Seared Tempeh Cobb Salad

Serves 4 to 6

The Brown Derby restaurant was so much more than its famous Cobb Salad, which was thrown together one night by owner Bob Cobb while searching the refrigerator for a snack. Herbert K. Somborn, a well-known gourmet who happened to be Gloria Swanson's husband, conceived the restaurant in 1925. The concept was simple: Serve fine American food made with the freshest and finest ingredients available, have it prepared by skilled chefs, create a unique atmosphere, and open in a great location—all of that over fifty years before the opening of Spago. According to Hedda Hopper, the Derby served trout from actor Noah Berry's mountain streams and the potatoes were grown on Wally Ford's ranch. Corn came from the Clark Gable–Carole Lombard acres, and the broccoli was from the Robert Taylor–Barbara Stanwyck farm. Only in early Hollywood could you eat from the farms of the famous.

COBB SALAD

1 tablespoon avocado oil or canola oil

1 shallot, finely chopped

8 ounces tempeh, crumbled

⅛ teaspoon smoked or regular paprika

⅛ teaspoon cayenne pepper

⅛ teaspoon chili powder

½ teaspoon kosher salt

¼ teaspoon freshly ground black pepper

1 teaspoon Worcestershire sauce

1 tablespoon Bragg Liquid Aminos

1 bunch watercress, finely chopped

1 heart of romaine, finely chopped

1 small bunch chicory, finely chopped

1 ripe avocado, peeled, pitted, and diced

2 hard-boiled eggs, peeled and diced

8 ounces prebaked tofu, cut into ½-inch cubes

2 ripe tomatoes, diced

4 ounces good-quality Roquefort or blue cheese, crumbled (optional)

2 tablespoons finely chopped fresh chives

DRESSING

¼ cup water

¼ cup red wine vinegar

1 tablespoon fresh lemon juice

1 teaspoon sugar

½ teaspoon kosher salt

¾ teaspoon vegetarian Worcestershire sauce

¼ teaspoon dried mustard

1 small shallot, finely chopped

2 tablespoons white miso paste

½ cup extra-virgin olive oil

⅓ cup avocado oil

To make the salad, heat the oil in a 12-inch skillet over medium-high heat. Add the shallot and cook until it begins to soften, about 2 minutes. Add the crumbled tempeh and cook an additional 2 minutes. Add the paprika, cayenne, chili powder, salt, pepper, Worcestershire sauce, and liquid aminos. Cook, stirring frequently, until the tempeh is coated with the seasonings and lightly browned, 3 to 4 minutes. Remove from skillet and let cool.

To make the dressing, combine the water, vinegar, lemon juice, sugar, salt, Worcestershire sauce, mustard, shallot, and miso in a blender. Start the blender and slowly add the oils through the top. Blend until smooth and emulsified.

Arrange the salad greens in a large bowl or on individual plates. Arrange the tempeh, avocado, eggs, tofu, tomatoes, and cheese in strips across the salad. Sprinkle the chives over the salad and serve with the dressing.

Arugula with Blood Oranges, Dates, and Walnuts

Serves 4 to 6

"Oranges for Health, California for Wealth" was the publicity slogan that brought fortune- and health-seekers to Southern California in the late 1880s. The Southern Pacific Railroad sent its first shipment of oranges from Southern California to St. Louis in the 1870s. Eventually the citrus growers became one cooperative, and by 1905 they had adopted the name California Fruit Exchange, later known as Sunkist. In the late 1920s, Hollywood's gossip queen Louella Parsons hosted a weekly radio program sponsored by Sunkist on which she interviewed movie stars. Blood oranges have been growing in California only for the last thirty-five years. They are particularly good in this salad, but when they're not in season you can substitute navel oranges.

SALAD

½ cup chopped walnuts

5 ounces prewashed baby arugula

½ red onion, thinly sliced

2 medium blood or navel oranges, peeled and sectioned, seeds removed

2 ounces dates, pitted and chopped

6 to 8 large thin prosciutto slices, preferably nitrate-free

DRESSING

2 tablespoons orange juice

2 tablespoons lemon juice

1 teaspoon honey

1 tablespoon Dijon mustard

¼ cup olive oil

1 tablespoon walnut oil

½ teaspoon kosher salt

Freshly ground black pepper to taste

Silent film star Mary Pickford drinking orange juice made with Sunkist fruit and juicer. (COURTESY OF SUNKIST PHOTO ARCHIVES)

Preheat the oven to 325°F. Spread the walnuts in 1 layer on a baking sheet. Roast for about 10 minutes, stirring once so they toast evenly. Remove from the baking sheet and set aside to cool.

To make the dressing, in a small bowl combine the orange juice, lemon juice, honey, mustard, salt, and pepper. Whisk in the oils until emulsified.

In a medium bowl toss the arugula and onion. Toss with about ¼ cup of the dressing. Place the salad greens on a large plate or platter. Garnish with the oranges sections, dates, prosciutto, and walnuts. Drizzle with more dressing if desired, and serve.

Wild Salmon and Artichoke Salad with Green Tea Ranch Dressing

Serves 4

The Spaniards brought artichokes to California in the late 1880s, but it was the Italian and French immigrants who first grew them commercially in the 1920s, near Castroville, the artichoke capital of the world. In 1948, Marilyn Monroe came to Castroville to promote diamond sales for a local jewelry store and promote her new movie career. Although her arrival had nothing to do with artichokes, some of the local artichoke growers asked the starlet to be the first California Artichoke Queen. She accepted, and the event is memorialized by a yellowed newspaper clipping of a smiling Marilyn looking indulgently at an artichoke, surrounded by a small crowd of embarrassed gentlemen.

WILD SALMON AND ARTICHOKE SALAD

2 lemons

12 baby artichokes (about 3 inches tall)

2 green onions, both white and green parts, thinly sliced

2 ribs celery, chopped

1 tablespoon fresh lime juice

¼ teaspoon diced jalapeño chile

⅛ teaspoon freshly ground black pepper

¼ teaspoon finely grated orange zest

1 teaspoon capers

1 head red leaf lettuce, torn into bite-size pieces

1 (6-ounce) can wild salmon

4 hard-boiled eggs, peeled and quartered

Lemon wedges (optional)

GREEN TEA RANCH DRESSING

1 cup light or vegan mayonnaise

½ cup plain soymilk

1 tablespoon fresh lemon juice

¼ teaspoon granulated garlic

1 teaspoon granulated onion

¼ teaspoon freshly ground black pepper

1 teaspoon green tea powder (matcha)

1 teaspoon sugar

2 green onions, both white and green parts, chopped

1 tablespoon chopped fresh dill

Cut the lemons in half and squeeze the juice into a large bowl filled with cold water; place the lemon halves into the water.

Working with 1 artichoke at a time, remove the top few layers of dark green leaves, exposing the tender yellow leaves below. With a sharp paring knife, pare away the tough, fibrous outer layer around the base of the artichoke, and then trim the tip of the artichoke off to flatten the top; you should still have about 2 inches of leaves above each heart. Drop the artichokes into the bowl of lemon water to keep them from darkening.

Steam the artichokes in a covered steamer basket placed above a pot of simmering water until tender when pierced with a knife, 12 to 15 minutes. Remove the artichokes and plunge them into a bowl of ice water to stop the cooking. Drain, cut into quarters, and set aside.

In a large bowl combine the green onions, celery, lime juice, jalapeño, pepper, orange zest, and capers. Add the salmon and, using a fork, mix the vegetables and fish together, breaking the salmon up into small flakes.

To make the dressing, purée the mayonnaise, soymilk, lemon juice, garlic, onion, pepper, green tea powder, sugar, green onions, and dill in a blender until smooth.

Divide the lettuce among individual serving plates. Arrange the salmon, hard-boiled eggs, and artichokes on top. Serve with lemon wedges, if you like, and the dressing on the side.

Grilled Eggplant Stack with Sprouts and Lemon-Tahini Dressing

Serves 4

he first Golden Temple I cooked at was the original one in India, where I learned how to make chapatis in a kitchen that served thousands daily. I then became the chef at the Golden Temple Conscious Cookery that was located across the street from CBS Studios. It wasn't unusual to spot Marilu Henner, Demi Moore, or Rene Russo all lunching on the same day. The restaurant was famous for its salad bar and lemon-tahini dressing. We also put that dressing on a sandwich similar to this salad, filled with deep-fried eggplant. I took the bread away, and now I bake the eggplant instead of frying it.

SALAD

1 eggplant (about 1¼ pounds), cut into ½-inch slices

1 teaspoon kosher salt, plus more for salting the eggplant

½ cup unbleached all-purpose flour

¾ teaspoon freshly ground black pepper

¾ teaspoon paprika

1 cup dry bread crumbs

½ teaspoon Italian seasoning

¾ cup plain soymilk

Olive oil or canola oil cooking spray

2 ounces mild sheep cheese such as Petit Basque, grated

2 large vine-ripened tomatoes, sliced

2 ounces (about 1 cup) alfalfa or sunflower sprouts

5 ounces mixed baby greens

LEMON-TAHINI DRESSING

½ cup light olive oil or canola oil

⅓ cup fresh lemon juice

2 tablespoons tamari or soy sauce

½ cup tahini

¼ red or green bell pepper, seeds removed and coarsely chopped

1 rib celery, chopped

2 green onions, all of white and half of green parts, chopped

½ cup water

Preheat the oven to 400°F. Slice the eggplant into 8 to 10 slices, place in a colander in the sink, sprinkle with salt, and let sweat for 10 minutes. Rinse off the salt and pat dry.

On a large plate combine the flour, ½ teaspoon of the salt, ¼ teaspoon of the pepper, and ¼ teaspoon of the paprika. On another large plate combine the bread crumbs, Italian seasoning, and the remaining ½ teaspoon salt, ½ teaspoon pepper, and ½ teaspoon paprika. Pour the soymilk into a medium bowl.

Line a baking sheet with parchment paper and brush with oil or coat with cooking spray. Coat the eggplant slices in the flour mixture, then dip in the soymilk, and lightly dredge in the bread crumbs. Place the eggplant slices on the prepared baking sheet and drizzle with about 2 teaspoons of olive oil. Bake the eggplant slices for 10 minutes, turn, and bake an additional 15 minutes. Remove from the oven, sprinkle with the grated cheese, return to the oven, and bake until the cheese melts, about 1 minute.

While the eggplant is baking, make the dressing by combining the oil, lemon juice, tamari, tahini, bell pepper, celery, green onions, and water in a blender and blend until smooth and creamy.

Assemble each "sandwich" by placing an eggplant slice on a plate, topped by a tomato slice, and followed by some sprouts. Repeat twice, starting with the eggplant and ending with the sprouts. Top each stack with an eggplant slice and garnish with sprouts. Surround each sandwich with the baby greens and drizzle with the dressing.

Long Life Chinese Chicken Salad with Hemp Seed Wontons

Serves 4

In 1960, Silvia Wu opened Madame Wu's Garden in Santa Monica with nine thousand dollars and encouragement from her friends, who loved her traditional Chinese fare. Known to all as Madame Wu, her celebrity clientele spanned nearly four decades of diners, from Frank Sinatra to Tom Cruise. Jack Benny was a fan of the shark fin soup because he said it preserved his vitality, while Cary Grant convinced her to put Chinese chicken salad on the menu after eating it at another restaurant. Wu was not the first to create the Chinese chicken salad, but like the Caesar and the Cobb, her clientele made it legendary. Chinese chicken salad is not a traditional Chinese dish, and since it was popularized in Los Angeles, the combination was most likely started when a customer asked for a salad in a Chinese restaurant. Like Wu's version, mine uses wontons and almonds for crunch, but I prefer to bake the wontons instead of frying them, and I use organic romaine hearts instead of iceberg. Try making this salad with a store-bought roasted chicken; it works great.

HEMP SEED WONTONS
12 square wonton wrappers
Canola cooking spray
1 egg white, lightly beaten
¼ teaspoon kosher salt
Freshly ground black pepper
¼ cup hemp seeds

DRESSING
1 tablespoon canola oil
2 tablespoons toasted sesame oil
2 tablespoons hoisin sauce

3 tablespoons rice vinegar

I tablespoon water

I teaspoon fresh ginger, peeled and grated

I teaspoon sugar

½ teaspoon dry mustard

SALAD

3 cups shredded cooked chicken (about two cooked 8-ounce breasts)

¼ teaspoon kosher salt

Freshly ground black pepper, to taste

½ cup thinly sliced green onions, both white and green parts

2 romaine lettuce hearts, shredded

I red bell pepper, cut into julienne strips

¼ cup toasted slivered almonds

For the hemp seed wontons, preheat the oven to 350°F. Cut each wonton square into 8 equal strips. Line two baking sheets with parchment paper and spray each with cooking spray. Place the wonton strips on the trays. Using a pastry brush, brush each strip with some egg white. Spray again with the cooking spray. Sprinkle with salt and pepper; top with hemp seeds. Don't worry about any hemp seeds that don't stick to the wontons, they will get tossed into the salad later. Bake for 6 to 8 minutes, watching carefully in the last minute because these burn easily. Set aside to cool.

To make the dressing, place the canola oil, sesame oil, hoisin, rice vinegar, water, ginger, sugar, and dry mustard in the container of a blender. Blend until smooth.

To assemble the salad, place the shredded chicken in a large bowl. Toss the chicken with the salt, pepper, and green onions. Add the shredded lettuce and red bell pepper. Add one tray of the wontons, including any loose hemp seeds. Toss in most of the dressing and mix lightly. Divide onto four plates. Garnish with the remaining wontons and toasted almonds. Add more dressing if desired.

8

Dinner at Eight

SEAFOOD, POULTRY, AND MEAT ENTRÉES

Gayelord Hauser and Adelle Davis promoted high-protein diets, and Marilyn Monroe was one of the many actresses who told *Los Angeles Times* beauty editor Lydia Lane that a diet of protein, green vegetables, and fruit was her key to losing weight. If you work as a private chef in Hollywood, you know all about diets like the Zone, Atkins, and South Beach.

Private chefs have been making dinner in Hollywood since the 1930s, when G. W. Milliers wrote *Servants and Stars,* which included a chapter titled "Favorite Dishes of the Movie Stars." Milliers was a former buffet man to Queen Victoria under Chef Francatelli, a celebrity chef in nineteenth-century London. Milliers claimed that the recipes in his book bearing the name of a movie star were his creations that he sold to each star for fifty dollars. Recipes included Greta Garbo's Salmon Loaf, Steak à la Charlie Chaplin, and Lievre à la Royale, a favorite rabbit dish of

King Edward VII, served by Douglas Fairbanks when he entertained British royalty. One thing I learned as a private chef was that, just because someone is famous, it doesn't mean they want a formal dinner every night. Once, after I catered a dinner for Al Pacino, he told someone, "I wish I could eat like this at home." I consider that the best compliment I ever got, and was thrilled that he enjoyed the simple rustic meal of roast chicken, pasta, and vegetables. Many of the recipes in this chapter are perfect for a simple dinner at home, and I have used many of them for catered events.

Most of the private and professional chefs I know agree that it is always better to cook with good-quality ingredients, and are fans of sustainable and organic products. Organic and eco-friendly seafood is widely available from companies like Emerald Organics, Johnson Sea Farms, EcoFish, Ocean Boy Farms, and Brave New Shrimp. I first served organic seafood from Emerald Organics and Johnson Sea Farms at the ChefDance dinners during the Sundance Film Festival—the seafood was the star of the evening.

A label on beef or poultry that reads "all natural" really doesn't mean anything unless it clearly states that no hormones and no antibiotics have been used. Organic poultry and beef mean that the animals grazed on organic land and only ate organic feed. Petaluma Poultry, Shelton's Poultry, Diestal Turkey Ranch, and Bell and Evans are great sources for good-quality poultry. Hormone- and antibiotic-free beef became widely available in the early 1980s with Coleman Beef, which I have used to cater many events. Other great beef companies include Niman Ranch and Organic Prairie. Along with the benefits of no hormones or antibiotics, I find that natural and/or organic beef and poultry are always more flavorful. All of the natural food stores and many supermarkets sell natural and organic beef and poultry, and there are many online sources as well.

Pumpkin Seed–Crusted Cod with White Peach Salsa

Serves 2

The Fairmont Miramar Hotel in Santa Monica was once the home of Santa Monica founder John P. Jones. The hotel has been an exclusive getaway for the film world since 1921. Greta Garbo lived there for four years, Jean Harlow rented one of the bungalows in the early 1930s, and Marilyn Monroe often retreated to the hotel to escape the media. Actress and environmentalist Blythe Danner, who was instrumental in implementing curbside recycling in Santa Monica, hosted the Green Power Baby Shower at the Fairmont. The meal, of course, was all organic, highlighted by the wonderful organic cod from Johnson Sea Farms. Pacific black cod would be another sustainable choice (see Resources).

NOTE: When peaches are not in season, try the salsa with mango or pear.

PUMPKIN SEED–CRUSTED COD
Canola cooking spray

2 teaspoons unsalted butter or olive oil

2 teaspoons toasted pumpkin seed oil

2 teaspoons finely grated fresh ginger

¼ teaspoon ground cumin

¼ teaspoon ground turmeric

½ teaspoon ground coriander

½ teaspoon paprika

Two 6-ounce black or organic cod fillets

Kosher salt and freshly ground black pepper

½ cup toasted pumpkin seeds, ground

Lime wedges for garnish

WHITE PEACH SALSA

1 medium white or yellow peach, peeled and cut into ¼-inch dice

¼ red bell pepper, cut into ¼-inch dice

1 serrano chile, minced

¼ cup finely chopped red onion

2 tablespoons fresh lime juice

2 tablespoons finely chopped cilantro

¼ teaspoon kosher salt

To make the cod, preheat the oven to 400°F. Spray baking sheet with oil or line with parchment.

Heat the butter and pumpkin seed oil in a 12-inch skillet over medium heat. Add the ginger, cumin, turmeric, coriander, and paprika. Cook for 1 minute and turn off heat.

Season the fish fillets with salt and pepper. Put the pumpkin seeds on a large plate or piece of parchment paper. Brush the fillets on each side with the spice butter and roll into the ground seeds. At this point the fish can be refrigerated for up to 2 hours. Bake on the prepared baking sheet for 8 to 10 minutes, turning halfway through.

To make the salsa, in a small bowl mix together the peach, bell pepper, chile, red onion, lime juice, cilantro and salt. You can make the salsa for up to 2 hours before serving, and keep covered and refrigerated. Garnish with lime wedges.

Chinese Black Bean and Miso Salmon

Serves 4

The Jack LaLanne Way to Vibrant Good Health (1960) was endorsed by Jack's friends and followers such as Bette Davis, Gary Cooper, and Merle Oberon, who all praised the LaLanne system for keeping them fit. In the book, Jack talked about eating out the healthy way and mentioned several Hollywood restaurants like Trader Vic's and Don the Beachcomber's. He also

The Godfather of Fitness

In his early nineties, Jack LaLanne still works out two hours every morning, as he has for over seventy-five years. His fans include Clint Eastwood, Arnold Schwarzenegger, and Richard Simmons, who once gave him a big kiss on television and told him he wouldn't be where he was if it hadn't been for Jack.

When Jack was a skinny, pimply fifteen-year-old kid with a sugar addiction, his mother took him to a Paul Bragg lecture. Inspired by Bragg, who called him a human garbage can, the sickly teenager gave up white sugar, white flour, red meat, and processed foods. He had entered high school a weakling, and after meeting Bragg he changed his diet, began lifting weights, and became a wrestling champ and captain of the football team.

LaLanne came to Hollywood in the 1930s and worked as a movie extra and an artists' model. He saved his money, and in 1936 opened a health club in Oakland, which was the first to include a health food store and a juice bar. Credited with owning the first coed gym, he also developed the first weight-loss instant breakfast meal–replacement drink, and was the first to sell exercise equipment and vitamins on television. If that weren't enough, he invented some of the first exercise equipment, and some say he invented the jumping jack, the exercise he began his show with every day. LaLanne is the only health and fitness guru to receive a star on the Walk of Fame in Hollywood, and he rightly deserves it. His exercise show was the first of its kind to go on the air in 1952, and by 1959 *The Jack LaLanne Show* was the first nationally syndicated show on exercise and nutrition.

In addition to his own show, Jack appeared as himself on TV's *Mister Ed, Here's Lucy, The Tonight Show,* Rowan & Martin's *Laugh-In, The David Letterman Show, The Simpsons,* and Howard Stern's radio show. He also appeared in several movies, including the 1966 big-screen version of *Batman.*

Breakfast for LaLanne is a soy protein shake, multigrain organic cereal with soymilk, and a large dose of vitamins and supplements. Lunch is cooked egg whites, fresh fruit, and a creamless soup. Dinner is usually brown rice, ten raw vegetables, and steamed or broiled fish. He drinks water during the day and organic wine in the evening. Fresh fruit and vegetable juices are part of the program—snacks are not—and he claims he hasn't had dessert since 1929. After seventy-five years of his regime, he is in better shape than most of us—he's still lecturing, writing books, and claims to have sold more juicers than George Foreman Grills. He has often been quoted saying, "I can't die, it will ruin my image."

talked about the fun of Oriental cooking and how he learned to steam fish from the Chinese. If you can find banana leaves, try them, otherwise parchment can be used. You can also bake this fish in the oven.

2 tablespoons preserved black beans (available in Thai and Chinese markets)
2 tablespoons white or yellow miso paste
2 green onions, white and most of green parts, thinly sliced on the diagonal
2 teaspoons finely grated fresh ginger
¼ teaspoon freshly ground black pepper
1 teaspoon toasted sesame oil
Fresh or frozen and thawed banana leaves (or parchment paper)
1½ pounds wild salmon, cut into four 6-ounce portions

Preheat the oven to 375°F if you're baking the fish.

Place the preserved black beans in a small bowl. Cover with very hot water and let sit for 10 minutes. Rinse in a colander and coarsely chop. In a small bowl mix the black beans with the miso, green onions, ginger, pepper, and sesame oil.

Cut a square piece of banana leaf big enough to wrap around each fish fillet. Lay each piece out on a work surface. Rub the miso mixture all over each salmon piece, wrap in the banana leaves, and secure with a toothpick, if needed. If you're baking the fish, place on a baking sheet and bake for 10 to 12 minutes. Unwrap and serve hot or at room temperature, or refrigerate and serve cold.

If you're steaming the fish, place in a covered bamboo steamer or a metal basket set over a pot of boiling water for 6 to 8 minutes.

"Banjo" Duck with Orange Hoisin Sauce

Serves 2 to 3

Internet sources claim that Danny Kaye made "duck à la orange stuffed with rice pineapple and sausage." Having no proof of that story, I decided to find out what Kaye was really cooking in his Chinese kitchen. Craig Clai-

Master Chef Danny Kaye (1913–1987)

If I could travel back in time it would be to have dinner at Danny Kaye's house. Ruth Reichl, Paul Bocuse, Roger Verger, and Jacques Pépin all dined with Kaye, who learned to cook Chinese cuisine at the still-existing Kan's restaurant in San Francisco. Kaye built a traditional, professional Chinese kitchen in his home and a similar one on the CBS lot for when he was making *The Danny Kaye Show*. His foodie friends included James Beard, award-winning author Marlene Sorosky, and Steve Wallace of Wally's, the best wine shop in Los Angeles. His foodie friends, known as the "cookers," often came with him on his shopping trips to Chinatown and the Farmers Market on Third Street and Fairfax, where he would search for the best ingredients. Kaye regarded cooking as theater, and his famous guests included Cary Grant, Shirley MacLaine, Luciano Pavarotti, Jack Lemmon, and Billy Wilder. He once told *Look* magazine, "There's no big mystery about cooking but you have to do it with love and affection."

borne wrote about Danny Kaye's cooking skills in the *New York Times* in 1975. He included Kaye's recipes for batter-fried scallops and lion's head and mentioned a Kaye specialty called "banjo duck." Later that year, the *Washington Post* reported that Kaye served his "banjo duck" at a recent dinner for Bob Wagner and Natalie Wood. Banjo duck was prepared by splitting a duck down the front and pegging it to resemble a long-necked banjo. The duck was then fan dried, coated with hoisin-garlic sauce, and roasted in a special vertical oven. I developed this recipe because I wanted to make a recipe that was as easy as possible, that didn't involve splitting the duck down the center or using a "special vertical oven." I used a vertical roaster instead, which works perfectly, and you can buy one at most kitchen supply stores. You can serve this duck with Bok Choy Stir-Fry (page 165).

"BANJO" DUCK

1 duck, about 5 pounds, cavities cleaned, excess fat trimmed, rinsed, and dried
  with paper towels

1 tablespoon plus 1 teaspoon kosher salt

1 teaspoon freshly ground black pepper

1 large orange, zest removed, juiced (reserve the orange skin, half the zest, and
   the juice from the orange for the sauce)

Prick the duck skin all over with a carving fork, being careful not to pierce the meat. Place the duck on a roasting rack or wire rack on a tray in the refrigerator and let it dry out, uncovered, overnight. (This step is optional but it helps produce crispier skin.)

Preheat the oven to 500°F. Rub the duck inside and out with the orange halves, then rub the duck inside and out with the salt and pepper. Sprinkle half of the orange zest inside the duck, reserving the other half for the sauce. Set the duck in a vertical roaster and place in a roasting pan. If you don't have a vertical roaster, place the duck on a rack in a roasting pan. Roast the duck for 30 minutes at 500°F, then lower the heat to 350°F. Once the temperature is down to 350°F, pierce the duck skin 2 to 3 times with a carving fork to release some of the fat.

Continue to roast for another hour to hour and a half, or until the juices run clear and an instant thermometer inserted in the thigh reads 175°F. The duck should be well browned and crispy. Let rest for 10 minutes before carving. Serve with the Orange Hoisin Sauce.

ORANGE HOISIN SAUCE

½ cup hoisin sauce

2 tablespoons orange liqueur

1 teaspoon grated peeled ginger

Reserved orange zest

Reserved orange juice

In a small pot combine all the ingredients and bring to a simmer. Cook for 2 minutes. Serve with the duck.

Ginger Shrimp with Brown Rice

Serves 4

I don't know what it is about Chinese food and actors, but the two seem to make a perfect marriage. Maybe it's because Asian cooking and acting both require lots of creativity, and restaurants, after all, are just another form of performance. First there was Arthur Wong, who came from Canton, China, when he was eight years old and worked his way up from dishwasher to restaurant owner of the now closed Far East Terrace near Universal Studios. Among Wong's movie credits are *Confessions of an Opium Eater*, starring Vincent Price. Restaurateur Michael Chow has been in many films, including *Rush Hour 1* and *2*, and *Lethal Weapon 4*. His first Mr. Chow restaurant opened in London in 1968, during the height of Beatlemania. John and Paul were regulars, along with Mick Jagger and Jackie O. The Beverly Hills Mr. Chow opened in 1974; thirty years later, it is still the hot spot for Chinese food in Los Angeles. The hot spot in Honolulu is Jackie's Kitchen, where martial arts movie star Jackie Chan's restaurant serves *Who Am I* Shu Mai Chicken and *Rush Hour* Ribs.

1 tablespoon sesame oil

2 tablespoons minced fresh ginger

1 clove garlic, finely chopped

8 ounces shiitake mushrooms, stemmed, wiped clean, and sliced

4 ounces oyster mushrooms, trimmed, wiped clean, and sliced

1 cup broccoli florets

1 small bunch asparagus, tops only, cut on the diagonal into 1-inch pieces

½ small green cabbage, chopped into 1-inch squares

8 ounces fresh shrimp, peeled and deveined, preferably trap-caught
    or organic

3 green onions, white and half of green parts, cut on the diagonal into
    ½-inch slices

½ red bell pepper, seeded and cut into 1-inch strips

½ cup snow peas, trimmed and cut in half

2½ cups cold cooked short-grain brown rice

3 tablespoons tamari or soy sauce

2 teaspoons toasted sesame oil

1 teaspoon sugar

¼ teaspoon freshly ground black pepper

¼ teaspoon freshly ground white pepper

Heat the sesame oil over medium-high heat in a wok or 12-inch nonstick skillet. Stir-fry the ginger and garlic for 30 seconds. Add the shiitake and oyster mushrooms and cook, stirring constantly, until tender. Add water or a small amount of oil if the mushrooms become too dry.

Add the broccoli and asparagus and cook, stirring constantly, for 30 seconds. Then add the cabbage and cook 1 minute, stirring constantly. Add the shrimp and cook 1 minute, stirring constantly. Add the green onions, bell pepper, snow peas, and brown rice, stir to combine, and cook for 1 minute until the rice is hot. In a small bowl, combine the tamari, toasted sesame oil, sugar, and pepper and stir until dissolved. Stir into the rice mixture in the pan and serve immediately.

Seared Pacific Halibut with Plum Tomatoes and Lemon

Serves 4

Health food supporter and actress Billie Burke once said, "Age is something that doesn't matter, unless you are a cheese." Billie was fifty-four when she played Glinda, the Good Witch of the North, in the screen classic *The Wizard of Oz* (1939), which makes me think her healthful diet paid off. Billie also starred in *Dinner at Eight* (1933) with Lionel Barrymore, John Barrymore, and Jean Harlow. In *Dinner at Eight*, Billie's scatterbrained character arranges a dinner party to benefit her husband's business. If you're stressed about having guests over for dinner, try this easy-to-make halibut, and serve it with Italian Broccoli with Pine Nuts and Garlic (page 231).

2 teaspoons plus 1 tablespoon extra-virgin olive oil

2 medium shallots, minced

4 plum tomatoes, peeled, seeded, and diced

½ teaspoon finely grated lemon zest

4 teaspoons capers

4 large fresh basil leaves, sliced lengthwise into long, thin strips

2 tablespoons fresh lemon juice

Four 6-ounce Pacific halibut fillets

¼ teaspoon kosher salt

¼ teaspoon freshly ground black pepper

Canola cooking spray

2 tablespoons chopped flat-leaf parsley for garnish

Lemon wedges for garnish

Heat 2 teaspoons of the oil in a small skillet over medium heat and add shallots. Cook for 2 to 3 minutes, add the tomatoes, lemon zest, and capers. Cook another minute, then remove from the heat. Add the basil and lemon juice.

Season the halibut fillets with the salt and pepper. Heat a large griddle pan or skillet over high heat, coat with cooking spray, and add the 1 tablespoon oil. Cook the halibut for 3 to 4 minutes per side. Sprinkle with the parsley. Serve with the sautéed tomatoes and lemon wedges.

Deviled Crab Bakes

Serves 6

When CBS moved to Los Angeles in January 1949, the first local sponsor to sign a CBS-TV contract was Earl B. Gilmore, owner of the city's Farmers Market. Gilmore sponsored a local cooking show hosted by market founder Fred Beck, author of *Farmers Market Cook Book* (1951). The show, which was launched in February 1949, was called *Fred Beck's Kitchen* and featured celebrities, professional chefs, the *Los Angeles Times*

★ The Farmers Market ★

One of the must-see tourist attractions in L.A. is the Farmers Market, which started in 1934 during the Great Depression on a vacant dairy farm in the middle of Los Angeles. Roger Dahlhjelm and Fred Beck approached the property owner, A. F. Gilmore, with an idea for creating a market of local vendors on his property. The market began with eighteen farmers selling produce from the back of their trucks, and rent was fifty cents a day. Fred coined the market's famous slogan "Meet me at 3rd and Fairfax" by writing it on the side of a broken-down Ford roadster and parking it down the street from the market on opening day. Fred Beck was the driving force behind the market for many years and together with his wife wrote about the market daily in the *Los Angeles Times*. They also wrote *The Farmers Market Cookbook*, published in 1951 with a foreword by M. F. K. Fisher.

Considering that CBS is located just north of the Farmers Market, it's no surprise that the *Los Angeles Times* once described the market as "the number one place in L.A. to spot stars." Long before the Dodgers moved to L.A., the Hollywood Stars baseball team (owned by Bing Crosby, Barbara Stanwyck, and Cecil B. DeMille) played baseball on the Gilmore Field, which is located on the same property. Movies were filmed at the market, stars were spotted, and, according to the market website, Walt Disney planned his initial drawings for Disneyland while sitting on the famed patio. Fan magazines ran pictures of Joan Crawford shopping at the market; gossip queens Hedda Hopper and Louella Parsons both shopped and wrote about whom they saw at the market. Farmers grew edelweiss for Greta Garbo, and Cary Grant once autographed some figs. At one charity event, film stars took over the stalls and Greer Garson sold flowers, while Boris Karloff and Rita Hayworth dished out pickles and sliced cheese.

The market is still the place to hang out, more popular than ever, and according to www.seeing stars.com, the market, with its shops, restaurants, and new mall, The Grove, is still the spot for star gazing in Los Angeles. David Letterman once drove into the parking lot of the market in a convertible filled with tacos. He then stopped a busload of tourists and offered them free lunch!

test cook Marion Manners, and amateur cooks. The chapter titled "The TV Collection" features recipes made on the show, including one for Deviled Crab.

Olive oil or canola cooking spray

1 tablespoon unsalted butter

2 tablespoons minced onion

2 tablespoons unbleached all-purpose flour

¾ cup plain soymilk

1 large egg, lightly beaten

1 tablespoon fresh lemon juice

2 to 3 drops hot red pepper sauce, to taste

1 teaspoon dried mustard

1 teaspoon Old Bay seasoning

⅛ teaspoon freshly ground white pepper

1 tablespoon finely chopped flat-leaf parsley

1 pound lump crabmeat, picked over for cartilage

¼ cup grated Parmigiano-Reggiano cheese

1 tablespoon minced chives for garnish

Preheat the oven to 350°F. Oil or coat six 4-ounce ramekins with cooking spray.

Melt the butter in a 10-inch skillet over medium-high heat. Add the onion and cook for 2 minutes, or until translucent. Add the flour and cook, stirring constantly, for another minute. Add the soymilk, and simmer, whisking constantly, for 1 minute, or until the sauce thickens. Stir a little of the sauce into the beaten egg, then add the egg mixture back to the sauce, along with the lemon juice, red pepper sauce, mustard, Old Bay seasoning, pepper, and parsley.

Remove from heat and transfer to a medium bowl. Fold in the crab meat. Transfer to the prepared ramekins and sprinkle with the cheese. Bake for 20 to 25 minutes. Let sit for 5 minutes, then turn out of the ramekins, garnish with the chives, and serve.

Orange-Pepper Scallops with Bok Choy Stir-Fry

Serves 4

C hances are, if you are buying exotic Asian vegetables in your local supermarket, they come from the California specialty produce company Melissa's. Melissa's distributes exotic items like lemongrass, galangal root, lotus root, and bitter melon. They also sell these great fresh water-packed tubs of baby corn, water chestnuts, and sliced bamboo shoots, which you may find in the produce section of your supermarket. Celebrity chef Martin Yan is a spokesperson of Melissa's, and the company is a frequent contributor to many Hollywood charity events. Chefs love to cook with Melissa's perfect vegetables, and the company is an official sponsor of the James Beard Awards, the Oscars of the professional food world.

BOK CHOY STIR-FRY

Canola cooking spray

2 teaspoons sesame oil

2 teaspoons minced garlic

¼ teaspoon crushed red chile flakes

2 bunches baby bok choy, washed, trimmed, and cut in half lengthwise

7.5-ounce tub water chestnuts, drained

7.5-ounce tub bamboo shoots, drained

One 4-ounce tub baby corn, drained

1 tablespoon black sesame seeds

Tamari or soy sauce to taste

ORANGE PEPPER SCALLOPS

16 large diver or large scallops

Kosher salt and freshly cracked coarse black pepper to taste

1 tablespoon sesame oil

4 teaspoons finely grated fresh ginger

2 shallots, minced

¼ cup orange juice

¼ teaspoon orange zest, finely grated

2 tablespoons tamari or other soy sauce

2 green onions, white and most of green parts, sliced thin on the diagonal

For the stir-fry, heat a large wok or 12-inch skillet over medium-high heat, coat with cooking spray, and add sesame oil. When the oil is hot, add the garlic and chili flakes and stir-fry just until they are aromatic, about 30 seconds. Add the bok choy, and stir-fry for 1 minute. Add the water chestnuts, bamboo shoots, baby corn, sesame seeds, and tamari, and cook another minute. Turn off heat and let sit while you prepare the scallops.

To prepare the scallops, season both sides of the scallops with salt and lots of pepper. In another 12-inch nonstick skillet heat the sesame oil over medium-high heat. Add the ginger and shallots and cook for 1 minute. Place scallops in skillet and cook on the first side for 2 to 3 minutes. Turn the scallops; add the orange juice, zest, tamari, and green onions. Cook another 2 minutes. Scallops should be browned and lightly glazed. Reheat the bok choy stir-fry, and serve immediately with the scallops.

Moroccan Fish Balls

Makes about 20 balls, or serves 6 to 8 as part of a buffet

Temple Israel of Hollywood was started in 1926 by a group of men who in one way or another were connected to the movie business. The temple's original tagline was "Temple Israel of Hollywood, Filmland's House of Worship." From 1942 to 1974 the temple was led by Rabbi Nussbaum, who officiated at many famous funerals, including those of Fanny Brice, Samuel Goldwyn, Al Jolson, and Edward G. Robinson. He also married several celebrities, including Elizabeth Taylor and Eddie Fisher. Rabbi Nussbaum was so well known that one evening in 1959 Ralph Edwards brought him out before millions on his TV show and announced, "Rabbi Max Nussbaum, This Is Your Life."

I served this dish at my daughter's bat mitzvah lunch at Temple Israel of Hollywood. Fish balls are traditionally served for the Jewish New Year or Passover dinners, but I like them anytime.

FISH BALLS

1½ pounds skinned whitefish fillets or wild salmon fillets

1 small onion, grated

1 large egg

⅓ cup matzo meal

2 teaspoons ground coriander

1 teaspoon ground cumin

¼ teaspoon ground turmeric

1 teaspoon finely grated fresh ginger

½ teaspoon kosher salt

½ teaspoon freshly ground black pepper

2 tablespoons minced fresh cilantro

Lemon wedges for serving (optional)

SAUCE

1 tablespoon extra-virgin olive oil

2 cloves garlic, minced

1 (14.5-ounce) can fire-roasted tomatoes with chiles

2 tablespoons tomato paste

1½ teaspoons sugar

1 teaspoon kosher salt

2 cups water

Chop the fish in a food processor. Remove to a large bowl and mix in the onion, egg, matzo meal, coriander, cumin, turmeric, ginger, salt, pepper, and cilantro. Mix well, cover, and refrigerate while you make the sauce.

To make the sauce, heat the oil in a 12-inch nonstick skillet over medium heat. Add the garlic and cook for 1 to 2 minutes. Add the tomatoes, tomato paste, sugar, salt, and water. Bring to a simmer, cover, and cook for 15 minutes.

Roll the fish mixture into walnut-sized balls. Place into the sauce one at a time and add additional water if needed to just cover the balls. Bring to a simmer and cover the pot. Simmer for 20 to 25 minutes, or until firm and the fish is cooked, turning over once. Let cool in the sauce. Serve hot, or refrigerate and serve chilled with lemon wedges.

Honey Glazed Chicken with Dried Plums and Apricots

Serves 6

Easy Rider (1969) star Peter Fonda won an Oscar for his role as a beekeeper in *Ulee's Gold* (1997). He claims he based his character on his father, Henry Fonda, who along with acting was a part-time beekeeper. Oscar-winning Henry Fonda is a Hollywood legend and was named the sixth greatest actor on the Fifty Greatest Screen Legends by the American Film Institute. Fonda gathered his honey in the backyard of his Bel Air mansion, which was filled with acres of flowers and groves of lemon, grapefruit, tangerine, mandarin apple, and orange trees, a virtual paradise for the bees. The honey was labeled Hank's Bel Air Hive and it was a Fonda tradition to bring honey as birthday gifts to friends like Jimmy Stewart. If you want a rich-tasting honey, look for varietal honeys in the natural food store or find a beekeeper at your local farmers' market. It's the honey that gives this chicken its delicious flavor.

1 whole chicken (about 2½ pounds), rinsed and cut into 8 pieces, or six 7-ounce chicken breasts, with or without bones

1½ teaspoons kosher salt

½ teaspoon freshly ground black pepper

⅓ cup minced shallots

2 teaspoons dried oregano

½ teaspoon dried thyme

3 tablespoons golden balsamic vinegar

2 tablespoons extra-virgin olive oil

2 bay leaves

½ cup dried plums

¼ cup dried apricots, cut in half

¼ cup pitted green California olives

¼ cup varietal honey, like sage, acacia, or avocado

¼ cup chopped fresh chervil or parsley

Place the chicken in a large bowl. Season with the salt and pepper. Add the shallots, oregano, thyme, vinegar, oil, bay leaves, dried plums, apricots, and olives. Mix well and place in a storage container or plastic freezer bag and refrigerate overnight.

Preheat the oven to 350°F. Place chicken pieces on an oiled baking sheet or in a large casserole dish. I like to tuck some of the fruit under the chicken so it remains soft and leave some exposed so it gets crisp. Spoon any remaining marinade around the chicken and drizzle with the honey.

Roast until an instant-read thermometer inserted into the deepest part of the breast registers 170°F and the juices run clear when pierced with a knife, about 45 minutes. Let rest for 10 minutes before serving. Serve hot or at room temperature, sprinkled with the chervil.

Cornflake-Crusted Chicken Tenders with Honey-Mustard Dipping Sauce

Serves 4

In 1925, breakfast mogul W. K. Kellogg purchased 377 acres in Southern California as the site of his Arabian horse ranch. Mary Pickford, Clara Bow, Gary Cooper, Olivia de Havilland, Tom Mix, and Loretta Young were among the Hollywood locals who came out to have their pictures taken with the horses. The most famous Arabian was Jardaan, who starred in six films, including Rudolph Valentino's last, *The Son of the Sheik* (1926). W. K. Kellogg dined at the Brown Derby, hung out on movie sets, and eventually hired many stars, including Loretta Young, to promote his cereals. When Kellogg's launched Corn Flake Crumbs in 1948, homemakers no longer had to crush whole cornflakes with rolling pins.

You can make your own cornflake crumbs by pulvarizing organic cornflakes in a food processor. Six cups of whole flakes makes about 2 cups of crumbs.

CORNFLAKE-CRUSTED CHICKEN TENDERS

½ cup plain soymilk or buttermilk

1 teaspoon fresh lemon juice

1 teaspoon finely grated lemon zest

1 teaspoon kosher salt

¼ teaspoon freshly ground black pepper

⅛ teaspoon freshly ground white pepper

¼ teaspoon paprika

1½ pounds chicken tenders (about 16 pieces)

Canola cooking spray or canola oil

2 cups cornflake crumbs

1½ teaspoons kosher salt

½ teaspoon freshly ground black pepper

¼ teaspoon dried thyme

1 teaspoon salt-free Spike seasoning

½ teaspoon paprika

⅛ teaspoon cayenne pepper

4 fresh egg whites or ½ cup liquid whites, whipped until frothy

1 tablespoon sesame oil or melted unsalted butter

HONEY-MUSTARD DIPPING SAUCE

½ cup whole-grain horseradish mustard

4 tablespoons sage honey

Pinch of crushed red chile flakes (optional)

In a small bowl whisk together the soymilk, lemon juice, lemon zest, salt, black and white pepper, and paprika in a large bowl. Add the chicken to the soymilk mixture, cover, and refrigerate for at least 30 minutes or up to 2 hours.

Preheat the oven to 425°F. Line a baking sheet with parchment paper and spray with cooking spray or brush with oil. Mix the corn flake crumbs, salt, pepper, thyme, Spike, paprika, and cayenne on a parchment-lined work surface or large plate. Pour the egg whites into a bowl. Drain the chicken pieces, then dip each piece in the egg whites. Roll the chicken pieces one by one in the corn flake mixture, patting the crumbs around the chicken pieces.

Arrange the chicken on the baking sheet and drizzle with the sesame oil. Bake the tenders 10 to 12 minutes, turning once.

While the chicken is in the oven, make the dipping sauce: In a small bowl mix together the mustard, honey, and chile flakes, if using.

Serve the chicken with the dipping sauce.

Thai Chicken and Daikon Curry

Serves 4

I consider celebrity chef Tommy Tang to be the Wolfgang Puck of Thai and Pacific Rim cuisine. When Tommy first came to the United States in 1972, he worked as a rock band manager and music producer, and then as the chef at Hollywood hangout Chan Dara. Together with his wife, Sandi, he opened restaurants and introduced the first Thai spices and sauces to the United States. In addition to his restaurants, television show, cookbooks, and Thai food line, Tang caters Hollywood parties using his authentic recipes. My Thai curry is untraditional, as it substitutes soymilk for some of the coconut milk, which sacrifices some of the fat but none of the flavor.

1 stalk fresh lemongrass

1 (14-ounce) can coconut milk

1 to 2 teaspoons red curry paste, to taste

½ teaspoon ground turmeric

1 tablespoon sugar

1 cup plain soymilk, plus more if needed

6 ounces fresh green beans, trimmed and cut into 1-inch pieces

12 ounces boneless, skinless chicken breast, cut into bite-size pieces

One 4-inch piece daikon radish, peeled, sliced in half, and cut into ⅛-inch slices

2 tablespoons fish sauce

2 Kaffir lime leaves (optional)

¼ cup whole Thai basil leaves

2 plum tomatoes, ends removed and cut into 4 wedges

Cut the top off the lemongrass and peel away 1 or 2 of the tough outer layers. Cut into 2-inch slices.

In a wok or 4-quart saucepot, heat the coconut milk over medium-high heat. Add the lemongrass, curry paste, turmeric, and sugar. Cook for 2 minutes, stirring frequently.

Add the soymilk and green beans and cook for about 8 minutes (the thinner the green beans, the faster they will cook). Add the chicken and cook an additional 5 to 7 minutes. Add the daikon, fish sauce, Kaffir lime leaves, and basil leaves and cook for 1 to 2 minutes.

Add the plum tomato wedges and additional soymilk if the curry seems too thick, and simmer until the tomatoes are hot, 1 to 2 minutes. If you wish, you can take out the lemongrass slices before serving. Serve hot with steamed rice.

Ginger-Brined Turkey "Ham" with Brown Sugar Crust

Serves 8 to 10

My friend Tracy Longsdale is rock and roll's favorite tour travel agent; she learned her art from her mom, who did many of the big rock tours of the '70s, such as Elton John's. Tracy cooks the best traditional English Christmas dinner and swears by Shelton Farms turkey. Shelton's Turkey Ranch began in 1924 when Mr. and Mrs. Shelton received one hen and one tom as a wedding gift. They began growing holiday turkeys in the Pomona Valley of Southern California and were one of the first companies to raise free-range poultry for the natural food industry. Today they sell their poultry nationwide. I swear by brined turkeys, as the brining makes them moist and full of flavor. All you need to do is remember to brine the turkey the night before you plan to cook it.

GINGER-BRINED TURKEY "HAM"

One 4- to 5-pound boneless turkey breast, with skin on, rolled in a net or tied with twine
4 quarts cold water
¾ cup coarse kosher salt
½ cup avocado or sage honey
¼ cup white balsamic vinegar
12 whole cloves
2 teaspoons black mustard seeds
1 tablespoon whole black peppercorns
2 tablespoons allspice berries
2 cinnamon sticks
2 bay leaves
¼ cup minced fresh ginger
2 shallots, chopped
1 orange, quartered
1 tablespoon avocado or canola oil
Freshly ground black pepper

BROWN SUGAR CRUST

1 cup packed light brown sugar
1 tablespoon dry mustard
½ teaspoon ground cinnamon
½ teaspoon ground ginger
¼ teaspoon ground cloves
2 to 3 teaspoons pineapple or orange juice

Put the turkey breast in a large colander and rinse under cold running water. In a 2-gallon stockpot combine the water, salt, honey, and vinegar. Add the cloves, mustard seeds, peppercorns, allspice berries, cinnamon sticks, bay leaves, ginger, shallots, and orange. Stir until the salt dissolves and add the turkey. (I have put larger turkeys in plastic roasting bags with the brine, but I find that I like this method best.) Cover and refrigerate, turning the turkey breast occasionally, for at least 12 hours and up to 24 hours.

The next day, preheat the oven to 350°F.

Remove the turkey from the brine, discard the brine, and put the turkey rounded breast side up on a heavy baking sheet or small roasting pan lined with parchment. Pat the turkey dry and rub on top and under the skin with the oil and sprinkle with pepper. Roast for about 1½ hours, or until deep golden brown and an instant-read thermometer inserted in the thickest part of the breast reads 165°F.

While the turkey is in the oven, make the brown sugar crust: mix the brown sugar, mustard, cinnamon, ginger, cloves, and pineapple juice in a small bowl. Use just enough pineapple juice to make the crust spreadable.

Remove the turkey from the oven and preheat the broiler. Transfer the breast to a pan that will fit under your broiler. Adjust the broiler rack to the lowest level. Cover the top and sides of the breast with the brown sugar mixture. Broil for 1 minute, rotate the pan and broil for 1 minute more. The crust should harden onto the breast. Let sit for 15 to 20 minutes, and slice as you would ham. You can also refrigerate and serve the turkey cold.

Short Ribs Braised with Chinese Flavors

Serves 4 to 6

When I got a call to cook for *American Idol* creator Simon Fuller, I was too busy to take on any more clients. I immediately called my friend Nikki Reiss, who is one of the best chefs I know. Nikki graduated from the

Culinary Institute of America and worked with super chefs Daniel Boulud and Jean-George Vongerichten when she lived in New York City. Fuller, of course, loves Nikki, who is also adored by Mariah Carey and Billy Bob Thornton. Whenever she has time, Nikki helps me cater events and is my lifesaver at the Sundance Film Festival—she can cook like nobody's business. I taught her to cook with soy, and she taught me how to make short ribs. She shared with me her recipe for these short ribs, which she likes to serve with sticky rice and Swiss chard.

Canola cooking spray

5 pounds short ribs on the bone, trimmed of fat and silver skin

Kosher salt and freshly ground black pepper

1 tablespoon canola oil

6 whole shallots, peeled and sliced ¼-inch thick

8 cloves garlic, peeled and chopped

⅓ cup peeled and sliced fresh ginger

2 tablespoons light brown sugar

5 whole star anise

4 whole cinnamon sticks

2 tablespoons pink peppercorns

4 whole red dried chiles

15 sprigs parsley

12 sprigs cilantro

1½ cups sake

½ cup low-sodium tamari or other soy sauce

3 cups water

Sliced green onions, for garnish

Preheat the oven to 325°F.

Season the short ribs with salt and pepper. Coat a large Dutch oven with cooking spray and place over medium-high heat. Add as many short ribs as can fit in a single layer to the pan. You will need to cook them in batches. Sear the ribs on both sides until well browned, then remove them from the pan and set aside. Repeat with the remaining short ribs coating with additionial cooking spray as needed.

Lower the heat to medium, add the oil, shallots, garlic, and ginger, and cook for 5 minutes. Add the sugar, star anise, cinnamon sticks, peppercorns, chiles, parsley, and cilantro sprigs. Sauté for 5 minutes more.

Deglaze the pot with the sake and add the tamari and water. Place the short ribs back in the pot, making sure they are submerged in the liquid. Cover and roast for 3 hours, or until the meat is tender and falling off the bone.

Remove the meat from the pot and set aside. Drain the fat off the cooking liquid and discard. Remove the meat from the bones and add back to the defatted sauce. Garnish with the sliced green onions.

Citrus Roasted Pork Chops with Rosemary Potatoes

Serves 4

Since their first movie premiere for *Popeye* in 1980, Along Came Mary Productions has produced elaborately themed parties for films like *Titanic, Batman Returns, Spider-Man 1* and *2,* and *Harry Potter: The Chamber of Secrets.* Irish chef Gavan Murphy used to work in the kitchens of Along Came Mary, whose founder, Mary Micucci, was dubbed by *Hollywood Reporter* the "Epicurean Steven Spielberg." Gavan helps me out when I have huge parties, since he is so much better than I am at running a kitchen that is preparing a sit-down dinner for 300. His real interest is in health, and he develops recipes using his simple approach to nutritious, healthy cooking. He shared with me his recipe for pork chops, which are so easy to make.

4 bone-in pork chops, 1½ inches thick, about 8 to 10 ounces each

Kosher salt and freshly ground pepper

3 cloves garlic, peeled and chopped

¼ cup olive oil

Juice of 2 large lemons

Zest of 2 large lemons

¼ cup chopped rosemary

Canola cooking spray

2 parsnips, peeled, cut in half diagonally, and chopped into 1-inch pieces

¾ pound small red potatoes, washed and quartered

10 ounces baby yellow onions, peeled

Season pork chops with the salt and pepper. In a nonreactive bowl, mix the chops, garlic, olive oil, lemon juice, lemon zest, and rosemary. Let marinate for at least two and preferably four hours.

Preheat the oven to 400°F. Heat a large skillet over medium-high heat and coat with canola cooking spray. Add chops and quickly sear on each side. Add the chops to a large roasting pan along with the marinade, parsnips, potatoes, and onions. Roast for 30 to 45 minutes, or until the internal temperature of the pork reaches 160°F.

9

Guess Who's Coming to Dinner?

VEGETARIAN DISHES

Since the early days, Hollywood has flocked to vegetarian restaurants, and not one of them has been without a celebrity following. Originally, vegetarians were usually motivated by health and religious convictions, but today many people become vegetarian or vegan as a statement for animal rights. In 1966, Broadway and television star Gretchen Wyler started her first animal shelter. In 1986, she founded the Genesis Awards to honor major news and entertainment media that present animal-protection issues with "courage, artistry, and integrity." The annual Genesis Awards presentation is heartbreaking and inspiring at the same time, and each year the red carpet is lined with stars stepping out for the cause.

When I first came to Los Angeles and worked at the Golden Temple, regulars like William Shatner, Michael Jackson, Sidney Poitier, and Mariel Hemingway came for the all-you-could-eat soup and salad bar. When I left the Golden Temple, I started working as a private chef, and my first clients included Barbra Streisand, Alana Stewart, and Carrie Fisher. I eventually had so many requests that I started a vegetarian meal delivery service, sending meals each week to Michael J. Fox, Dana Delany, Judith Light, and mega producer, writer, and director James Cameron.

This chapter includes some of my favorite vegetarian recipes, all inspired by Hollywood's love of healthy ingredients. The comfort dishes, like the Tempeh-Tofu Loaf and Blue Corn Shepherd's Pie, are great for dinner at home. I like to serve the Cornmeal Crusted Chiles Rellenos as part of a Mexican buffet, and the Dandelion Buckwheat Crepes make a great vegetarian entrée for a sit-down dinner. Vegetarian dishes have come a long way since 1896, when nut roast, lima bean stew, and rice with raisins were menu items on LA's first vegetarian restaurant. During this time, movies were not yet an industry, and Hollywood was still a small community built by H. H. Wilcox, who sold property to wealthy Midwesterners who wished to winter in California. Because of the early work of health crusaders like Clark Irvine, Paul Bragg, and Otto Carque, vegetarian restaurants and health food stores started opening, and by the 1930s and '40s, juice bars and vegetarian cafés could be found up and down Hollywood Boulevard.

California Health News, the forerunner to *Let's Live,* reported in 1936 on the Health Cafeteria, newly opened on Hollywood Boulevard. "Not only has Hollywood taken to meatless roasts, raw salads, palatable health desserts in the tantalizing cafeteria section, but the health food store has been accepted, and many film notables have become followers of the health movement overnight. Movie people, who must take every means to preserve their health, are flocking to the cafeteria." In 1941, *California Health News* reported that the Golden Shower restaurant on Hollywood Boulevard was a place "where residents and tourists, sipping luscious juices and relishing health meals, rub shoulders with movie stars, directors, radio artists, international celebrities and many doctors." At today's popular vegetarian restaurants, you can "rub shoulders" with the same kind of crowd.

Pad Thai with Tofu Tenders

Serves 2 to 3

No one has more energy than Patricia Bragg, who carries on the Bragg family tradition of crusading for health. Patricia has been a health consultant to royalty, athletes, residents, and film stars and has more energy than most people half her age. Bragg Liquid Aminos is a one-of-a-kind product made from soybeans and purified water. It tastes like a light soy sauce and makes a great substitute for fish sauce in this recipe.

7 ounces dried rice noodles (about ¼-inch wide)

¼ cup Bragg Liquid Aminos

2 tablespoons firmly packed brown sugar

2 tablespoons ketchup

2 tablespoons tamarind paste

¼ teaspoon crushed red chile flakes

4 teaspoons sesame oil or canola oil

4 ounces Chinese long beans, or thin green beans,
   cut on the diagonal into ½-inch-long pieces

½ head broccoli, cut into florets

8 ounces baked tofu tenders or cutlets, cut into ½-inch squares

2 shallots, minced

2 cloves garlic, minced

2 green onions, halved lengthwise and cut crosswise into
   1-inch pieces

2 cups bean sprouts

2 tablespoons water

⅓ cup crushed roasted peanuts

2 limes, cut into wedges

Fresh cilantro sprigs for serving (optional)

★ Paul Bragg (1881-1976) ★

"Health adviser to the stars," author, athlete, media personality, and more, it is no doubt that Paul Bragg was one of the founders of America's health movement. He is known for the promotion of deep breathing techniques, fasting, organic foods, juicing, and exercise. Like many of the health crusaders, Bragg overcame health problems as a teenager with natural cures and proper diet. He came to Los Angeles in 1921 and worked as a physical director at the YMCA. By the late 1920s, he was director and owner of Bragg's Health Center, where he taught exercise classes and operated a health food store and a cafeteria. Bragg was often photographed with young actresses while demonstrating new gadgets like the electric juicer. It was Bragg who inspired Jack LaLanne to change his diet, and LaLanne always thanked Bragg profusely and retold the story of their fateful meeting many times.

Paul Bragg's Health Builder *magazine, 1946, with Rita Hayworth on the cover.*
(COURTESY OF BRAGG HEALTH BUILDER ARCHIVES)

Bragg introduced new "products like pineapple or tomato juice and was the first to distribute honey nationwide. Prior to that, honey was available only at farmers' roadside stands. He worked with Luther Burbank in California to develop new varieties of healthful, organically grown fruits and vegetables. He was a regular at the film studios and an adviser to film stars such as Gloria Swanson, Robert Cummings, and Clint Eastwood, the Beach Boys, and giants of American business, such as J. C. Penney, Del E. Webb, Dr. Scholl, and Conrad Hilton.

Hollywood loved Bragg, who became an even bigger celebrity and a television personality when his show *Health and Happiness from Hollywood* premiered in 1959. Patricia Bragg cohosted the show, which included exercises, cooking demonstrations, and guest appearances by famous people. Today, she continues to run the family business, carrying on the tradition of spreading the word about diet and exercise. Patricia still publishes the Bragg books, including *The Bragg Healthy Lifestyle, Apple Cider Vinegar Miracle Health System,* and *The Miracle of Fasting.* And the Paul Bragg legacy lives on with Bragg Apple Cider Vinegar, Organic Olive Oil, and Bragg Liquid Aminos, which sell in natural food stores nationwide.

In a medium saucepan, bring 4 cups of water to a boil. Remove from heat and add noodles to the water. Let stand 8 to 10 minutes, stirring occasionally, until noodles are soft and tender. Drain well in a colander. In a small bowl make the sauce by mixing together the Liquid Aminos, brown sugar, ketchup, tamarind, and chile flakes.

Heat 2 teaspoons of the oil in a wok or nonstick skillet over medium-high heat until hot. Add the long beans and broccoli and cook for 2 minutes, or until bright green and crisp-tender, adding 2 to 3 tablespoons of water near the end of cooking. Add the tofu and cook, stirring constantly, for another minute. Transfer to a bowl.

In the same skillet heat the remaining 2 teaspoons oil, then add the shallots and garlic and cook until lightly browned, about 1 minute. Add the reserved sauce, noodles, green onions, half the bean sprouts, the water, and reserved vegetables and tofu. Cook for 3 to 5 minutes, stirring constantly, until heated through.

Mound on a platter and garnish with the remaining sprouts, peanuts, lime wedges, and cilantro sprigs, if using.

Blue Corn Shepherd's Pie

Serves 6

One of the best restaurants in Los Angeles for great star spotting and even better food is the Newsroom Café on Robertson Boulevard. The chef/owner is Eddie J. Caraeff, a great visionary and one of my best friends. Before Eddie was cooking, he was snapping photos of some of the biggest names in the music industry. When he was a teenager, he attended the Monterey Pop Festival and stood up on a chair to take the legendary photo of Jimi Hendrix on his knees with the burning guitar. Three *Rolling Stone* covers later and thousands of shots of rock and roll's finest, Eddie left the business to begin a cooking career. Rumor has it that Jennifer Lopez orders the blue corn waffle, but my favorite Newsroom special is the inspiration for this recipe.

BLUE CORN CRUST

1¼ cups unbleached all-purpose flour

¼ cup blue cornmeal

1 teaspoon sugar

1 teaspoon fine sea salt

½ cup canola oil

2 tablespoons cold plain soymilk

FILLING

2 teaspoons olive oil

1 large zucchini, cut into ½-inch pieces

Kernels from 1 large ear of yellow or white corn (or 1 cup frozen corn kernels, thawed)

2 poblano chiles, roasted, peeled, seeded, and cut into ½-inch strips

2 red bell peppers, roasted, peeled, seeded, and cut into ½-inch strips

4 green onions, white and half of green parts, sliced

½ teaspoon kosher salt

BEAN PUREE

1 tablespoon extra-virgin olive oil

3 cloves garlic, sliced

1 teaspoon ground cumin

1 (22-ounce) jar cannellini beans, rinsed and drained

½ teaspoon kosher salt

¼ teaspoon freshly ground black pepper

Pinch crushed red chile flakes

3 tablespoons water

Paprika for topping

To prepare the crust, preheat the oven to 425°F. In a large bowl combine the flour, cornmeal, sugar, and salt. Whisk the oil and soymilk together in a small bowl and add to the flour mixture. Mix lightly until a dough forms. Press the dough into a 9-inch pie plate. Cut a piece of parchment paper or foil slightly larger than crust and fit into the unbaked shell. Fill the parchment liner about a quarter full with pie weights or dried beans. Bake for about 15

★ Books and Cooks ★

Film stars' favorite recipes first appeared in fan magazines like *Motion Picture* and *Photoplay*. Books like *Photoplay's Cook Book: 150 Favorite Recipes of the Stars* (1928), *Betty Crocker's Let the Stars Show You How to Take a Trick a Day with Bisquick* (1935), and *Swingers and Singers in the Kitchen* (1966) all included "recipes of the stars." Film and television stars, producers, screenwriters, singers, and famous health gurus have all written cookbooks, and ever since Julia Child and James Beard, cookbook authors have become celebrities.

Many of the Hollywood health gurus wrote bestselling cookbooks, but Pasadena's Helen Evans Brown was the one who took California ingredients to the next level. If Helen had not died in 1964 at the early age of sixty, she might have become as famous as her friends James and Julia. Her most important work was the *West Coast Cook Book*, published in 1952. The recipes included healthy ethnic ingredients such as fresh ginger, bean sprouts, passion fruit, cherimoya, pomegranates, fermented tofu, tortillas, hot peppers, and cactus. She introduced mainstream readers to such recipes as Chinese-style "Bass with Bean Sprouts and Ginger," a Syrian "Barbequed Eggplant," Italian "Risotto," and "Tostados," her version of nachos. Along with her husband and editor, Phillip Brown, she wrote numerous cookbooks, contributed to magazines such as *Sunset* and *McCall's*, and wrote newsletters for local gourmet grocery stores. The Browns drew inspiration from their extensive cookbook library, and were close friends with James Beard, who put Helen on the same level as M. F. K. Fisher. Her fabulous Mexican meals and other goings-on with Beard were often reported in the *New York Times*, who dubbed Helen "the West Coast cooking authority" in 1953.

minutes. Remove the parchment and beans and bake an additional 5 minutes. Remove from the oven and let cool while you make the filling and topping. Reduce the oven temperature to 375°F.

To make the filling, heat the oil in a 12-inch nonstick skillet over medium-high heat. Add the zucchini, corn, chiles, bell peppers, green onions, and salt. Cook for 5 to 6 minutes, stirring frequently. Transfer into a bowl and set aside.

Using the same skillet, make the bean puree: Heat the oil over medium heat, add the garlic and cumin and cook for 1 to 2 minutes. Transfer to a food processor, add the beans, salt, pepper, chile flakes, and water, and puree until smooth.

Fill the cooked pie shell with the vegetables and top with the bean puree. Sprinkle with paprika. Bake for 25 minutes. Remove from the oven, cool for 10 minutes, and serve.

Green Chile Soy Mac and Cheese

Serves 4 to 6

Follow Your Heart started in full "flower-power bloom" in the spring of 1970 as a seven-seat juice and sandwich bar in the back of Johnny Weissmuller's American Natural Foods. Weissmuller, an Olympic swimming champion, star of the early Tarzan films, and a Kellogg follower, licensed his name to a maker of vitamins who owned a chain of health food stores. Locals referred to the original store as "Johnny's." Today the store and restaurant is always packed, and whenever I am in the neighborhood I stop by for some vegetarian comfort food. Follow Your Heart makes Vegan Gourmet, a vegan soy cheese that actually melts and tastes great, especially in this mac and cheese recipe.

Canola cooking spray or oil

8 ounces white spelt or other elbow macaroni

2¾ cups plain soymilk

1 bay leaf

2 tablespoons canola oil or nonhydrogenated soy spread

½ medium onion, minced

3 tablespoons white spelt or unbleached all-purpose flour

2½ cups grated cheddar-style or nacho-flavored soy cheese (about 10 ounces)

½ teaspoon paprika

1¾ teaspoons kosher salt

¼ teaspoon freshly ground black pepper

2 poblano chiles, roasted, peeled, seeded, and cut into ½-inch dice, about ¾ to
   1 cup (optional)

½ cup fine whole-wheat or spelt bread crumbs

¼ teaspoon paprika

⅛ teaspoon freshly ground white pepper

⅛ teaspoon dried thyme

⅛ teaspoon dried oregano

2 teaspoons olive oil

Preheat the oven to 350°F. Oil or coat a 2-quart baking dish with cooking spray.

Bring a large pot of salted water to a boil. Add the macaroni and cook until al dente. Drain in a colander and rinse under cold running water. Drain well. Meanwhile, heat the soymilk with the bay leaf in a medium saucepan over medium heat until the milk scalds (small bubbles will appear around the edges), about 5 minutes. Remove from the heat and set aside for 5 minutes while you cook the onions. Remove the bay leaf.

Heat the canola oil in a 2-quart saucepan over low heat. Add the onion and cook about 5 minutes, or until translucent. Add the flour and cook, stirring constantly with a wooden spoon, for 3 minutes more, being careful not to let the flour burn. Add the hot soymilk in a steady stream, whisking constantly, until thick and smooth. Cook the sauce at a simmer for 2 to 3 minutes, then remove from the heat and add the cheese, paprika, 1½ teaspoons of the salt, and the black pepper.

If the cheese is not completely melted, puree the sauce in a food processor until smooth and creamy. In a large bowl mix the sauce with the macaroni and the chiles, if using. Pour into the prepared dish. In a small bowl mix together the bread crumbs, paprika, remaining ¼ teaspoon salt, the white pepper, thyme, oregano, and olive oil. Sprinkle over the macaroni.

Bake for 20 minutes, or until bubbling and browned on top.

Millet "Om" Croquettes

*Makes ten
2½-inch croquettes*

Yogananda had many famous students, such as the legendary dancer Ruth St. Denis (teacher to Martha Graham) and Luther Burbank, the botanist and scientist who developed over 800 varieties of new fruits, plants, and flowers. Yogananda student Dennis Weaver (*Gunsmoke* and *McCloud*) co-founded LIFE (Love Is Feeding Everyone) and founded the Institute of "Ecolonomics" to find solutions for a sustainable ecology and economy. At Yogananda's India Café restaurant on Sunset Boulevard, they used to make Hindu-style Calcutta Croquettes. Om Burgers were served at a little café near Yogananda's Encinitas center, which overlooks Swamis, a surfing beach. They are great served with Tomato Chutney (page 58).

1½ cups water or vegetable broth

½ cup whole millet

½ teaspoon kosher salt

1 tablespoon extra-virgin olive oil, plus more for the pan

1 medium onion, finely chopped

1 rib celery, finely chopped

1 red bell pepper, seeded and finely chopped

1 medium carrot, finely grated or ground in a food processor

1 small zucchini, finely grated or ground in a food processor

3 green onions, both white and green parts, minced

4 ounces extra-firm tofu, drained, patted dry, and mashed well

2 teaspoons Madras curry powder

½ teaspoon kosher salt

¼ teaspoon freshly ground black pepper

2 tablespoons tamari or soy sauce

½ cup rolled oats, ground in a food processor

Preheat the oven to 350°F.

Bring the water, millet, and salt to a boil in a 1-quart saucepan. Reduce the heat to a simmer and cook, covered, for 20 minutes, or until all the water is absorbed. Turn off the heat and let sit for 10 minutes.

Meanwhile, heat the oil in a 10-inch nonstick skillet over medium heat. Add the onion and cook for 5 minutes, or until softened. Add the celery and bell pepper and cook for 2 minutes more.

In a large bowl combine the cooked millet, onion mixture, carrot, zucchini, green onions, mashed tofu, curry powder, salt, pepper, tamari, and ground oats. Mix well.

Line a baking sheet with parchment and brush it with oil or spray with cooking spray. Using a 4-ounce scoop or a measuring cup, form the mixture into ten 2½-inch-round croquettes and place on the parchment. Bake for 45 minutes, or until crisp and lightly browned. Serve immediately. Leftovers can be frozen.

Grilled Eggplant Parmigiana

Serves 4

One of my absolute favorite experiences as a private chef was working for Barbra Streisand. She always kept an incredible organic garden full of delicious fresh vegetables, which, of course, inspired my creativity. One day I came up with this recipe in an attempt to lighten up traditional eggplant parmigiana. The secret to this dish is using firm Japanese eggplants, fresh basil, ripe plum tomatoes, and the best-quality extra-virgin olive oil and Parmigiano-Reggiano you can find.

Olive oil cooking spray or olive oil

5 medium Japanese eggplants

Kosher salt

2 tablespoons extra-virgin olive oil

6 tablespoons grated Parmigiano-Reggiano cheese

3 tablespoons finely chopped fresh basil

1 clove garlic, minced

3 plum tomatoes, cut vertically into ¼-inch slices

Freshly ground black pepper

Preheat the oven to 375°F. Spray a 10-inch round casserole dish with cooking spray or coat with oil.

Cut the tops off of each eggplant and slice lengthwise about ⅓ inch thick. Sprinkle each slice with salt and layer in a colander set in the sink. Let sweat for 10 to 15 minutes, then rinse and pat dry with paper towels.

Heat an electric grill or stovetop grill pan and spray with cooking spray. Brush the grill with olive oil and grill eggplant slices on both sides until tender, about 4 to 5 minutes total.

In small bowl toss the cheese, basil, and garlic together. Place half the eggplant in a single layer on the bottom of the prepared dish, top with half the tomatoes, a sprinkle of pepper, and half of the cheese mixture. Repeat with the remaining ingredients, ending with the cheese.

Bake for 30 minutes. Serve hot or at room temperature.

Dandelion Buckwheat Crêpes
with Leeks and Wild Mushrooms

Serves 6;
makes 12 crêpes

Oxnard Beach was once a hideaway for Hollywood's luminaries, and it was the location where Rudolph Valentino filmed *The Sheik* (1921). Valentino eventually bought a vacation home in Oxnard, and Clark Gable made movies in the area. The McGrath Family Farms began farming lima beans in Oxnard more than 100 years ago, and the organic strawberries grown on their property may very well be sold in your local supermarket or natural food store. McGrath Farms sells their produce to celebrity chefs at Spago and other top restaurants in Los Angeles, and they are my first stop at the Hollywood and Santa Monica Farmers Markets. Their fresh dandelion greens can't be beat.

DANDELION BUCKWHEAT CRÊPES

1 large egg

½ cup liquid egg whites or 4 fresh egg whites

1½ cups plain soymilk

¼ cup water

½ teaspoon fine sea salt

¾ cup unbleached all-purpose or white spelt flour

¼ cup buckwheat flour

¾ cup finely chopped dandelion greens

Vegetable cooking spray and melted unsalted butter for cooking

FILLING

2 tablespoons unsalted butter

1 leek, white and pale green parts, halved lengthwise, cleaned, and thinly sliced

1 pound shiitake mushrooms, stemmed, cleaned, and sliced

1 pound wild mushrooms, stemmed, cleaned, and sliced

2 cups finely chopped dandelion greens

1 teaspoon fresh thyme leaves

½ teaspoon kosher salt

¼ teaspoon freshly ground white pepper

TO ASSEMBLE

1 cup low-fat ricotta or soft goat cheese

¼ cup Dijon mustard

1 cup shredded Gouda or goat cheese

Vegetable cooking spray and melted unsalted butter, for cooking

To prepare the crêpes, lightly beat the egg with the egg whites in a medium-size bowl. Whisk in the soymilk, water, and salt. In a separate bowl combine the spelt and buckwheat flours. Whisk in the liquid ingredients. Add the chopped dandelion leaves. Transfer to an airtight container and refrigerate for at least 30 minutes or longer while you make the filling.

To make the filling, heat the butter in a 10-inch skillet over medium heat. Add the leeks and cook for 5 minutes. Add the shiitake and wild mushrooms and cook until tender. Add the dandelion greens, thyme, salt, and pepper, and cook for an additional 3 to 5 minutes, or until the greens are wilted. Set aside.

To cook the crêpes, heat a nonstick crêpe pan or skillet over medium-low heat. Coat the pan with cooking spray and brush the pan lightly with butter. Stir the crêpe batter and pour ¼ cup of the batter into the center of the hot pan, swirling the pan so the bottom is evenly coated with batter. Cook the crêpe until the top appears dry, about 1 minute. If the first crêpe looks too thick, thin the batter with a tablespoon or two of water. Using a small spatula, gently lift the crêpe, flip it, then cook another 40 to 60 seconds. Transfer the crêpe to a parchment- or wax-paper-lined plate. Repeat with the remaining crêpe batter, layering each crêpe with a paper towel.

To assemble the crêpes, mix the ricotta and mustard in a small bowl. Spread some of the ricotta, followed by some of the Gouda and some of the mushroom-dandelion mixture along the lower third of a crêpe. Fold the bottom edge away from you to just cover the filling, then fold the 2 sides in to the center. Roll the crêpe away from you a couple of times to make a bundle, ending with the seam side down. Repeat with remaining crêpes and filling. To finish cooking the prepared crêpes, heat a nonstick crêpe pan or skillet over medium-high heat and coat with cooking spray and a brush of melted butter. Cook each crêpe, fold side down first, 2 to 3 minutes each side, until cheese is melted and crêpe is a bit crispy. Keep crêpes warm in a 200°F oven while you are finishing the crêpes. Serve immediately.

Tempeh-Tofu Meatless Loaf

Serves 6,
with leftovers

Vegetarian meatless loafs have been popular in Hollywood since the 1930s, when the Hollywood Health Cafeteria opened on Hollywood Boulevard. Many years later, the entertainment industry flocked to a hip little place in West Hollywood called the Artful Balance. The now defunct Artful Balance was the perfect dark, low-key Hollywood hangout in the 1980s and served the best vegetarian meatless loaf with mashed potatoes and gravy. Today, vegetarians such as Tobey Maguire, Joaquin Phoenix, and Alicia Silverstone flock to Real Food Daily for the TV Dinner, a tempeh-based loaf also served with mashed potatoes and gravy. I like to serve my version with Parsnip-Truffle Puree with Wild Mushroom Sauce (page 216).

Vegetable cooking spray or olive oil

1½ tablespoons canola oil

1 large onion, finely chopped

2 shallots, minced

2 cloves garlic, minced

2 ribs celery, finely chopped

½ pound extra-firm tofu, drained and patted dry

1 pound tempeh

½ cup walnuts, finely ground in a food processor

1 teaspoon kosher salt

1 tablespoon poultry seasoning

½ cup minced fresh parsley

2 tablespoons plus 1 teaspoon vegetarian
   Worcestershire sauce

½ teaspoon freshly ground black pepper

1 teaspoon paprika

1 tablespoon Dijon mustard

½ cup ketchup, plus ⅓ cup for topping

1 teaspoon minced jalapeño or serrano chile (optional)

Preheat the oven to 350°F. Spray or oil a 9 x 5 x 3-inch loaf pan.

Heat the canola oil in a 10-inch nonstick skillet over medium-high heat. Add the onion and shallots and cook until translucent and fragrant, about 10 minutes. Add the garlic and celery and cook another 1 to 2 minutes.

In a large bowl mash the tofu with a potato masher or with your hands. Don't be tempted to use a food processor—you don't want a puree. With a handheld grater, grate the tempeh into the tofu. Add the onion mixture, ground walnuts, salt, poultry seasoning, parsley, 2 tablespoons of the Worcestershire sauce, pepper, paprika, mustard, and ½ cup of the ketchup. Mix well and transfer to the prepared loaf pan. Mix the remaining ⅓ cup ketchup, the remaining 1 teaspoon Worcestershire sauce, and the jalapeño, if using. Spread the mixture over the top of the loaf.

Bake for 40 to 45 minutes, until the loaf is firm. Let sit for 15 minutes before serving.

Smothered Spinach and Tofu

Serves 4

Every year I cater events at Natural Products Expo West in Anaheim, California. Expo West is part of New Hope Natural Media, a company created in Malibu twenty-five years ago by my friend Doug Greene. Doug is one of the true pioneers of the modern-day natural food movement, and is one of the reasons you can buy organic and natural foods everywhere in the world—even in Moscow! One year I brought Isaac Hayes to Expo West and he loved meeting the founders of his favorite products. Isaac was the guest of honor at one of the dinners I catered, where I served this recipe, traditionally called *sag* in northern India.

2 tablespoons plus 2 teaspoons clarified butter

1 teaspoon ground cumin

★ "Health Foods" ★

Dr. John Harvey Kellogg was the first to develop the concept of packaging natural foods on a large scale and began to use the term "health food" in the late 1800s, about the same time he established the Battle Creek Sanitarium, making packaged foods for his patients. In the late 1800s, Newberry's grocery store in Los Angeles sold his Battle Creek products, which included granola, gluten meal, bran, graham flour, fruit crackers, graham crackers, whole wheat and rye wafers, and granose—the first ready-to-eat flaked wheat cereal.

By the 1950s and 1960s, Los Angeles health food stores were becoming larger and were starting to carry organically grown produce along with canned, packaged, and bottled products. The emerging counterculture and the "back to nature" movement of the late 1960s brought organic foods to a whole new generation. Gayelord Hauser once said, thank God for the hippies, they brought back natural foods, and we can thank Hauser for bringing them to Hollywood.

By the 1970s and 1980s, natural food stores were bigger than ever, and the natural food superstores were starting to replace mom-and-pop health food shops. In 1977, a kindergarten teacher named Sandy Gooch opened Mrs. Gooch's and she went on to build a chain of successful natural food superstores in Southern California. Gooch's rules—no sugar, white flour, chocolate, and coffee—were so stringent that any product she approved of became known as "Goochable," and set a standard for the entire natural foods industry. Rumor has it that Gayelord Hauser sent her flowers after visiting her store, with a card that read: "You did it."

Mrs. Gooch's Beverly Hills store was the place to spot celebrities or their private chefs shopping for groceries. Twenty to thirty years ago, there were very few large-scale natural food supermarkets in the country besides Mrs. Gooch's. There was Bread and Circus in Boston, Whole Food Company in New Orleans, Nature's in Oregon, and Whole Foods Market in Texas. Peter Roy of Whole Food Company and John Mackey of Whole Foods Market met at one of the first Natural Product Expos in Anaheim, California. Roy and Mackey became friends, and Roy became the visionary behind the merging of his store and the other large natural food chains into Whole Foods Market, the largest retailer of natural and organic supermarkets in the world. When Whole Foods Market bought out Mrs. Gooch's in 1993, the "Goochable" rules were lifted, and grocery shopping became a lot more fun, as natural foods stores began selling organic versions of "junk" foods like Oreo-style cookies made with organic unbleached flour and sugar.

Today, mega supermarkets like Safeway feature large natural food sections and organic produce. Safeway has even added a Safeway Select organic line that includes milk, eggs, bread, coffee, cereal, soymilk, and frozen fruits and vegetables. Kellogg would have been amazed at it all, but most likely still upset about the sugar in the cornflakes.

2 teaspoons ground coriander

1 large onion, finely chopped

2 cloves garlic, thinly sliced

1 tablespoon minced fresh ginger

½ teaspoon kosher salt

1½ pounds baby spinach, washed

2 medium tomatoes, peeled and chopped

1 cup water

2-inch piece of fresh ginger, peeled and cut into thin matchsticks

4 ounces extra-firm tofu, cut into ½ by 1-inch cubes

¼ teaspoon kosher salt

⅛ teaspoon crushed red chile flakes

⅛ teaspoon freshly ground black pepper

Heat 1 tablespoon of clarified butter in a 12-inch skillet over medium-high heat. Add the cumin, coriander, onion, garlic, minced ginger, and salt. Cook for about 5 minutes, or until the onions begin to sweat from the salt. Add the spinach, tomatoes, and water. Bring to a boil. Reduce the heat to medium-low and simmer, covered, for about 15 minutes, or until the onion is tender. Let cool and roughly pulse in a food processor until almost smooth.

Clean the skillet and reheat the pan over medium-high heat. Add 1 table-spoon of clarified butter and the ginger matchsticks. Sauté the ginger for a few minutes, until it begins to wilt and turn golden, making sure that it doesn't burn. Remove the ginger with a slotted spoon, leaving the clarified butter in the pan, and set aside.

Add the tofu cubes, salt, chile flakes, and black pepper to the pan, adding the remaining clarified butter. Cook the tofu, turning lightly a few times so each side is lightly browned. Add the spinach mixture and the ginger to the pan and simmer over medium heat for about 15 to 20 minutes, for the flavors to blend. I like to serve this dish as part of a buffet with the Oven-Roasted Curried Cauliflower (page 221), Ginger-Spiced Beets (page 224), and steamed basmati rice.

Squash-Topped Spinach Pie

Serves 8

As a teenager in the late 1930s, Joe Gold worked out at Muscle Beach, the place that launched America's fitness craze. In 1954, Joe was recruited by Mae West to join her all-male chorus line nightclub act, which toured America for five years. In 1965, Joe founded Gold's Gym in Venice, California, where Arnold Schwarzenegger was featured in the 1976 documentary *Pumping Iron*. When Gold's began selling pasteurized liquid egg whites for protein shakes, Los Angeles–based Eggology Egg Whites were put on the map. One-quarter cup liquid egg whites substitutes for one whole egg, and they work great in this recipe.

Vegetable cooking spray or olive oil

1 kabocha or butternut squash (about 3½ pounds)

1 cup liquid egg whites or 8 fresh egg whites, beaten until frothy

1½ teaspoons kosher salt

½ teaspoon freshly ground white pepper

2 teaspoons extra-virgin olive oil

2 leeks, white and pale green parts only, halved lengthwise, cleaned, and thinly sliced

1½ pounds baby spinach

¼ cup plus 3 tablespoons grated Parmigiano-Reggiano cheese

8 ounces ricotta or soft goat cheese such as chèvre

⅛ teaspoon freshly grated nutmeg

Preheat the oven to 375°F. Spray or oil a 13-inch oval ceramic or glass casserole dish.

Cut the squash into 8 pieces and scrape out the seeds. Place the squash in a roasting pan with 2 inches of water. Bake the squash until very soft, 45 minutes to 1 hour. Allow the squash to cool, then scrape the flesh from the skin. Place in a food processor and puree until smooth. Transfer to a large bowl and whisk in the ½ cup of the egg whites, ¾ teaspoon of the salt, and ¼ teaspoon of the pepper.

Heat the olive oil in a 12-inch nonstick skillet over medium-high heat. Add the leeks and cook for 5 to 7 minutes, or until the leeks have softened.

Place the spinach in a large stockpot over medium heat. Cook until wilted, 5 to 6 minutes. Drain the spinach and rinse under cold running water. Use your hands to squeeze out the excess water. Transfer to a work surface and finely chop.

In a large bowl mix the spinach with the leeks, ¼ cup of the Parmigiano-Reggiano, the ricotta, remaining egg whites, the remaining ¾ teaspoon of salt,

★ Mae West (1893–1980) ★

Before Marilyn or Madonna there was Mae West, who in 1926 wrote a play called *Sex* that landed her in jail for ten days. She wrote many of her own films, including *My Little Chickadee* (1940) with W. C. Fields, and *She Done Him Wrong* (1933), which was nominated for an Oscar and made Cary Grant a star. Her first movie role was a small part in *Night After Night* (1932), but her scene is legendary. When a coat check girl says, "Goodness! What lovely diamonds!" as she eyes Mae's jewelry, Mae replies, "Goodness had nothing to do with it." Mae exercised every day, and was one of the original Muscle Beach groupies. She started her day with a poached egg, fresh fruit, and a slice of Jack LaLanne's high-protein bread. During the day she ate fresh fruit, and dinner was a high-protein meal with lots of vegetables.

the remaining ¼ teaspoon pepper, and the nutmeg. Transfer the spinach mixture to the prepared casserole dish. Carefully cover the spinach with the squash mixture. Sprinkle with the remaining 3 tablespoons Parmigiano-Reggiano. Bake for 40 minutes, or until slightly puffed and browned. Serve immediately.

Almond Eggplant Balls

*Serves 4; makes
20 eggplant balls*

Cookbook author, radio personality, and columnist Mildred Lager wrote a column for *Let's Live* magazine that often included recipes. In December of 1942, she wrote that meat rationing had hit the stomach of America, and that the following recipe was the simplest and best meatless recipe she knew of. I had my doubts, but it is truly amazing. This dish is great for vegetarians following a low-carb diet, and is equally good without the spaghetti.

One 12-ounce eggplant, peeled and cut into ½-inch slices

⅛ teaspoon kosher salt, plus more for salting the eggplant

Vegetable cooking spray

2 tablespoons extra-virgin olive oil

2 cups raw almonds, ground in a food processor, plus more as needed

½ teaspoon Spike or other seasoned vegetable salt

1 tablespoon Bragg Liquid Aminos

1 shallot, minced

⅛ teaspoon garlic powder

¼ teaspoon dried basil

¼ teaspoon dried oregano

¼ teaspoon freshly ground black pepper

2 to 3 cups of your favorite jarred marinara sauce (preferably organic or good quality)

8 ounces spelt or durum semolina spaghetti (optional)

8 large fresh basil leaves, finely slivered

½ cup grated Parmigiano-Reggiano or Pecorino Romano cheese

Sprinkle each eggplant slice with salt and layer in a colander placed in the sink. Let the eggplant sweat for 15 minutes, then rinse off the salt and pat dry. Heat an electric or stovetop grill, spray with cooking spray, and brush with 1 tablespoon of the oil. Grill the eggplant slices until completely tender on both sides. Let cool, then blot dry with paper towels to remove excess moisture.

Very finely chop the eggplant and place it in a large bowl. Add the ground almonds, Spike, Liquid Aminos, shallot, garlic powder, basil, oregano, the ⅛ teaspoon salt, and the pepper, and mix well. The mixture should be stiff and you should be able to form it into balls easily. Add a bit more ground almonds if necessary and adjust the seasonings, adding more salt and pepper if needed. Roll the mixture into twenty 2-inch balls. Heat the remaining 1 tablespoon oil in a 12-inch nonstick skillet over medium heat. Add the balls and cook until browned on both sides. Add the tomato sauce to the skillet and bring to a low simmer while you make the pasta.

Cook the spaghetti according to the package directions, if using. Serve the spaghetti with the almond eggplant balls and sauce. Top with the basil and cheese and serve immediately.

Cornmeal-Crusted Chile Rellenos with Goat Cheese and Tomatillo Sauce

Serves 4

Back in the 1930s, Buster Keaton, Bob Hope, Mary Pickford, and Lionel Barrymore used to dine at the Spanish Kitchen, once the place to hang out and eat Mexican dishes like enchiladas and chiles rellenos. In 1961 the restaurant closed mysteriously. It never reopened until forty years later, when celebrity hair stylist Laurent Dufourg opened Privé Salon and Ona Spa. Once they cleared the ghosts and cobwebs from the building with a feng shui master, the former Spanish Kitchen once again became a Hollywood hangout.

TOMATILLO SAUCE

1 pound fresh tomatillos, skin removed

1 (14.5-ounce) can fire-roasted tomatoes

1 small onion, chopped

4 cloves garlic, chopped

¼ cup chopped fresh cilantro

1 jalapeño or serrano chile, finely chopped

1 teaspoon kosher salt

¼ teaspoon freshly ground black pepper

¼ cup water

CHILES

1½ cups unbleached all-purpose flour

2 teaspoons kosher salt

¼ teaspoon freshly ground black pepper

¼ teaspoon paprika

1½ cups yellow cornmeal

2 cups plain soymilk

6 ounces Monterey jack cheese or goat Gouda, cut into ½-inch squares

3 ounces soft goat cheese, crumbled

8 poblano chiles, roasted, peeled, and seeded, leaving the stem ends intact (try not to split the sides)

½ cup canola oil

To make the sauce, place the tomatillos in a 2-quart saucepan and cover with cold water. Bring to a boil, then reduce the heat to a simmer and cook for 5 minutes. Drain and place in a blender or food processor. Add the tomatoes, onion, garlic, cilantro, chile, salt, pepper, and water. Pour the sauce into a small saucepan, bring to a simmer, and cook for another 10 minutes. Set aside.

To make the chile rellenos, combine the flour, 1 teaspoon of the salt, the pepper, and paprika on a large plate. On a separate plate combine the cornmeal and remaining 1 teaspoon salt. Pour the soymilk into a medium bowl.

Line a baking sheet or large platter with parchment. Mix the 2 cheeses together in a small bowl. Make an incision through the length of each chile and stuff some of the cheese filling into each one, threading them together with toothpicks. Roll each stuffed chile into the flour, then dip in the soymilk, and then roll in the cornmeal. Place side by side on the prepared baking sheet. Let sit for 30 minutes.

Heat the oil in a large, deep skillet or cast-iron pan over medium-high heat. Fry the chiles, turning once, to brown on each side. Transfer to paper towels or paper bags to drain any excess oil. Serve with the warmed tomatillo sauce.

Pappardelle with Edamame, Asparagus, and Spinach Sauce

Serves 4

Edamame are the fresh green soybeans in the pod that you normally find in sushi bars. Henry Ford started canning green soybeans back in the 1930s when he had a soy factory next to his automobile factory. Ford was fascinated by soy, and he even had a suit made out of it. Gayelord Hauser often mention the Fords in his magazine *Diet Digest,* and Mrs. Ford attended lectures in Detroit when Hollywood health gurus like Paul Bragg or chiropractor Dr. Harry Finkel came to town. Dr. Finkel gave Mrs. Ford cooking classes, and Paul Bragg sold her an electric juicer. Look for shelled edamame in the freezer section of your supermarket or natural food store.

NOTE: This recipe is great with Grilled Eggplant Parmigiana (page 188).

2 cups vegetable stock

1 bunch asparagus, tough part of the stalks cut off, remaining stalk and tips cut on the diagonal into 1-inch lengths

1 cup frozen shelled edamame

2 teaspoons extra-virgin olive oil

2 teaspoons unsalted butter

2 shallots, finely chopped

1 clove garlic, minced

5 ounces baby spinach

¼ cup coarsely chopped fresh basil

¼ cup grated Pecorino Romano cheese, plus more for serving

¼ teaspoon freshly ground black pepper

1½ teaspoons white truffle oil

8 ounces pappardelle or fettuccine

Bring the vegetable stock to a boil in a 2-quart saucepan. Add the asparagus pieces and blanch for 1 minute. Remove with a slotted spoon to an ice water bath to cool. Remove the asparagus with a slotted spoon and set aside in a bowl.

Bring the stock back to a boil, add the edamame, and cook for 8 to 10 minutes, or until tender. Remove the edamame with a slotted spoon and set aside in a bowl. Reserve the stock.

Heat a 12-inch nonstick skillet over medium heat. Add the oil, butter, shallots, and garlic. Cook until the shallots are softened, about 2 minutes. Add the spinach and cook until it wilts, about 1 to 2 minutes.

Place the spinach, half the asparagus, half the edamame, and ¾ cup of the reserved stock, the basil, cheese, pepper, and truffle oil in a food processor or blender and puree until very smooth and creamy.

Cook the pasta according to the package directions. Before serving, add the reserved asparagus and edamame to the sauce and toss or ladle over the pasta. Serve with additional grated cheese.

Padre's Goat Cheese Enchiladas

Serves 4

The *Farmers Market Cook Book* (1951) tells the story of the legendary and still bustling Farmers Market in Los Angeles. The book was written by Neill and Fred Beck and includes a foreword by M. F. K. Fisher. Among the many food stories is one about the little yellow cottage in Santa Monica, where

Señora Castillo made her signature enchiladas and whose daughter Consuelo eventually opened a Castillo Spanish Kitchen at the Farmers Market. The story goes on to say that the original enchilada contained no meat and was served by the mission padres on holy days. In those days the padres raised goats for milk and cheese, and enchiladas were made with fresh white goat cheese. The book, which is over fifty years old, laments that the making of good goat cheese is one of the lost arts of California. Fortunately for us, it has long been revived and can easily be found to make this recipe.

Olive oil or olive oil cooking spray

6 dried ancho chiles, stemmed and seeded

1 (14.5-ounce) can fire-roasted tomatoes

3 plum tomatoes, coarsely chopped

3 cloves garlic, minced

3½ cups water

Pinch of freshly ground black pepper

¼ teaspoon ground cumin

1 teaspoon dried oregano

½ teaspoon kosher salt

11 ounces soft chèvre-style goat cheese

½ large white onion, finely chopped

¾ cup sliced black California olives

8 corn tortillas

2 green onions, both white and green parts, chopped, for garnish

2 tablespoons chopped fresh cilantro, for garnish

Preheat the oven to 350°F. Oil or spray a 13 x 9-inch casserole dish.

Put the chiles, fire-roasted tomatoes, plum tomatoes, garlic, water, pepper, cumin, oregano, and salt in a 2-quart saucepan over medium-high heat. Bring to a boil, then reduce to a simmer and cook, uncovered, for 30 minutes. Remove from the heat and let cool for 10 minutes. Puree the sauce in a blender or food processor in 2 batches. Pass through a strainer to remove the skins of the tomatoes and the chiles, and place back in the saucepan.

Crumble enough goat cheese to make 1 cup, reserving the rest of the cheese. Place in a small bowl and add the onion and olives. Spread ½ cup of the sauce in the prepared casserole. Dip each tortilla in the hot sauce to coat both sides. Spoon some of the goat cheese filling on the lower third of a tortilla, roll up and place in the dish. Repeat with remaining tortillas, lining the rolled enchiladas up side by side in the dish. Pour the remaining sauce over the enchiladas, and crumble the remaining goat cheese on top. Bake for 15 to 20 minutes, until the cheese is melted and the enchiladas are heated through. Garnish with the green onions and cilantro and serve immediately.

Barbecued Franks and Beans

Serves 6 to 8

Malibu was once a private ranch of 17,000 acres, but by the late 1920s, property in the "Malibu Colony" was being leased to film stars. Early residents included Clara Bow, Bing Crosby, and Ronald Colman, star of *Lost Horizon* (1937). Colman was friends with surf king and Olympic winner Duke Kahanamoku, who was often spotted surfing in the Malibu Colony. The Duke was a film star as well, and made over a dozen films, including *Mister Roberts* (1955), with Henry Fonda and Jack Lemmon. Malibu is the place to hang on July 4th, and whether I am catering a party or going to one, this dish is always on the menu.

Canola cooking spray or canola oil

1 tablespoon canola oil

1 large onion, finely chopped

2 cloves garlic, minced

1 (14.5-ounce) can crushed tomatoes

½ cup ketchup

1 teaspoon hot red pepper sauce

2 tablespoons molasses

½ teaspoon vegetarian Worcestershire sauce

1 tablespoon sage or orange blossom honey

½ teaspoon celery salt

¼ teaspoon freshly ground black pepper

1 tablespoon dry mustard

1 teaspoon smoked paprika

2 (15-ounce) cans small white beans

6 tofu hot dogs, cut into ¾-inch pieces

Preheat the oven to 325°F. Spray or oil a 13 x 9-inch casserole dish. Heat the canola oil in a Dutch oven or heavy 4-quart stockpot over medium heat. Add the onion and cook for 10 minutes, or until translucent and fragrant. Add the garlic and cook for 1 to 2 minutes more. Add the tomatoes, ketchup, red pepper sauce, molasses, Worcestershire sauce, honey, celery salt, pepper, mustard, paprika, beans, and hot dogs. Cook for 5 minutes, and turn into the prepared casserole dish.

Bake, uncovered, for 45 minutes.

Mama Vespa's Tomato Tart

Makes one 10-inch tart; serves 4

WireImage cofounder, artist, and photographer Jeff Vespa's work includes the bestselling Paris Hilton books, legendary red carpet shots, and his signature graffiti-strewn images of Madonna, Nicole Kidman, Nicolas Cage, and other film icons. Jeff is a popular fixture at the Sundance Film Festival, where he captures the portraits of all attending stars at his WireImage Celebrity Portrait Studio. At Sundance 2005, celebrity chef Rocco DiSpirito dubbed Jeff's mom "Mama Vespa." In real life, she is Marlene Meyer, owner of Life of the Party, a catering company in Baltimore. Jeff loves his mom's cooking so much, she is now his official caterer at Sundance. Marlene shared with me her tomato tart recipe, one of her signature dishes. Marlene says to always serve this warm; you can also serve it as an appetizer, cut into wedges or small squares. The tart also can be made up to two days ahead. Reheat at 400°F for 15 minutes just before serving.

1 recipe Pie Crust (page 77), rolled into a round 10-inch false-bottom tart pan
    and chilled for 20 minutes
8 to 12 fresh, ripe Italian plum tomatoes, all the same size if possible
2 heaping tablespoons Dijon mustard
12 ounces grated mozzarella cheese
Extra-virgin olive oil
½ teaspoon dried thyme
½ teaspoon dried parsley
½ teaspoon dried oregano
½ teaspoon granulated garlic
Freshly ground black pepper

Preheat oven to 350°F. Line the tart crust with parchment paper or foil and fill with pie weights, rice, or dried beans. Bake until the crust is set, about 10 minutes. Remove the parchment paper and weights and bake until golden brown, about 8 to 10 minutes more. Remove crust from the oven and let cool. Raise the oven temperature to 400°F.

While the crust is cooling, slice the tomatoes into ½-inch slices. Spread the mustard on bottom of the cooled crust, covering the surface. Fill the tart with the shredded cheese. Place the tomatoes on the cheese, overlapping each slice about halfway, placing them in circles on top of the cheese.

Brush the tomatoes lightly with the olive oil. Mix the thyme, parsley, oregano, and garlic together in a small bowl, then sprinkle tomatoes with herb mixture and season with pepper. Bake at 400°F for 45 minutes. Serve warm.

Swiss Chard–Stuffed Mushrooms

Serves 4

Swiss chard–stuffed mushrooms were one of the entrées on the Source restaurant menu. California surfer girl Gabrielle "Ganga" Barrett helped Jim Baker open the Source on Sunset Strip in 1969. She remembers writer/director/actor Paul Mazursky (*Bob & Carol & Ted & Alice*) holding court at the Source every day at lunchtime, and said that "people came not just for the food, but because it was a cool place to hang out." After her stint at the Source, Ganga, who always traveled with a case of California avocados, taught healthy California cooking classes across America, and she eventually opened the chain of Golden Temple restaurants in the early 1970s.

Canola cooking spray or olive oil

4 large portobello mushrooms, stems removed

1 tablespoon plus 2 teaspoons extra-virgin olive oil

½ teaspoon kosher salt

½ teaspoon freshly ground black pepper

1 tablespoon tamari or soy sauce

2 bunches red or green Swiss chard

1 large leek, white part only, cleaned and finely chopped

1 shallot, peeled and finely chopped

1 clove garlic, minced

⅓ cup grated fresh pecorino cheese (Pecorino Fresco)

4 teaspoons grated Pecorino Romano cheese

1 tablespoon finely chopped fresh basil

Preheat the oven to 375°F. Spray, oil, or line a baking sheet with parchment paper.

Using a knife or spoon, scrape out and discard the brown gills from the bottom of the mushroom caps. Brush the mushrooms on both sides with the

1 tablespoon oil, and season with ¼ teaspoon each salt and pepper. Preheat an electric or stovetop grill pan and brush with olive oil or coat with cooking spray. Grill the mushrooms about 5 minutes each side, or until browned and tender. Place on the prepared baking sheet.

Tear the Swiss chard leaves from their thick white stalks. Coarsely chop the leaves and finely chop the stalks. Simmer the stalks in a 4-quart saucepan of boiling salted water until tender, 5 to 10 minutes, and drain in a colander. In a 12-inch skillet, heat the remaining 2 teaspoons oil over medium heat. Add the leek, shallot, and garlic and sauté until translucent. Add the chard leaves and cook until tender. Add the chard stalks, cook 1 to 2 minutes more, and season with ¼ teaspoon salt and ¼ teaspoon pepper.

Fill each mushroom cap with the chard mixture. Top with the fresh pecorino and Pecorino Romano cheese. At this point the stuffed mushrooms can be refrigerated until ready to serve. Bake the mushrooms for 10 to 15 minutes. Serve hot or at room temperature, garnished with the fresh basil.

Little Soybean Casseroles

Serves 6

In 1943 soybeans made their way into the wartime edition of America's favorite cookbook, *The Joy of Cooking*. Fresh soybeans were a popular victory garden crop, and *Joy* author Marion Rombauer Becker was a fan of organic gardening. She also read Adelle Davis, which may explain why the 1951 edition of *Joy* praises brown rice and whole grains. That edition also includes a recipe for "soybean cheese" (tofu), which was early for a mainstream American cookbook. When Gypsy Boots opened his Health Hut restaurant in the late 1950s, Soybean Casserole was on the menu. Perhaps he got his recipe from the Soybean Loaf in the 1943 edition of *Joy*, which inspired me to make this dish. The leftovers make a great sandwich.

Vegetable cooking spray or olive oil
6 tablespoons plus ½ cup minced onion

★ *Gypsy Boots* (1914–2004) ★

Paul Bragg and Gypsy Boots.
(COURTESY OF THE PAUL C. BRAGG ARCHIVE)

One of Hollywood's greatest health food crusaders was the one and only Gypsy Boots. When I told Gypsy I was writing a book on the history of healthy eating in Hollywood, he told me, "Honey, you should put me on the cover, standing under a fruit tree." That will sell books! Born Robert Bootzin to Russian immigrant parents, he was influenced by the German *Naturmenschen* movement in the 1930s, and in the early 1940s Gypsy was running around with a pack of bearded, half-naked vegetarians known as the "Nature Boys." They were outdoor-loving guys who lived in the Tahquitz Canyon of Palm Springs and sometimes camped out under the Hollywood sign. Gypsy eventually married and settled in Los Angeles, and in 1958 he opened the Back to Nature Health Hut in Hollywood. The publicity was immediate, and soon the restaurant had a celebrity following: Gloria Swanson and Indra Devi came for lunch and regulars included Angie Dickinson, Jim Backus, Red Buttons, and George Hamilton.

After the restaurant closed, Boots started delivering fresh organic produce to actors like Kirk Douglas and Efrem Zimbalist Jr. In the early 1960s, Gypsy was quite a sight with his long hair and sandals, delivering sandwiches and healthy cookies to Beverly Hills hair salons. His big television break came when hairstylist Jay Sebring (Sharon Tate's boyfriend) introduced him to Steve Allen. He became a regular on the *Steve Allen Show,* swinging in on a vine and feeding Steve dates, nuts, sprout sandwiches, and juices. He became so popular that he had fan clubs in twenty-five cities. He was a paid performer at the Monterey Pop Festival, along with acts like the Grateful Dead, the Jefferson Airplane, and the Jimi Hendrix Experience. Gypsy even made a few appearances in films, and in

1968 he recorded a song called "We're Having a Love-In." Gypsy wrote two books, *Bare Feet and Good Things to Eat* and *The Gypsy in Me*. Along with eden ahbez, Gypsy was a living link between the German *Naturmenschen* movement and the flower children of the late 1960s.

In the 1970s, Gypsy had groupies of young health-conscious girls and was a regular on the sidelines at USC football games, where he wore a cardboard crown and chanted "Don't panic, go organic, get in cahoots with Gypsy Boots." Gypsy was the original promoter of Kyolic odorless garlic, feeding it to the Los Angeles Lakers and the Dodgers, and his annual birthday parties were legendary, especially the one Michael Douglas threw for him at Paramount Studios. He died eleven days short of his ninetieth birthday, and he was still doing book signings, promoting health, and selling fruit at the Farmers Market up until about six weeks before he died. Seeing Gypsy at the Farmers Market was always a treat—he would always show me who had the best figs and I would get to buy some of his organic almonds, which were the best.

1 tablespoon unsalted butter

1 rib celery, minced

2 cloves garlic, minced

½ cup tomato sauce

2 (15-ounce) cans soybeans, rinsed and drained

1 cup dry whole-grain or spelt bread crumbs

2 large eggs, beaten

1 teaspoon kosher salt

½ teaspoon curry powder

½ teaspoon paprika

¼ teaspoon dried thyme

¼ teaspoon celery salt

¼ cup chopped fresh parsley

Preheat the oven to 350°F. Spray or oil six 4-ounce ceramic ramekins. Place 1 tablespoon of the minced onion in each ramekin.

Heat the butter in a 12-inch skillet over medium heat. Add the ½ cup onion and cook for 5 minutes, or until translucent and fragrant. Add the celery and garlic and cook for 1 to 2 minutes more. Add the tomato sauce, bring to a simmer, and turn off the heat.

Pulse the soybeans in a food processor until ground but not pureed. You can also pass the soybeans through a grinder. Transfer to a large bowl and add the bread crumbs, eggs, salt, curry powder, paprika, thyme, celery salt, parsley, and onion-tomato mixture. Mix well and divide equally among the prepared ramekins. Place the ramekins on a baking sheet and bake for 45 minutes. Remove from the oven and let rest for 5 to 10 minutes. Run a butter knife around the edge of each ramekin, turn them out onto plates, and serve.

10

Fried Green Tomatoes

VEGETABLE SIDES

Most diets call for lots of vegetables, and no diet guru has ever disputed their goodness. Adelle Davis once said, "The principle weakness in American cooking lies in the preparation of vegetables." In *Let's Cook It Right* (1947), she claimed that vegetables should be gathered immediately before being cooked, or purchased as fresh as possible, with shoppers choosing the ones that are trimmed the least. A vegetable side dish is an important part of every dinner, and seasonal organic vegetables from the farmers market are always my first choice.

This chapter is full of tasty, good-for-you vegetable dishes like Oven-Roasted Curried Cauliflower, Pineapple Yam Bake, and Oven-Fried Green Tomatoes, which may please even the pickiest eaters. Silent film star Mary Pickford might have enjoyed my No-Creamed Spinach, since she often dieted on spinach and milk when she was making a movie. Her spinach likely came from the garden, and the milk came from her very own cows. Since Los Angeles was originally an agricultural town, it's not surprising that many of Hollywood's famous residents lived on small farms or planted vegetable gardens in their backyards. In *Cooking for Healthy Living* (1996), Jane Fonda reminisces about her father's Victory Garden; even in his later years, he grew his own fruits and vegetables and kept chickens for fresh eggs and bees for honey. Today, four-time Oscar nominee and two-time Golden Globe–winning actress Marsha Mason practices "spiritual agriculture" at Resting on the River Organic Farm, her organic farm in New Mexico, where she grows herbs and flowers to make a signature line of wellness products.

Actor Robert Cummings was a known health advocate and is best remembered for *The Bob Cummings Show* (aka *Love That Bob*) and Hitchcock's *Dial M for Murder* (1954). In his 1960 book *Stay Young and Vital,* he mentions the importance of eating vegetables, and writes about Louis Bromfield, who shared with Bob his sustainable and organic farming practices. Bromfield was a best-selling author, Pulitzer Prize winner, and one of the first writers whose books became screenplays. Mae West, Lana Turner, and James Cagney all starred in Bromfield films, but his real passion was his Malabar Farm in Ohio, where he lectured on sustainable farming methods and philosophies. Humphrey Bogart and Lauren Bacall were secretly married at the farm in 1945, with Bromfield as the best man. The farm is still thriving today and is a popular tourist attraction, wedding location, restaurant, and camping ground.

Before Alice Waters planted the edible schoolyard, actor Eddie Albert pioneered the Eddie Albert Farm Program, which set up gardens for city kids to expose them to organic farming and environmental concerns. At his home in Los Angeles, he always kept an organic vegetable garden, the real life version of *Green Acres,* his long-running television show with Eva Gabor. Albert was also an early supporter of environmental causes—Earth Day is held on April 22 partly because it was his birthday.

Oven-Fried Green Tomatoes

Serves 3 to 4

Occasionally a film comes along that captures the food moments so well that you just have to go eat what you just saw in the film. *Fried Green Tomatoes* was one such movie—it just left you desperate for a big plate of fried green ones. Most recipes call for frying the tomatoes in butter or lard, so I decided to try baking them, and trust me—I had my doubts. Instead of using cornmeal, which I didn't think would get crisp in the oven without lots of fat, I opted for cornflakes that I made in the food processor using store-bought organic cornflakes (as well as regular bread crumbs).

Canola cooking spray or olive oil
2 cups cornflakes, pulverized into crumbs in a food processor
1 cup fine dry bread crumbs
⅓ cup grated Pecorino Romano cheese
1 teaspoon paprika
¼ teaspoon dried thyme
Pinch of freshly ground white pepper
⅛ teaspoon cayenne pepper
½ cup unbleached all-purpose flour
1 teaspoon kosher salt
¼ teaspoon freshly ground black pepper
½ cup liquid egg whites, or 4 fresh egg whites
¼ cup plain soymilk
3 green tomatoes, ends removed and cut into ½-inch slices
1 tablespoon melted unsalted butter or olive oil

Preheat the oven to 400°F. Line a baking sheet with parchment and spray or oil it.

On a large plate combine the cornflake crumbs, cheese, paprika, thyme, white pepper, and cayenne. On another plate mix the flour, salt, and pepper. In a medium bowl whisk the egg whites and soymilk together.

Coat the tomato slices in the flour mixture, followed by the soymilk mixture, and then coat with the cornflake crumbs.

Place the tomatoes on the prepared baking sheet and drizzle with the butter. Bake for 10 minutes, then turn and bake an additional 10 minutes. Serve hot.

★ Food and Film ★

When Julia Child began her PBS television show *The French Chef* (1962–1963), she created a whole new genre of television personality—the celebrity chef. Considering the popularity of today's star chefs like Emeril Lagasse, it's not surprising that Anthony Bourdain's *Kitchen Confidential* (2000) is being produced for Fox by Darren Star (*Sex and the City*) and that Mark Burnett (*Survivor*) is producing *The Apprentice: Martha Stewart*.

Ever since Lucy worked in the chocolate factory and drank "Vitameatavegamin," TV segments concerning food have been popular. Black-and-white cookies, muffin tops, chocolate babka, and the Soup Nazi's soup were all featured on *Seinfeld* (1990–1998), but meals on the set were catered by the queen of low-fat cooking, chef Beth Ginsberg.

Fans of movies about food can never get enough of *Like Water for Chocolate* (1992), *Big Night* (1996), and other films where cuisine is the star. Who can resist eating fried chicken and homemade pies while watching Joan Crawford in her Oscar-winning role, *Mildred Pierce* (1945)? In real life, Crawford avoided carbohydrates and lunched on green salads with roast chicken and yogurt dressing. In 1959, she told *Los Angeles Times* beauty editor Lydia Lane that her favorite weight-loss drink was a fat-burning vinegar "highball" made from two tablespoons of cider vinegar in a glass of water.

The Oscar goes to cookbook author and television star Madhur Jaffrey, who has appeared in numerous films, including Merchant-Ivory's *Cotton Mary* (1999). Many of Jaffrey's recipes have been the inspiration for my Indian-themed events, complete with tunic-garbed waiters. Jaffrey directed *Cotton Mary* with the late Ismail Merchant, who, along with producing award-winning films, wrote four cookbooks. Cooking show fan Martin Scorsese often put his mother, Catherine Scorsese (*The Scorsese Family Cookbook*, 1996), in his films like *Goodfellas* (1990). Scorsese compared movie-making and cooking in a 1997 *Details* interview: "A lot of the inspiration you need in cooking—the creativity, the improvisation—is very similar. In a movie, every shot is like making a good meal. But since you do maybe ten shots a day, that's like preparing and cooking ten good meals a day. And you have a lot of pots simmering."

Parsnip-Truffle Puree with Wild Mushroom Sauce

Serves 6

In *How America Eats* (1960), Clementine Paddleford said, "California eats better at home and in her restaurants than any other state, or so it seems to me." If you want to know what the celebrity chefs of Los Angeles are cooking, check out the Santa Monica Farmers Market on Wednesdays for some of the best produce California has to offer. Chef Josie LeBalch of Josie's offers a Wednesday Farmers Market Dinner, and KCRW's *Good Food* host and chef Evan Klieman of Angeli Caffe creates her special Thursday-night dinners with produce from the market. I often head for the "mushroom man," who seasonally has morels and other kinds of wild mushrooms. Around Thanksgiving time, he offers domestic white truffles, which I shave into this puree of parsnips and potatoes.

PARSNIPS

2½ pounds parsnips, peeled and cut into 1-inch chunks

½ pound yellow Finnish or Yukon Gold potatoes, peeled and cut into 1-inch chunks

1 tablespoon extra-virgin olive oil or unsalted butter

1 tablespoon white truffle oil

¾ cup plain soymilk, scalded

Kosher salt and freshly ground white pepper

MUSHROOM SAUCE

3½ cups homemade, canned, or boxed vegetable stock

1 ounce dried morel or porcini mushrooms

1 tablespoon unsalted butter or canola oil

¼ cup minced shallots

2 tablespoons dry sherry

8 ounces fresh wild mushrooms such as shiitake or chanterelle, cleaned, stems
   removed, and thinly sliced

¼ teaspoon dried thyme

4 tablespoons white rice flour

½ cup cold water

Kosher salt and freshly ground black pepper to taste

To make the parsnips, place the parsnips and potatoes in a 4-quart saucepan and add enough cold water to cover by 1 inch. Bring to a boil, then reduce the heat to a simmer and cook, uncovered, until the parsnips and potatoes are tender when pierced with a fork, 25 to 30 minutes. Drain, then return the parsnips and potatoes to the same pot. Add the olive oil and mash with a potato masher until most of the lumps are gone. Place the potatoes and parsnips in a food processor, along with the truffle oil and hot soymilk, and process until smooth. Season with salt and pepper to taste.

If you are not serving immediately, place in a casserole dish, cover, and reheat in a 200°F oven before serving.

While the parsnips are cooking, make the sauce: Heat the vegetable stock in a 2-quart saucepot until almost boiling and turn off the heat. Add the dried mushrooms and let soak for 30 minutes. Drain the dried mushrooms, reserving the stock. Mince the dried mushrooms and set aside.

Heat the butter in a 12-inch nonstick skillet over medium-low heat. Add the shallots and cook, stirring, until softened, 5 to 10 minutes. Add the sherry, fresh mushrooms, and thyme and cook for 5 to 10 minutes, or until the mushrooms are tender. Add the dried mushrooms and cook an additonal 5 minutes. Add the reserved stock and bring to a simmer.

In a small bowl mix the rice flour with the water until the flour dissolves. Add the rice flour mixture to the sauce, whisking, and simmer for 2 minutes longer. Season with salt and pepper, to taste, and serve the warmed parsnip puree with the sauce on top.

Pineapple Yam Bake

Serves 4 to 6

Donna Reed and Paul Bragg, sometime in the 1950s.
(COURTESY OF THE PAUL C. BRAGG ARCHIVE)

Paul Bragg taught thousands about optimum health, but since he lived near Hollywood, many of his students were famous. Actress Donna Reed, who starred in Frank Capra's *It's a Wonderful Life* (1946) with Jimmy Stewart, shared her recipes with Bragg, and he inspired her to plant an organic garden at her Beverly Hills home. Bragg once visited a pineapple cannery and noticed the juice running off as the pineapples were canned. He had the factory can some of the juice for him, and when he realized how tasty and nutritious it was, he began sharing his discovery with his students.

NOTE: What we call yams are really sweet potatoes, since a true yam is sold only in Latin America or Africa. I prefer a garnet yam for this dish, but it also works with yellow-fleshed sweet potatoes.

Canola cooking spray or unsalted butter

3 pounds garnet or jewel yams

½ cup light brown sugar

2 tablespoons white spelt or unbleached all-purpose flour

1 teaspoon finely grated orange zest

1 teaspoon finely grated lemon zest

¼ teaspoon kosher salt

½ teaspoon ground cinnamon

2 teaspoons ground ginger

¼ teaspoon freshly grated nutmeg

1 tablespoon unsalted butter (optional)

1 cup chopped fresh or canned pineapple (cut into ½-inch dice)

1 cup pineapple juice

Preheat the oven to 350°F. Spray or butter a 13 x 9-inch casserole dish.

In a large pot of boiling salt water, boil the yams in their jackets until tender but firm, about 10 minutes. Cool on a baking sheet or work surface, and when cool enough to handle peel and slice into ¾-inch rounds.

In a small bowl combine the brown sugar, flour, orange and lemon zest, salt, cinnamon, ginger, and nutmeg. If using the butter, cut into the mixture until coarse crumbs form. Place half of the yams in the prepared casserole dish. Cover with half of the seasoned sugar mixture. Add the remaining half of the yams and cover with the chopped pineapple. Sprinkle with the remaining seasoned sugar mixture. Pour the pineapple juice over everything and bake for 45 minutes.

Japanese Eggplant with Miso Glaze

Serves 4

Two of my favorite people are Pierce Brosnan and his wife, Keely, who is an expert organic gardener and wonderful creative cook. Whenever I cater parties for them, Keely will have great suggestions for the menus, like her idea of adding chopped cashews to this eggplant dish. The best part is walking out to her organic garden to clip some fresh herbs for cooking. One day I am going to get her to teach me how to garden, because everything out of Keely's garden is amazing.

Vegetable cooking spray

4 Japanese eggplants, halved lengthwise

1 teaspoon kosher salt

1 teaspoon toasted sesame oil

1 tablespoon brown rice miso

2 teaspoons fresh lime juice

1 teaspoon finely grated fresh ginger

2 teaspoons light brown sugar

1 tablespoon canola oil

1 teaspoon toasted black sesame seeds

1 green onion, all of white and three-quarters of green, thinly sliced

2 tablespoons finely chopped toasted cashews

Preheat the oven to 400°F. Spray a 13 x 9-inch casserole dish.

With a sharp knife, make a few slits crossing each other on the cut side of each eggplant half. Sprinkle with the salt, place in a colander in the sink, and let sweat for about 15 minutes. Rinse and pat dry.

Meanwhile, make the sauce by combining the toasted sesame oil, miso, lime juice, ginger, and brown sugar in a small bowl.

Preheat an electric or stovetop grill pan, coat with cooking spray, and brush the eggplants and the pan with sesame oil. Grill the eggplant until tender on both sides. Remove and place on the prepared casserole dish. Spread the miso sauce over each eggplant half, and bake for 10 minutes. Garnish with the sesame seeds, green onion, and cashews. Serve warm or at room temperature.

Oven-Roasted Curried Cauliflower

Serves 4

Variety magazine called Haskell Wexler "the most widely known and honored of today's U.S. cinematographers" and he is one of the six cinematographers to have been awarded a star on the Hollywood Walk of Fame. He won Oscars for *Who's Afraid of Virginia Woolf* (1966), and *Bound for Glory* (1976), and was nominated for *Blaze* (1989) and *One Flew Over the Cuckoo's Nest* (1975). His work also includes *Medium Cool* (1969), *The Thomas Crown Affair* (1968), *In the Heat of the Night* (1967), *Coming Home* (1978), and *Mulholland Falls* (1996). Haskell and his wife, actress Rita Taggart, were two of my first clients when I started working as a personal chef, and we have been friends ever since. When I worked as a personal chef, I made food deliveries twice weekly all over Los Angeles. This curry was always on my menu, and contains less fat than a traditional curry because I finish the cooking in the oven.

Olive oil or vegetable cooking spray

2 tablespoons clarified butter or canola oil

2 inches fresh ginger, cut into thin matchsticks

1 onion, sliced in half and then cut into ¼-inch half-moons

1 clove garlic, minced

½ small serrano or Thai chile, seeded and minced

⅛ teaspoon crushed red chile flakes

¼ teaspoon ground turmeric

¾ teaspoon cumin seeds

2 teaspoons ground coriander

½ teaspoon garam masala

½ teaspoon amchoor (dried mango powder)

I head cauliflower, broken into large pieces, thicker stems removed

½ teaspoon kosher salt

¼ teaspoon freshly ground black pepper

¼ cup water

¼ cup fresh cilantro leaves for garnish

Preheat the oven to 400°F. Oil or spray a 13 x 9-inch casserole dish or baking sheet.

Heat the clarified butter in a 12-inch skillet over medium heat. Add the ginger and onion, cover, and cook until softened, about 5 minutes. Add the garlic and chile and cook until fragrant, about 30 seconds. Add the chile flakes, turmeric, cumin seeds, coriander, garam masala, and amchoors. Cook an additional 30 seconds. Add the cauliflower, salt, pepper, and water and cook another 3 to 4 minutes, stirring occasionally. If the curry becomes dry, add more water as needed.

Spread the cauliflower over the prepared casserole dish and roast for 30 minutes, or until tender and lightly browned. Sprinkle with the cilantro leaves, and serve.

No-Creamed Spinach

Serves 4

When Shirley Temple met Gayelord Hauser, she immediately told him she didn't like spinach. Shirley's dislike for spinach was well known and a constant source of argument with her parents at the dinner table. In 1934, a prop man gave Shirley a little magnet and she played with it at the studio, picking up nails on the stage. One night at dinner, when her father told her how much iron spinach contained, she dragged her little iron-grabbing magnet through her spinach to see what would happen. She then proudly told her family that there was no iron in the spinach. The spinach argument was revisited in *Poor Little Rich Girl* (1936), when Jack Haley (the Tin Man of Oz) sang to Shirley, "You've Gotta Eat Your Spinach."

1½ pounds (four 6-ounce bags) prewashed baby spinach

2 cups plain soymilk

1 bay leaf

1 tablespoon unsalted butter or olive oil

1 tablespoon minced shallots

4 tablespoons unbleached all-purpose flour

1½ teaspoons kosher salt

Freshly ground black pepper

Pinch of freshly grated nutmeg

Place the spinach and ½ cup water in a large saucepan or stockpot over medium heat. Cook, covered, until the spinach is wilted, 4 to 5 minutes. Drain in a colander and let cool. Press or squeeze out the excess water from the spinach and finely chop. Set aside in a medium bowl.

In a 2-quart saucepan heat the soymilk with the bay leaf to just below the boiling point and set aside. In another 2-quart saucepan heat the butter over medium-high heat, add the shallots, and cook for 2 to 3 minutes, until softened. Reduce the heat to medium, stir in the flour, and cook, stirring with a wooden spoon, until the flour is lightly browned, about 2 minutes. Slowly whisk in the warm soymilk and bring the sauce to a boil. Reduce the heat to a simmer, stirring often to prevent lumps from forming, and cook for 3 to 4 minutes, until the consistency of a cream sauce. Remove the bay leaf.

Mix in the chopped spinach. Season with the salt, pepper to taste, and the nutmeg.

Ginger-Spiced Beets

Serves 4

When Yogi Bhajan came to Los Angeles in 1969, some of his first students were singer Johnny Rivers and photographer Lisa Law, author of *Flashing on the Sixties,* a book and documentary, that includes interviews with Peter Coyote, Dennis Hopper, and Peter Fonda. Law, a California native, experienced and recorded Haight-Ashbury, the commune scene, and Woodstock, where she helped feed 160,000 people with Wavy Gravy and the Hog Farm. I learned about curried beets from Yogi Bhajan, who was quite innovative with food and was always coming up with unique fusion-style dishes combining Eastern and Western ingredients.

1 large bunch red beets (about 1 pound), greens removed, washed well, and reserved

1 large bunch yellow beets (about 1 pound), greens removed, washed well, and reserved

Olive oil for coating the beets

2 teaspoons clarified butter or olive oil

1 teaspoon black mustard seeds

2 cloves garlic, finely chopped

2 tablespoons finely grated fresh ginger

2 large leeks, pale green and white parts only, cleaned and cut into matchsticks

½ teaspoon kosher salt

⅓ cup water

Preheat the oven to 400°F. Line a large baking sheet with parchment paper. Wash and scrub the beets. Dry the beets and rub lightly with olive oil. Place the beets on the prepared baking sheet. Tightly seal the top with foil. Roast for 1 hour, or until tender when pierced with a fork. Remove the beets from the oven, unwrap, and cool to room temperature.

While the beets are cooling, cut the greens into ½-inch slices. When the beets have cooled, peel and cut them into 1-inch squares or ½-inch-wide pieces.

Heat the clarified butter in a 12-inch nonstick skillet over medium-high heat. Add the mustard seeds and cook for about 30 seconds, or until they pop and sizzle. Add the garlic and ginger and cook 1 to 2 minutes, until fragrant. Add the leeks and cook until softened. Add the salt, reserved chopped beet greens, and the water. Reduce the heat, cover, and cook 5 minutes more. Add the beets and cook 1 minute more, to warm through.

Serve hot or at room temperature.

Edamame Puree

Serves 4

The *Los Angeles Times* first wrote about edamame (fresh green soybeans) in 1942 in an article about soy products including tofu, soy sauce, and bean sprouts. But Hollywood created the real boom for edamame when the popularity of the 1980 TV miniseries *Shogun,* based on the novel by James Clavell, created an interest in Japanese culture among Americans, who began to frequent sushi bars. Many people first sampled edamame served with sake and beer in Japanese restaurants. I like to serve this with Chinese Black Bean and Miso Salmon (page 155).

2 cups shelled frozen edamame

1 shallot, minced

1 tablespoon olive oil or unsalted butter

¼ teaspoon kosher salt

⅛ teaspoon freshly ground white pepper

Bring 4 cups of salted water to a boil in a large stockpot over high heat. Add the edamame and shallot and boil for 5 to 6 minutes, or until the edamame are tender. Drain, reserving the cooking liquid. Place the edamame and ¼ cup of the cooking liquid in a food processor, along with the oil, salt, and pepper, and puree until smooth. Add more cooking liquid for a lighter puree.

Serve immediately or reheat with a little water or additional cooking liquid if needed.

Carrots with Honey-Mustard Glaze

Serves 4

Bernarr Macfadden was a colorful character and one of the first promoters of diet and exercise in America. A few scenes from the 1916 silent film *His Picture in the Papers* are filmed in a restaurant called Macfadden's Vegetarian Restaurant. During that period Macfadden did have several health food restaurants, known as Penny Restaurants, because he wanted to prove to the public that vegetarian food was tasty and affordable. His Penny Restaurants became very popular, and by 1910 he owned nearly twenty of them. According to many sources, Macfadden's favorite food was carrots.

1¼ pounds peeled baby carrots

2 teaspoons Dijon or horseradish mustard

2 teaspoons varietal honey such as avocado

2 teaspoons white miso paste

1 tablespoon tamari or soy sauce

¼ teaspoon freshly ground black pepper

2 teaspoons water

1 tablespoon olive or sesame oil

1 teaspoon mustard seeds

1 red onion, cut in half, and then into ¼-inch half-moons

Blanch the carrots in a large pot of rapidly boiling salted water for about 5 minutes, or until tender. Remove with a strainer and plunge into an ice-water bath to stop the cooking. Drain, and set aside.

In a small bowl mix together the mustard, honey, miso, tamari, pepper, and water and set aside.

★ Bernarr Macfadden (1868–1955) ★

Like many other health pioneers, Bernarr Macfadden was a sickly child who was restored to health with diet and exercise. In 1899 he launched a magazine called *Physical Culture.* The first issue sold for five cents and focused on bodybuilding. *Physical Culture* later contained articles on diet and health and included many Hollywood stores, as the West Coast editor was Arnold Pike, "Mr. Media of Nutrition." Macfadden didn't live in Hollywood, but he promoted himself and his empire in true Hollywood style.

With the success of *Physical Culture,* Macfadden began to launch bodybuilding competitions, and his contestants included Pudgy Stockton, the "Iron Woman of Muscle Beach" and Charles Atlas, who won his "Most Perfectly Developed Man" contest. In 1915 and 1916 he tried unsuccessfully to make films about exercise and superhuman activity, and eventually gave up on filmmaking after having lost millions. In 1919 he launched a second magazine, *True Story,* based on the letters he received from readers who had overcome personal difficulties. *True Story* is still published today, almost eighty-five years later. Macfadden started the fan magazines *Movie Weekly* and *Movie Mirror,* and in 1934 bought *Photoplay* and *Shadow Play.* By 1931 he was worth 30 million dollars and by 1935 his magazine empire had a combined circulation of more than seven million.

His bad business deals and legal problems led to his financial demise. Macfadden died at eighty-seven in 1955, and was healthy and alert almost to the end. His Hollywood friends included Paul Bragg and *Let's Live* publisher Clark Irvine, who often hiked up Mount Hollywood with him. Actor Bob Cummings wrote about him in his book *Stay Young and Vital* (1960) and called him a "rebel with a cause." Bernarr Macfadden was the first health and fitness guru to become a millionaire, and the first to own and fly his own plane, *Miss True Story,* even at the age of eighty. He wrote over 100 books, including the *Physical Culture Cookbook* (1928), published many magazines and newspapers, and some credit him for the invention of tabloid journalism. *Time* and *Newsweek* wrote about him, and when meeting the press he would show off his muscles and give interviews standing on his head. If he were alive today, I am sure he would be producing reality TV shows along the lines of *Survivor* and *Fear Factor.*

Heat the oil in a 12-inch skillet over medium heat. Add the mustard seeds and cook for about 30 seconds, or until they begin to sizzle and pop. Add the onion and cook for another 5 to 6 minutes, until the onion begins to soften and is slightly translucent.

Add the carrots and mustard mixture to the skillet and cook for an additional 2 minutes. Serve hot or at room temperature.

Cauliflower-Chive Puree

Serves 3 to 4

In the 1960s, chives were sold frozen in little white plastic cups, since fresh herbs were not packaged as they are today. P.R. whiz Leo Pearlstein worked with the California Chive Institute promoting chives, and had James Beard, Phyllis Diller, Vincent Price, and Jack LaLanne all promoting the savory long green herb. The big coup came when Pearlstein teamed up chives with Frank Sinatra Jr., who cross-promoted chives with his album *Spice* and penned a small cookbook titled *Frank Sinatra Cooks His Way,* which included chive-based recipes.

1 head cauliflower
1 tablespoon unsalted butter
½ teaspoon kosher salt
⅛ teaspoon freshly ground white pepper
2 ounces soft goat cheese
¼ cup grated Parmigiano-Reggiano cheese
1 to 2 tablespoons chopped fresh chives, to taste

Break the cauliflower into large florets and place them in a vegetable steamer set over water. Bring the water to a boil, cover the cauliflower, and steam for 15 minutes, or until soft. Puree the cauliflower, butter, salt, pepper, goat cheese, and Parmigiano-Reggiano in a food processor until smooth and creamy. Fold in the chives just before serving.

★ Celebrity Stew ★

In 2000, Leo Pearlstein celebrated his fiftieth year in the public relations business. In Pearlstein's book *Celebrity Stew* (2002) he tells the story of how he helped promote California-grown products with Johnny Carson, Bob Hope, Steve Allen, Bing Crosby, and Jayne Mansfield. Film star Eddie Bracken gave Leo his start. In 1947, Bracken was in advertising as well as the movie business. Leo got a job at Bracken's advertising agency, and when Bracken closed his agency in 1950 he gave Leo all the food accounts, and Lee and Associates was born. As Leo put it, "I made a career out of combining food with recognizable faces." He put healthy foods together with celebrities to promote movies, television shows, charitable causes, and food events. He worked with home economists, chefs, doctors, teachers, and dieticians, promoting everything from chives to turkeys. He literally invented product placement before the term existed. When *TV Guide* wanted to know about product placement in TV and movies, they went to Leo, who became the subject of a feature article in 1978.

Jayne Mansfield, the star of *Will Success Spoil Rock Hunter?* (1957) and *The Girl Can't Help It* (1956), was known as the new "Queen of Sex" in the late 1950s and '60s. At one point the press gave Jayne the title of "World's No. 1 Sex Symbol," and Jayne appeared on the covers of more than 500 magazines throughout her lifetime. Her Mediterranean mansion on Sunset Boulevard was known as The Pink Palace; Jayne loved pink so much that she even had a custom pink marble-topped barbecue.

When Leo was working with the California Turkey Advisory Board in 1957, he cut a deal with Jayne's manager to trade turkeys for a photo session with Jayne. With a little coaxing from Leo, Jayne donned a sexy bikini top and took photos with a barbecued turkey for the camera. The stunt was a huge success, and when Jayne married Mickey Hartigay she told *Life* magazine that she loved turkeys, especially on the barbecue, and that she would be cooking them not just for holidays, but all the time. Leo did not stop with Jayne, and his turkey promotions went on for nearly twenty years. In Leo's book *Celebrity Stew* he includes turkey shots with famous television families like *Ozzie and Harriet, My Three Sons,* and *Lassie,* hugely popular shows of the day.

Along the way Leo got Groucho Marx to pose with California White Potatoes, and had everyone from James Beard to Joan Rivers promoting prunes. Leo had Doris Day eating pretzels, and Bob Hope promoted grapefruits at the annual Bob Hope Classic in Palm Springs. Bob even provided Leo with his favorite grapefruit recipe, grapefruit halves topped with honey-stewed figs. Bob Hope contributed the quote "Leo Pearlstein is the P. T. Barnum of food and even more" to the jacket of *Celebrity Stew.* He couldn't have put it better.

Glazed Brussels Sprouts with Dried Plums and Chestnuts

Serves 6

Back when dried plums were still called prunes, they had quite a run in Hollywood, thanks to P.R. maven Leo Pearlstein, author of *Recipes of the Stars* (2004). Leo placed prunes on popular shows like *What's My Line?, The Dating Game,* and *Dinah!* Prunes eventually made their way to a series of radio commercials, and since they were known as the "funny fruit," it's no surprise that funny lady Joan Rivers helped promote them. Joan's commercials were the highlight of the radio spots; she even lent some of her recipes to the campaign.

12 ounces yellow pearl onions

1¼ pound Brussels sprouts

1 tablespoon extra-virgin olive oil

1 tablespoon white balsamic vinegar

1 teaspoon honey

2 tablespoons Marsala

1 cup pitted dried plums

7 ounces peeled cooked chestnuts (jarred or frozen and thawed)

½ teaspoon kosher salt

¼ teaspoon freshly ground black pepper

2 tablespoons chopped fresh flat-leaf parsley

Blanch the pearl onions by placing them into a large pot of rapidly boiling salted water. Cook for about 1 minute, remove the onions from the water with a strainer, then plunge the onions into an ice bath to stop the cooking. Remove from the ice bath and drain. Remove the skins by slicing off the root ends and pinching the onions from the skin.

Blanch the Brussels sprouts in the same water for 5 to 7 minutes, or until tender. Remove with a strainer and plunge into an ice bath to stop the cooking. Remove from the ice bath and drain. Reserve ¾ cup water from the pot.

Heat the oil in a 12-inch skillet over medium heat. Add the pearl onions and the vegetable water and cook, covered, for 10 minutes, then uncover and cook an additional 5 minutes. Add the vinegar, honey, and Marsala, and cook for 2 to 3 minutes more. Add the dried plums, chestnuts, Brussels sprouts, salt, and pepper and cook to heat through, adding 1 to 2 tablespoons cooking water if needed. Garnish with the chopped parsley. You can also make this dish ahead of time and reheat for 15 minutes in a 350°F oven.

Italian Broccoli with Pine Nuts and Garlic

Serves 4

In *Christmas in Connecticut* (1945), Barbara Stanwyck plays a single New York food writer, who can't cook but is known as "America's Best Cook." Her editor (who believes her lies) invites himself and a war hero to her "farm" for a Christmas dinner with her perfect family, which doesn't exist. Stanwyck must come up with a farm, a husband, a baby, and the perfect holiday dinner meal on short notice. Ironically, in real life Stanwyck lived on a farm with husband Robert Taylor and sold her farm-grown broccoli to the Brown Derby Restaurant.

2 bunches (about 2 pounds) rapini (also called broccoli rabe, or Italian broccoli), bottoms trimmed and stems peeled

2 teaspoons extra-virgin olive oil

★ Vegetables, Fruits, and Nuts ★

When I told my father I was moving to California, he asked me why I wanted to go to the "land of the fruits and nuts." I think he meant the people, but I was thinking about the fruits and nuts. Considering that horticulture was the number-one industry at the turn of the century, it's not surprising that the various California fruit and vegetable commissions and organizations are largely responsible for the promotion of cooking with California-grown ingredients like lemons, oranges, grapefruits, avocados, almonds, walnuts, olives, apricots, dates, dried plums (prunes), raisins, and figs. Promotional books including recipes from grower organizations helped to promote the use of California fruits and vegetables. In P.R. king Leo Pearlstein's books *Celebrity Stew* and *Recipes of the Stars,* he tells the story of how he helped promote California-grown products with Johnny Carson, Bob Hope, Steve Allen, Bing Crosby, and Jayne Mansfield. Leo was truly a master at the art of food and celebrity publicity, unrivaled even today.

Many of the country's largest specialty and organic produce companies started in California. In the early 1960s, produce seller Frieda Caplan of Frieda's introduced many new fruits and vegetables to California and America, including kiwifruit, button mushrooms, alfalfa sprouts, spaghetti squash, jicama, shallots, mangos, doughnut peaches, and a wide variety of Latin and Asian specialties. The media has dubbed Frieda's the "company that changed the way America eats," since they did it first.

When I was the chef at the Golden Temple restaurant in the early 1980s, a farmer from Santa Barbara named Albert used to come to the back door with a pickup truck full of organic vegetables for sale. In 1983 he established Albert's Organics, which today is part of United Natural Foods, the largest wholesale distributor of natural and organic products in America. Even though they are up in Carmel Valley, Earthbound Farms comes down to support Hollywood events like Envrionmental Media Awards and the Green Power Baby Shower, where moms learn about organic baby clothes, earth-friendly bathtub cleaners, and fresh organic vegetables. You may get lucky and spot Clint Eastwood in Carmel, but I like to visit the Earthbound Farmstand, which is one of my favorite spots in the state.

2 cloves garlic, chopped

¼ teaspoon kosher salt

⅛ teaspoon freshly ground white pepper

1 tablespoon chopped fresh basil

3 tablespoons pine nuts, toasted

Roughly chop the rapini bunches and drop into a large stockpot of rapidly boiling salted water. Cook for about 1 minute, then drain. Heat the oil in a 12-inch skillet over medium heat. Add the garlic and cook for 1 minute. Add the rapini, salt, and pepper and cook an additional 2 to 3 minutes, or until the rapini stems are tender.

Season with salt, pepper, and basil. Garnish with pine nuts.

11

Chocolat

CAKES, PIES, COOKIES, AND OTHER SWEETS

When I first started working as a chef at the Golden Temple in Los Angeles, my partner in crime was Mani Niall, author of *Sweet and Natural Baking* (1996) and *Covered in Honey* (2003). Mani, who pioneered the art of healthy homestyle desserts, opened Mani's Bakery in Los Angeles in 1989, and used natural sweeteners like concentrated fruit juice, maple syrup, and honey in his baked goods. The media soon dubbed him "baker to the stars" and Danny DeVito, Dwight Yoakum, Faye Dunaway, Marilu Henner, and the Red Hot Chili Peppers all became fans of Mani's "Fauxnuts" (see page 30), cookies, cakes, and pies.

Desserts made with healthful ingredients have historically had a bad rap. Mani was the first natural food chef to create desserts from a traditional baking perspective rather than solely focusing on ingredients. My first whole-wheat honey cakes were lead bricks, and it took a few years of experimentation to get it right. Baking is a science, and creating wheat-free, dairy-free, or vegan desserts can be complicated, but it certainly is possible.

There are many theories on what defines a "healthy" dessert: wheat-free, dairy-free, low-carb, fat-free, sugar-free, and 100 percent organic are all possibilities. All of the various ingredients needed to make healthy desserts are now available organically grown, which is a huge milestone for the natural food industry.

Many of the recipes in this chapter are dairy free, and baking delicious dairy-free desserts is easy using plain soymilk, which is low in fat, lactose free, contains no cholesterol, and adds a nutritional punch to baked goods. Cup for cup, unsweetened or plain soymilk can replace cow's milk in any recipe, and you won't be able to tell the difference. I add 1 teaspoon of lemon or orange juice per 1 cup of soymilk to replace buttermilk.

Billy Bob Thornton turned me on to spelt flour when I started catering holiday parties for him. Spelt is an ancient grain and a high-protein cousin to wheat. Spelt is not gluten free, but it is considered wheat free, and it is easier to digest than wheat. For Billy's parties I created desserts like Pralines and Crème Carrot Cake and Sweet Potato Pie, using white spelt flour and soymilk. The results were superb, and because of Billy, I became a spelt flour convert. Of course, you can use unbleached flour in any recipe that calls for spelt flour, if you prefer.

Instead of white sugar, try light blond organic sugar, which is available in most supermarkets and natural food stores. Turbinado sugar and coarse granulated sugar will not work in certain recipes, and sucanat or dark brown sugar will make every dessert taste like molasses, which won't work when you want a light flavor. I also like to bake with honey, especially mild-flavored varieties like sage or acacia. Maple syrup adds a lot of flavor to baked goods, and give maple sugar a try—it's amazing in the Maple Pecan Butter Cookies.

Honey–Goat's Milk Flan

Serves 8

In the beginning days of Rancho La Puerta, founders Deborah and Edmond Szekely kept their own goats for milk and cheese and bees for honey. In the early days they didn't serve a lot of desserts, but when they did, they were sweetened with honey. I learned how to make flan from my friend Nancy Zaslavsky's cookbook, *Meatless Mexican Home Cooking* (1997). In 1971 Edmond wrote *The Book of Living Foods* and included a recipe for Mexican Honey Custard and, like me, he recommends goat milk and sage or acacia honey.

⅔ cup sugar

¼ cup water

7 large eggs

⅓ cup sage or acacia honey

1 quart goat's milk or cow's milk

1 teaspoon ground cinnamon

1 teaspoon pure vanilla extract

¼ teaspoon kosher salt

Preheat the oven to 350°F.

Place the sugar in a saucepan and add the water—do not stir. Place over high heat and heat until the sugar begins to melt. Swirl the pan over the heat until the syrup darkens to a medium amber color, about 10 minutes—don't stir.

When the liquid is caramel colored, pour it into the bottom of a 12 x 4½ x 2½-inch loaf pan or 2-quart ceramic soufflé dish or deep casserole pan. Bring a kettle of water to a boil for the water bath and keep it hot.

In a free-standing heavy-duty electric mixer or in a large bowl using electric beaters, whisk the eggs and honey until just blended. Heat the goat's milk in a medium saucepan over medium-low heat until it scalds (tiny bubbles will appear around the sides). Pour the goat's milk very slowly into the egg mixture, whisk-

★ Rancho La Puerta and the Golden Door ★

Deborah Szekely has been influencing Hollywood and the rest of the world on the value of diet and exercise for the past sixty-five years. Her fate was sealed in 1926, when her vegetarian parents decided to move her entire family to Tahiti. In Tahiti the family met Edmond Szekely, a Hungarian scholar and philosopher who had come to the island to study the Polynesians. When Deborah was seventeen she married Szekely, and in 1940 they hosted a "health camp" three hours south of Los Angeles near Tecate, Mexico.

Edmond, a Hungarian scholar, philosopher, and "natural living experimenter," had been teaching health and wellness for many years. In the beginning they called their retreat the Essene School of Life, based on Edmond's studies of the Essenes as the world's first agriculturists and natural healers. Eventually they named their retreat Rancho La Puerta. The first summer they charged $17.50 per week, guests brought their own tents, and everyone helped out with cooking and gardening and other ranch chores, such as milking goats for cheese, making sprouts, and baking bread, a task performed by Burt Lancaster in the 1950s. Grains were bought from local sources such as El Molino Mills, yogurt cultures were imported from Paris, and fruits were dried in the sun. Salads were made

Burt Lancaster baking bread at Rancho La Puerta. (COURTESY OF RANCHO LA PUERTA ARCHIVES)

with vegetables they grew from what was the first modern-day organic garden on the West Coast, based on the same *Agricultural Testament* by Sir Albert Howard that had inspired J. I. Rodale in his work. Many of the recipes came from Deborah's mother, who spent many years helping them develop the natural food dishes they originally served at the Ranch. From the first day Deborah was the secretary and activities and exercise director. She soon began to hire dance instructors and assembled as many activities as possible into one day, hiking, water exercise, yoga, volleyball, and exercising to jazz (the most popular class) among them. They literally pioneered the modern health spa program in food and exercise.

In 1958 they opened the Golden Door, in response to suggestions from the Ranch's celebrity guests, who wanted a spa with more privacy and amenities closer to Los Angeles. The Golden Door introduced aromatherapy, herbal baths, and other ancient healing practices to the West. Both resorts are still booked year round, and are the forerunners to the health resorts and spas now found in California and all of America.

ing constantly. Add the cinnamon, vanilla, and salt, and whisk to combine. Pour the mixture into the prepared pan. Set the pan into a larger baking pan.

To create the water bath, pour the hot (not boiling) water into the larger pan to come about 1 inch up the sides of the mold; be careful not to get water into the flan. Carefully transfer to the oven, and bake for 30 to 45 minutes, or until a knife inserted in the middle comes out fairly clean (a few small clumps on the knife are okay). Cool to room temperature in the water bath, then remove the flan, cover with plastic, and refrigerate for at least 4 hours or overnight.

When you are ready to serve, run a butter knife around the inside of the mold to loosen the flan. Place a platter on top of the flan and invert to pop it out.

Crispy Fruit Crumble

Serves 6 to 8

Tony award winner and three-time Emmy winner Shirley Knight is known for her fabulous parties and delicious fruit crumbles. Since starring with Paul Newman in *Sweet Bird of Youth* (1962), she has appeared in more than eighty-five movies, and is currently a frequent guest on ABC's hit drama *Desperate Housewives*. Our mutual friend, actress Julie Janney, shared one of Shirley's crumble recipes with me. I first used crispy rice cereal in a crumble topping at a ChefDance dinner I catered with Wild Oats Marketplace during the Sundance Film Festival in Park City, Utah. I was a "Desperate Chef" myself, needing something to help the topping crisp up at that high altitude. The recipe works even better at sea level.

4 pounds medium peaches, nectarines, or pears, peeled, pitted, and cut into 1-inch slices (about 5 cups)

¼ cup sugar

1 tablespoons unbleached flour, plus 1 cup for the topping

Zest of 1 lemon

1 tablespoon fresh lemon juice

¾ cup packed light brown sugar

½ cup rolled oats

½ teaspoon cinnamon

¼ teaspoon fine sea salt

6 tablespoons cold unsalted butter, cut into small pieces

½ cup crispy brown rice cereal

Preheat the oven to 375°F.

In a large bowl, combine the fruit, sugar, 1 tablespoon flour, lemon zest, and lemon juice. Place the mixture in a 9-inch pie pan or similar-sized round baking dish.

In another bowl, combine the remaining 1 cup flour, brown sugar, oats, cinnamon, and salt. Add the cold butter and mix with your fingertips until the topping resembles coarse meal. Mix in the brown rice cereal.

Spread the topping over the fruit. Bake for 30 to 35 minutes, or until the topping is browned and the fruit begins to bubble. Let cool for 15 minutes, serve warm or at room temperature. The crumble is great with the Strawberry-Lavender Goat's Milk Gelato (page 269).

Coconut Meringue Custards

Serves 6

From opening day in 1929, department store Bullock's Wilshire's Tea Room baked coconut cream pie on a daily basis. Actors Ingrid Bergman, Bob Hope, and Katharine Hepburn, as well as fashion designers Gianni Versace and Donna Karan, dined at the Tea Room. Even "health nuts" Mae West and Greta Garbo were spotted dining in the cabbage-rose wallpapered garden-style room. My version is made without a crust and meringue is used instead of whipped cream—same great taste, less fat, and dairy-free.

CUSTARD

½ cup shredded unsweetened coconut

⅔ cup sugar

⅓ cup cornstarch

3 cups plain soymilk

2 large eggs

1 teaspoon pure vanilla extract

COCONUT MERINGUE TOPPING

2 egg whites

¼ teaspoon cream of tartar

¼ cup sugar

¼ cup shredded unsweetened coconut

To make the custard, have ready six 4-ounce ceramic ramekins and preheat the oven to 300°F. Spread the coconut over a small baking sheet or cake pan. Place in the oven and toast, stirring occasionally, until golden brown, 5 to 10 minutes. Remove from the oven and increase the oven temperature to 325°F.

Place the sugar and cornstarch in a heavy 2-quart saucepan. Gradually whisk in the soymilk until the cornstarch dissolves. Whisk in the eggs until thoroughly incorporated. Place over medium heat and bring the mixture to a simmer, stirring constantly with a heatproof rubber spatula or wooden spoon. Remove from the heat, scrape the pan with the spatula, and whisk again until smooth. Return to the heat and cook at a bare simmer for 1 minute. Remove from the heat and add the toasted coconut and vanilla. Place the ramekins on a baking sheet or in a large casserole dish and fill each with the hot custard. Cover with plastic wrap while you make the meringue.

To make the meringue, place the egg whites in the bowl of a freestanding heavy-duty electric mixer or a large bowl (make sure it's dry and grease-free). Beat the egg whites on medium speed until frothy. Add the cream of tartar and beat until soft peaks form. Gradually beat in the sugar and continue whipping until the egg whites are stiff but not dry.

Cover each custard with some meringue, making sure the entire top is covered, adhering the meringue to the rim of the ramekin. Sprinkle with the shredded coconut. Bake for 8 minutes, or until lightly browned on top.

Lemon-Almond Pudding

Serves 6

I found this recipe in *Sunkist Lemons Bring Out the Flavor* (1939) and added the almonds for texture and taste. The absolute best almonds I have ever had were from Gypsy Boots (page 209), who sold them to me at the Hollywood Farmers Market. Gypsy appeared on Steve Allen's *Tonight Show* twenty-five times, reaching a national audience of over 30 million viewers and receiving tons of fan mail. He would come in swinging on a vine and make Steve fresh juice or a smoothie. He also appeared in a bizarre cult movie called *Mondo Hollywood* (1967) with Ram Dass and Frank Zappa, and had roles in other films like *A Swingin' Summer* (1965), *Confessions of Tom Harris* (1969), and *The Game* (1997) with Michael Douglas.

Canola cooking spray

2 tablespoons unsalted butter, softened

¾ cup sugar

2 tablespoons unbleached all-purpose flour

2 large eggs yolks, beaten

¼ cup fresh lemon juice

I teaspoon finely grated lemon zest

I cup plain soymilk

2 large egg whites

2 tablespoons finely chopped or sliced almonds

Preheat the oven to 375°F. Coat six 4-ounce ceramic ramekins with cooking spray. In a freestanding heavy-duty electric mixer or with hand beaters, cream the butter, sugar, and flour. Whisk in the egg yolks, lemon juice, lemon zest, and soymilk. Bring a kettle of water to a boil for the water bath and keep it hot.

In a dry and grease-free bowl, beat the egg whites until stiff but not dry. Lightly fold the egg whites into the lemon mixture.

Place the ramekins in a 13 x 9-inch casserole dish. Evenly divide the pudding among the ramekins. Sprinkle each with 1 teaspoon of the almonds.

Create a hot water bath by filling the casserole dish halfway with the hot water. Bake for 25 minutes, or until the puddings are firm to the touch and lightly browned. The pudding will have a cake-like top and a layer of lemon custard below. Serve immediately.

Wild Honey Rice Pudding

Serves 6

In the 1950s, P.R. genius Leo Pearlstein called Capital Records to see if they would promote National Honey Week with their new John Arcesi record, *Wild Honey*. Capital suggested a "honey and feather" party at the Garden of Allah Hotel in Hollywood—the place that was once home to Ernest Hemingway, F. Scott Fitzgerald, Dorothy Parker, Errol Flynn, and Humphrey Bogart. Miss Wild Honey was "tarred" with honey and covered with real feathers at the party, and although she was a mess, the publicity for all involved was huge.

Canola cooking spray

⅓ cup short-grain white rice such as Arborio or sushi

1½ cups water

⅛ teaspoon kosher salt

⅛ teaspoon ground cinnamon

⅛ teaspoon ground cardamom

⅛ teaspoon freshly grated nutmeg, plus more for garnish

⅓ cup raisins

4 large eggs

5 tablespoons sugar

2 tablespoons sage honey

2 cups plain soymilk

¼ cup soymilk creamer

1 teaspoon pure vanilla extract

Preheat the oven to 325°F. Coat six 4-ounce ceramic ramekins with cooking spray. Place the rice, water, and salt in a 2-quart saucepan over medium-high heat and bring to a boil. Cover, reduce the heat to medium, and cook at a low boil for 15 minutes. Drain and put into a medium bowl. Add the cinnamon, cardamom, nutmeg, and raisins. Place the ramekins in a 13 x 9-inch baking dish. Divide the rice mixture equally among the ramekins. Bring a kettle of water to a boil for the water bath and keep it hot.

In a separate bowl, whisk together the eggs, sugar, and honey. Bring the soymilk and soymilk creamer to a bare simmer in a small saucepan. Remove from the heat, add vanilla, and very slowly whisk into the egg mixture. Fill each ramekin with the soymilk mixture. Grate a little fresh nutmeg over each ramekin. Create a hot water bath by filling the casserole dish 1 inch up the sides of the ramekins with the hot water. Bake for 40 to 45 minutes. Serve warm or cold.

Neil's Apricot Soufflé with Raspberry Coulis

Serves 6

*N*eil Zevnick came to California from New York to further his acting career. Actors must eat, and what better way than to become a chef, which is exactly what Neil did. Neil works as a private chef and his clients, like Elizabeth Taylor and Pierce Brosnan, love his Apricot Soufflé, which he has served at numerous dinners over the years. He shared the recipe with me, which is easy to make and if there is any left over, as he says, "it's even great cold." I agree. If you can afford the calories, top the soufflé with fresh organic whipped cream.

APRICOT SOUFFLÉ

Canola cooking spray

2 tablespoons sugar, plus more for dusting

3 ounces (½ cup) chopped dried apricots

¾ cup water

¼ teaspoon almond extract

3 large egg whites

⅛ teaspoon fine sea salt

¼ teaspoon cream of tartar

RASPBERRY COULIS

1 pint fresh raspberries

2 tablespoons mild honey such as sage or acacia

1 teaspoon fresh lemon juice

To make the soufflé, preheat the oven to 350°F. Coat a 1-quart soufflé dish with cooking spray and dust with sugar. Place the apricots in a small saucepan over medium heat with the water. Bring to a simmer and cook until tender, about 10 minutes. Cool. Place apricots and liquid in a food processor with the almond extract and process until smooth.

In a dry and grease-free glass or metal bowl, beat the egg whites on medium speed with a handheld or freestanding electric mixer until frothy. Add the cream of tartar and salt; beat until soft peaks form. Gradually beat in the sugar and continue whipping until the egg whites hold stiff glossy peaks.

Fold in a quarter of the whites into the apricot mixture, then fold the apricot mixture back into the egg whites. Spoon into the soufflé dish. (The mixture can be refrigerated at this point for up to 1 hour.) Bake for 18 minutes, or until set in the center.

While the soufflé is baking, make the sauce: Puree the raspberries, honey, and lemon juice in a blender or food processor until smooth. Strain through a fine-mesh strainer, adding a little more honey or lemon juice if needed.

Cappuccino Cream Pie with Chocolate Cookie Crust

Serves 8

Thanks to Paul and Nell Newman, you can now make this entire pie with organic ingredients. Newman's Own started in 1982; since then the company has given more than 150 million dollars to charity. Nell Newman heads up Newman's Own Organics, another company with the same spirit of giving. Newman's Own makes Tops & Bottoms, chocolate wafers that contain no trans fats and are made with nonhydrogenated palm oil. You can substitute soymilk for the cow's milk, but don't skip the whipped cream—it makes the pie.

CRUST

1 (8-ounce) package chocolate wafer cookies (such as Newman's Tops & Bottoms) pulverized to crumbs in a food processor

5 tablespoons unsalted butter or nonhydrogenated vegetable shortening,
  melted

¼ cup sugar

FILLING

⅔ cup sugar

¼ cup cornstarch

2½ cups cow's milk, preferably organic

1 tablespoon finely ground espresso beans

⅛ teaspoon fine sea salt

3 large eggs

2 tablespoons unsalted butter, cut into small pieces

2 teaspoons pure vanilla extract

TOPPING

1 cup heavy cream, preferably organic

2 tablespoons powdered sugar

1 teaspoon pure vanilla extract

¼ of an 8-ounce espresso-flavored organic chocolate bar, such as Newman's
  Organics Sweet Dark Chocolate Espresso Bar, grated

Preheat the oven to 350°F. To make the crust, combine the crumbs, butter, and sugar in a medium bowl and mix well. Firmly press the crumb mixture evenly into the bottom and up the sides of a 9-inch pie plate. Bake for 8 minutes. Remove from the oven and cool.

To make the filling, place the sugar and cornstarch in a heavy 2-quart saucepan. Gradually whisk in the milk, making sure that the cornstarch dissolves. Add the espresso beans and salt, then whisk in the eggs, mixing well until no sign of yolk remains. Place over medium heat and bring the mixture to a simmer, stirring constantly with a heatproof rubber spatula or wooden spoon. Remove from the heat and scrape the pan with the spatula, then whisk again until smooth. Return to the heat and cook at a bare simmer for 1 minute. Remove from the heat and strain through a wire mesh strainer into a medium bowl. Whisk the butter and vanilla into the filling and pour into the cooled pie crust. Cover with plastic wrap or wax paper and refrigerate for at least 4 hours.

To make the topping, whip the cream with the powdered sugar and vanilla using an electric mixer or handheld beaters. Cover the pie with the whipped cream and top with the grated chocolate.

Raspberry Tart with Cashew Crème and Coconut-Date Crust

Makes 4 tarts

Hollywood's first queen of raw cuisine was Vera Richter, who "cooked" her raw pies in a solar oven back in the 1920s. Today's raw chefs use dehydrators to create pie crusts, but here I wanted to make a raw pie that didn't require a dehydrator and wouldn't take 2 to 3 days of soaking, blending, and drying. Woody Harrelson is one of Hollywood's leading raw-food advocates, and he wrote the foreword to *Living Cuisine: The Art, Science, and Spirit of Raw Foods,* by Renee Underkoffler (2004), whose recipes inspired me to create this one.

CRUST

½ cup finely shredded unsweetened coconut

¼ cup almond meal or raw almonds ground in a food processor

¼ cup pitted and coarsely chopped dates

2 teaspoons fresh orange juice

CASHEW CRÈME

1 cup raw cashews

6 Medjool dates, pitted

1 teaspoon finely grated lemon zest

5 tablespoons fresh lemon juice

5 tablespoons raw honey

Scraped seeds from half of a vanilla bean
Pinch of fine sea salt

BERRIES
2 teaspoons raw honey
1 teaspoon fresh lemon juice
1 pint fresh raspberries or other seasonal berries

Preheat the oven to 200°F.

Fit four 4-inch removable-bottom tart pans with parchment rounds.

To make the crust, pulse the coconut, almond meal, dates, and orange juice in a food processor until a "dough" is formed. Using your fingertips, press the mixture about ½-inch thick onto the bottoms of the prepared tart pans. Turn off the oven, place the tarts on a baking sheet, and leave in the oven for 1 hour to dehydrate.

Meanwhile, make the cashew crème: Soak the cashews in cold water to cover for 30 minutes. Drain and reserve the soaking water. Put the cashews, dates, lemon zest, lemon juice, honey, the vanilla bean seeds, and salt in a food processor and process until thick and creamy, adding 1 tablespoon of the reserved cashew water if needed. Refrigerate until you are ready to assemble the tarts.

To make the berries, mix the honey and lemon juice in a medium bowl. Add the berries and let sit for 15 minutes.

To assemble the tarts, remove the dehydrated crusts from the tart pans, peeling off the parchment from the bottoms. Place each crust on a dessert plate and fill them with the cashew crème. Top with the berries, and serve immediately.

Fresh Plum Tart with Honey Crème Anglaise

Serves 8

Dorothy Chandler made the cover of *Time* in 1964 for her outstanding work in campaigning for the arts in Los Angeles. Her fundraising efforts saved the Hollywood Bowl from closing in 1950, and she then headed the campaign that raised the money to build the Los Angeles Music Center, home to the new Walt Disney Concert Hall. Her father-in-law was Harry Chandler, a "health seeker" who came to Los Angeles in the late 1880s to cure his lung problems. Chandler grew fruit and produced honey before he became the publisher of the *Los Angeles Times,* where he first started a health column in 1899.

When plums and peaches are out of season you can substitute 4 cups peeled and sliced apples sautéed in 1 tablespoon unsalted butter for 10 minutes.

CORNMEAL CRUST

1 cup plus 2 tablespoons unbleached flour

¼ cup yellow cornmeal

½ teaspoon fine sea salt

8 tablespoons unsalted butter or nonhydrogenated vegetable shortening, chilled

2 to 3 tablespoons ice water, as needed

FILLING

4 cups sliced firm plums or peaches

2 tablespoons sage or acacia honey

1 teaspoon finely grated lemon zest

5 tablespoons ground toasted almonds (ground in a food processor)

¼ cup fruit-sweetened strawberry or apricot jam

HONEY CRÈME ANGLAISE

3 large eggs or ¾ cup fat-free liquid egg product

¼ cup sage or acacia honey

2 tablespoons cornstarch

2 cups plain soymilk

2 teaspoons pure vanilla extract

To make the crust, combine the flour, cornmeal, and salt in a medium bowl. Cut in the butter and work into the dry ingredients until the mixture is crumbly and resembles coarse meal. Add the ice water, 1 tablespoon at a time, until the dough begins to cling together and forms a ball. Transfer the dough to parchment or wax paper and flatten into a 6-inch disk. Wrap in plastic and refrigerate for 1 hour before rolling out.

Preheat the oven to 400°F. Roll the dough into a 10-inch removable-bottom tart pan and prick the dough with a fork 2 or 3 times. Bake the crust for 10 minutes, remove to a rack and let cool. Reduce the oven temperature to 350°F.

To make the filling, combine the plums, honey, and lemon zest in a medium bowl. Sprinkle the bottom of the cooled pie crust with the ground almonds. Top with the jam and arrange the fruit on top. Place on a parchment-lined baking sheet and bake for 45 minutes, or until the juices bubble and the fruit is lightly caramelized.

To make the crème anglaise, in a medium bowl whisk the eggs, honey, and cornstarch until the cornstarch dissolves. In a heavy 2-quart saucepan over medium heat, heat the soymilk until scalding (tiny bubbles will appear on top).

Slowly drizzle in ½ cup of the hot soymilk into the egg mixture, whisking constantly. Pour the egg mixture back into the saucepan with the remaining milk. Set over low heat and cook until thick and creamy, about 2 minutes, stirring constantly with a wooden spoon. The mixture should register 170°F on an instant-read thermometer. Strain into a bowl and stir in the vanilla. Serve warm or cold. Make sure the sauce is completely chilled before covering, as condensation may cause it to thin. Serve tarts with crème anglaise on the side.

Sweet Potato Pie

Serves 8

I once made Thanksgiving dinner for 300 while on a rock and roll tour in Australia. The best part about the event was that the whole band helped me and made all their favorite dishes. Sweet potato pie, of course, was on the menu, and fortunately sweet potatoes are available in Australia. Finding cranberries was a whole different story—I think we had to fly them in. My favorite Thanksgiving dinners are the ones I spend at Billy Bob Thornton's house, and this pie is often on the menu.

1 recipe Spelt Pie Crust (recipe follows)

¾ cup sugar

¼ cup firmly packed light brown sugar

2 teaspoons cornstarch

1 teaspoon ground cinnamon

1 teaspoon ground ginger

½ teaspoon freshly grated nutmeg

¼ teaspoon fine sea salt

6 egg whites or ¾ cup liquid egg whites

2 pounds cooked garnet yams or sweet potatoes, peeled and pureed, to make
    about 1¾ cups

1 cup plain soymilk

Preheat the oven to 425°F.

To make the crust, roll the dough into a 9- or 10-inch pie pan and place in the freezer while you make the filling.

In a large bowl mix the sugar, brown sugar, cornstarch, cinnamon, ginger, nutmeg, and salt. Whisk to remove any lumps from the cornstarch.

In a large bowl whisk the egg whites. Add the pureed yams and then add the sugar mixture. Slowly whisk in the soymilk and pour into the prepared crust.

Bake for 15 minutes, then reduce the oven temperature to 350°F and bake for 40 to 50 minutes, or until a toothpick inserted in the center comes out clean. Cool the pie to room temperature. It can be made several hours ahead, or up to one day in advance.

Spelt Pie Crust

1½ cups white spelt flour

2 teaspoons sugar

½ teaspoon fine sea salt

8 tablespoons cold nonhydrogenated vegetable shortening or unsalted butter

2 to 3 tablespoons ice water, or as needed

Place the flour, sugar, and salt into a medium bowl. Cut in the shortening and work into the dry ingredients until the mixture is crumbly and resembles coarse meal. Add the ice water 1 tablespoon at a time, until the dough begins to cling together and form a ball. Transfer the dough to parchment or wax paper and flatten into a 6-inch disk. Wrap and refrigerate for 1 hour before rolling out.

Sundance Chocolate Torte

Serves 8

Hollywood should really be using Alice Medrich as a consultant when they make movies like *Chocolat* (2000) because no one knows more about chocolate than Alice. If she lived in Los Angeles, I'm sure she would be the "chocolatier to the stars," though to me she is, since I use her recipes all the time. This is my wheat-free, soy-enhanced version of Alice's Chocolate Walnut Torte from *Chocolate and The Art of Low-Fat Desserts* (1994). When I catered my first events at the Sundance Film Festival, in 2003, I took this recipe along, knowing the altitude wouldn't really affect the texture. It was a huge hit at all of the parties, and I have been serving it every year.

Canola cooking spray

⅓ cup chopped hazelnuts or almonds

3 tablespoons spelt or barley flour

2½ ounces semisweet chocolate, finely chopped

⅓ cup Dutch process cocoa

1 cup sugar

⅓ cup plain soymilk

1 tablespoon rum or Kahlúa

1 egg yolk

½ teaspoon pure vanilla extract

4 fresh egg whites or ½ cup liquid egg whites

¼ teaspoon cream of tartar

CHOCOLATE GLAZE

4 ounces good quality semisweet chocolate, chopped into 1-inch pieces
  (about ⅔ cup)

3 tablespoons soymilk creamer

Preheat the oven to 350°F. Line an 8-inch round springform pan or removable-bottom cake pan with parchment paper and spray with cooking spray. Grind the nuts with the flour in a food processor until very fine.

Combine the chopped chocolate, cocoa, and ¾ cup of the sugar in a medium bowl. Heat the soymilk and rum in a small saucepan to scalding. Remove from the heat, pour it over the chocolate, and whisk until the mixture is completely smooth. Stir in the egg yolk and vanilla.

With a handheld or freestanding heavy-duty electric mixer, beat the egg whites with the cream of tartar on medium speed until soft peaks form. Gradually add the remaining ¼ cup sugar, and continue to beat until stiff but not dry. Fold the nut mixture into the chocolate. Fold a quarter of the egg whites in with a rubber spatula to lighten the mixture, then fold in the rest. Scrape the batter into the prepared pan and smooth to the edges with the rubber spatula. Bake for 25 to 30 minutes. Don't overbake, or it will dry out. Cool the torte on a rack. Slide a butter knife around the sides to release the torte. Remove the sides from the pan, invert the pan, remove the paper liner from the bottom, and turn the torte right side up onto a cake platter or large plate.

In a double boiler or stainless steel bowl set over gently simmering water (the water should not touch the bottom of the bowl) melt the chocolate, stirring. Turn off the heat and let stand over the warm water until ready to use.

Scald the soymilk in a small saucepan over medium heat. Pour into the melted chocolate and whisk together.

Pour the chocolate glaze over the cake and let cool before serving.

Pralines and Crème Carrot Cake

Makes one 8 x 8-inch square or 10-inch round cake; serves 8 to 10

She was born Leona A. Male, but in true Hollywood style, she changed her name to Prudence Penny. Prudence was a huge fan of carrots in cakes, breads, and cookies, and in *Prudence Penny's Cook Book* (1939) she includes a recipe for carrot cake, one of the earliest seen in Los Angeles. Prudence played herself in three movies, including *Remedy for Riches* (1940), where she judges a bake-off at the county fair. The film stars Oscar winner Jean Hersholt, who helped start the Motion Picture Relief Fund. The Jean Hersholt Humanitarian Award, presented at the Academy Awards, is named in his honor.

CARROT CAKE
½ cup canola oil, plus more for the pan
1½ cups unbleached all-purpose flour, plus more for the pan
1½ teaspoons baking soda
½ teaspoon baking powder
½ teaspoon fine sea salt

1 ¾ teaspoons ground cinnamon

1 teaspoon ground ginger

¼ teaspoon freshly grated nutmeg

1 cup sugar

2 tablespoons packed light brown sugar

¾ cup plain soymilk or low-fat buttermilk

1 ½ teaspoons pure vanilla extract

1 ½ teaspoons finely grated orange zest

1 tablespoon orange juice

2 cups shredded carrots (about 4 large carrots)

¾ cup drained crushed or chopped pineapple

½ cup shredded unsweetened coconut

½ cup chopped walnuts or pecans

CREAM CHEESE ICING

1 cup (8 ounces) tofu or low-fat dairy cream cheese

¼ cup nonhydrogenated vegetable shortening or unsalted butter

2 ½ cups powdered sugar, sifted

½ teaspoon pure vanilla extract

PECAN PRALINE

Canola cooking spray or canola oil

1 cup sugar

6 tablespoons water

⅛ teaspoon cream of tartar

1 cup toasted pecans

Preheat the oven to 350°F. Grease and flour an 8 x 8-inch square or 10-inch round baking pan. Sift the flour, baking soda, baking powder, salt, cinnamon, ginger, and nutmeg into a large bowl.

In a medium bowl whisk the sugar, brown sugar, and oil for 1 minute. Whisk in the soymilk, vanilla, orange zest, and orange juice until emulsified. Add the wet ingredients to the dry, using a rubber spatula, stirring just enough to blend. Fold in the carrots, pineapple, coconut, and walnuts, mixing just until combined.

Transfer the batter to the prepared pan, smoothing to edges. Bake for 35 to 40 minutes, or until springy to the touch and a toothpick inserted in the center comes out clean. Cool the cake in the pan on a wire rack to room temperature.

To make the frosting, beat the cream cheese and shortening until smooth in a freestanding heavy-duty electric mixer or using hand beaters. Beat in the powdered sugar and salt until the mixture is of frosting consistency, then beat in the vanilla. Set aside.

To make the praline, coat a baking sheet with cooking spray or lightly oil a clean marble slab. Heat the sugar, water, and cream of tartar in a 1-quart heavy saucepan, over low heat until the sugar is dissolved—do not stir. Brush down the sides of the pan with a pastry brush. Bring to a boil and cook without stirring until it reaches 356°F on a candy thermometer (medium caramel stage). Add the pecans and stir quickly with a wooden spoon. Remove from the heat and pour the syrup on the prepared surface. Let cool completely. Break into pieces and pulverize with a food processor or crush with a rolling pin. You will use one-third to one-half of this to decorate the top cake.

Ice the cake with the cream cheese frosting and sprinkle the top with about half of the crushed pralines. Freeze the rest and use it to decorate another cake or to sprinkle on ice cream.

Orange Chiffon Cake with Citrus Compote and Vanilla-Scented Fromage Blanc

Serves 12 to 16

Harry Baker was an insurance salesman who invented the chiffon cake in Los Angeles in 1927. He converted a spare room in his apartment and baked forty cakes a day, which he sold to the Brown Derby Restaurant for two dollars each. They eventually put his cake on the menu, which became well known as the Grapefruit Cake. His cakes appeared in movies and were sold to Barbara Stanwyck, Eleanor Roosevelt, and the MGM and RKO commissaries. His secret recipe, with a magic ingredient (vegetable oil), eventually sold to General Mills for an unreported sum in 1947. Betty Crocker introduced the new cake as the "Chiffon Cake," and claimed it to be the "first new cake in a hundred years." This recipe is taken from the Betty Crocker version, but I use white spelt flour, which works beautifully.

At the Brown Derby, this cake was layered with cream cheese and grapefruit icing. I think the presentation is much better this way.

ORANGE CHIFFON CAKE

2¼ cups white spelt flour or cake flour

1½ cups sugar

1 tablespoon baking powder

1 teaspoon fine sea salt

½ cup canola oil

4 egg yolks

¼ cup fresh grapefruit juice

½ cup fresh orange juice

2 teaspoons pure vanilla extract

2 tablespoons finely grated orange zest

1 teaspoon finely grated lemon zest

8 fresh egg whites or 1 cup liquid egg whites

½ teaspoon cream of tartar

CITRUS COMPOTE

4 navel or blood oranges

3 ruby grapefruits

Sugar, if needed

VANILLA-SCENTED FROMAGE BLANC

8 ounces fromage blanc or ricotta cheese

½ teaspoon pure vanilla extract

½ vanilla bean, seeds scraped from the pod

½ cup powdered sugar

To make the cake, preheat the oven to 325°F. Have ready but *don't grease* a 10-inch tube pan with a removable bottom. Sift the flour, sugar, baking powder, and salt into a large bowl. In another bowl whisk the oil, egg yolks, grapefruit and orange juices, vanilla, and orange and lemon zests. Make a well in the center of the flour mixture and add the liquid ingredients. Mix until smooth with a wire whisk.

In a freestanding heavy-duty electric mixer or using a handheld mixer, whip the egg whites until foamy. Add the cream of tartar and beat until stiff peaks form. Gradually pour the yolk mixture over the beaten whites, lightly folding in with a rubber spatula until just combined—do not stir or overblend.

Pour the batter into the ungreased tube pan and bake for 55 minutes, or until the top of the cake springs back when lightly touched and a toothpick inserted in the center comes out clean. Remove the cake from the oven and immediately invert the pan on the top of a funnel, or rest the inverted pan on 4 glasses and cool for 1½ to 2 hours. (Inverting the pan is essential for proper cooling.)

Meanwhile, make the citrus compote. Finely grate the outer rind of the oranges and grapefruit to make 2 tablespoons of zest. Peel and section the fruit and combine in a medium bowl. Taste and add a little sugar if the fruit is not sweet enough. Refrigerate until ready to use.

To make the fromage blanc, puree the fromage blanc, vanilla, vanilla bean seeds, and powdered sugar in a food processor until smooth and creamy.

When the cake has cooled, turn the pan right side up and run a butter knife around the edges and around the tube, pressing the knife against the pan to avoid tearing the cake. Lift the tube upward to lift the cake from the pan, then slide the knife under the cake to detach it from the bottom. Place the cake on a serving platter, slice it, and serve with the citrus compote and fromage blanc.

Avocado Coffee Cake

Makes 1 cake, 12 to 16 slices

The original *Oceans Eleven* (1960) starred Rat Pack members Frank Sinatra, Dean Martin, Sammy Davis Jr., and Peter Lawford. Sinatra played Danny Ocean, the role played by George Clooney in the 2001 remake. Beatrice Ocean (called Tess Ocean in the 2001 remake with Julia Roberts) was played by actress Angie Dickinson, one of the few female Rat Pack buddies. Along with the Rat Pack, Dickinson defined sexy and cool in the 1960s, and is best known for her 1970s role as Sgt. "Pepper" Anderson, on TV's *Police Woman*. In 1963 Universal Studios had Dickinson's legs insured for a million dollars; in 1981 her famous legs were featured on a billboard and print campaign for California Avocados. The campaign showed Angie holding a slice of avocado with the message "17 calories per slice . . . would this body lie to you?" Avocados have been sexy and cool ever since, and replace the butter and sour cream that would normally be in this coffee cake recipe.

FILLING

⅔ cup walnuts

¼ light brown sugar

1 teaspoon ground cinnamon

½ cup finely chopped semisweet chocolate

CAKE

2 cups unbleached all-purpose flour, plus more for dusting the pans

1 teaspoon baking powder

1 teaspoon baking soda

½ teaspoon fine sea salt

⅓ cup avocado or canola oil

1 cup pureed ripe avocados, about 2 large Hass avocados

1 cup sugar

2 large eggs

2 teaspoons vanilla extract
½ cup plain soymilk or low-fat milk
1 tablespoon orange juice

Position a rack in the lower third of the oven and preheat the oven to 325°F. Spray or oil a 9-inch round tube pan and dust with flour. Tap to remove excess flour.

To make the filling, place the walnuts, sugar, and cinnamon in the bowl of a food processor fitted with the steel blade. Pulse 6 to 8 times, or until the nuts are chopped into small pieces. Transfer to a bowl and add the chopped chocolate. Set aside.

To make the cake, sift the flour, baking powder, baking soda, and salt. Set aside.

With a freestanding heavy-duty electric mixer or in a bowl with handheld beaters, cream together the oil and mashed avocado for 1 minute. Slowly add the sugar and beat until creamy. Add the eggs one at a time, at 1-minute intervals, scraping the sides of the bowl if necessary. Blend in the vanilla. Remove the bowl from the mixer.

Mix the soymilk and the orange juice. Add the dry ingredients to the avocado mixture alternately with the soymilk mixture, dividing the dry ingredients into three parts, starting and ending with the flour. Mix just until incorporated after each addition.

Smooth half of the batter into the bottom of the pan. Sprinkle half of the filling over the batter. Spoon another half of the batter into the pan, spreading the batter from the center out, and top with remaining filling.

Center the pan on the rack and bake in the preheated oven for 35 to 40 minutes, or until the cake is golden brown on top and begins to come away from the sides of the pan. A toothpick inserted in the center should come out clean. Remove the cake from the oven and cool in the pan. After the cake has completely cooled, loosen the cake from the sides of the pan with a table knife and remove the center core of the pan from the sides. Loosen the bottom and center core with a spatula or sharp knife. Invert onto a greased wire rack and reinvert onto a serving plate.

Mystery Cupcakes with Chocolate Cream-Cheese Icing

Makes 12 cupcakes

In 1928, Chef Mabelle Wyman, the *Los Angeles Times* test-kitchen director, demonstrated a recipe for Mystery Cake in a cooking class she taught, claiming it to be a "culinary idea" of her own skill. In 1957, Clementine Paddleford wrote in the *Los Angeles Times* that no one really knows where the recipe for Mystery Cake came from, but in the early 1920s housewives were sending tomato soup cake recipes to soup canners, who eventually started testing the recipes and handed out samples on plant tours. Paddleford wrote that the recipe was first published in 1922, so it may not have been Mrs. Wyman's original idea after all. Paddleford made hers into a chiffon cake, M. F. K. Fisher suggested chopped figs, and James Beard baked his in a loaf pan and frosted it with chocolate cream-cheese icing. My version takes the tomato soup idea one step further and includes an entire can of diced tomatoes, which are rich in lycopene, an antioxidant.

CUPCAKES
Canola cooking spray

2 cups unbleached all-purpose flour

1 teaspoon baking powder

½ teaspoon fine sea salt

1 teaspoon ground cinnamon

½ teaspoon ground ginger

½ teaspoon ground allspice

¼ teaspoon ground nutmeg

⅛ teaspoon ground cloves

½ cup canola oil

1 large egg

1 cup sugar

1 teaspoon pure vanilla extract

1 teaspoon baking soda

1 (14-ounce) can salt-free diced tomatoes, pureed in a blender until smooth

CHOCOLATE CREAM-CHEESE ICING

¼ cup tofu or low-fat cream cheese

¼ cup nonhydrogenated vegetable shortening

1 cup powdered sugar

3 tablespoons Dutch process cocoa

Pinch of fine sea salt

½ teaspoon pure vanilla extract

⅓ cup chopped toasted pecans

To make the cupcakes, preheat the oven to 350°F. Fill a 12-cup muffin pan with paper liners and coat with cooking spray. Sift the flour, baking powder, salt, cinnamon, ginger, allspice, nutmeg, and cloves into a large bowl. In another large bowl whisk together the oil, egg, sugar, and vanilla until emulsified.

Combine the baking soda and tomato puree in a medium bowl and whisk lightly. Add the dry ingredients to the liquid ingredients alternating with the tomato puree two times, starting and ending with the dry ingredients. Mix lightly after each addition.

Divide the batter equally among the muffin cups. Bake for 20 to 25 minutes, or until springy to the touch and a toothpick inserted into the center of a cupcake comes out clean. Cool the cupcakes on a wire rack to room temperature. Remove from the pan.

To make the icing, beat the cream cheese and shortening for about 1 minute in a freestanding heavy-duty electric mixer, or in a bowl using a hand beater. Sift in the powdered sugar, cocoa, and salt and beat until the mixture is a spreadable consistency. Beat in the vanilla. Add a little more powdered sugar if needed. Frost the cupcakes with the icing and sprinkle with the chopped pecans.

Vegan Brownies

Makes 16
2 x 2-inch
brownies

The best vegan party of the year in Los Angeles is the annual Ark Trust Genesis Awards, hosted by stage and screen star Gretchen Wyler. Gretchen starred in the original Broadway productions of *Guys and Dolls* and *Damn Yankees* and has been advocating for animal rights since 1968. The Genesis Awards, held at the International Ballroom of the Beverly Hilton Hotel, where the Golden Globes happen, are always a sell-out. Gretchen still stars in one of the best shows in town, and she created the first award show to feature an all-vegan menu.

⅓ cup nonhydrogenated vegetable shortening, plus more for the pan

¾ cup all-purpose unbleached flour, plus more for the pan

4½ ounces unsweetened chocolate, chopped (about ¾ cup)

½ teaspoon baking powder

¼ teaspoon fine sea salt

¾ cup plain soymilk

1½ cups sugar

1 teaspoon pure vanilla extract

½ cup chopped walnuts or pecans

Powdered sugar for garnish

Preheat the oven to 350°F. Grease and flour an 8 x 8-inch baking pan.

In the top of a double boiler placed over simmering water, melt the chocolate with the vegetable shortening, stirring. Remove from heat and let cool for 5 minutes.

Combine the flour, baking powder, and salt in a medium bowl. Puree the soymilk, sugar, and vanilla in a food processor. Add the melted chocolate and puree until smooth.

Fold the chocolate mixture into the flour mixture, mixing lightly. Fold in the chopped nuts. Transfer to the prepared pan and bake for 20 minutes. Remove from the oven and set on a rack to cool. Sift some powdered sugar over the top before serving.

These brownies freeze really well on the off chance you have leftovers.

Maple Pecan Sandies

Makes about 5 dozen cookies

I was inspired to create these cookies when I worked as Carrie Fisher's private chef. I first baked them on her antique stove, which somehow made them taste even better. I would always take this recipe with me on rock and roll tours; they seemed to be everyone's favorite. They have since become a favorite of all my clients, and one year I made them as Christmas gifts, as the cookies stay crisp when it's cold out. Use the best maple syrup you can afford—the flavor will be worth it.

I cup pecans, whole or pieces
1¾ cups unbleached all-purpose flour
¼ cup whole-wheat flour
½ teaspoon fine sea salt
½ teaspoon baking soda
I cup unsalted butter, softened
¼ cup maple sugar or light brown sugar
¾ cup pure maple syrup
I teaspoon pure vanilla extract

Preheat the oven to 325°F. Line two baking sheets with parchment paper and set aside. Spread the pecans over a small baking sheet or cake pan. Toast in the oven, stirring occasionally, until golden brown, 6 to 8 minutes. Remove from the oven, cool, then finely chop the pecans. Increase the oven temperature to 350°F.

Whisk the all-purpose flour, whole-wheat flour, salt, and baking soda together in a medium bowl.

With a freestanding heavy-duty electric mixer or in a bowl with a hand-held mixer, cream the butter with the maple sugar for about 2 minutes. Slowly add the maple syrup and beat until creamy. Beat in the vanilla.

Add the dry ingredients to the wet ingredients with a rubber spatula and mix lightly until the flour is blended in. Fold in the pecans.

Drop by heaping teaspoonfuls onto the prepared cookie sheets. Bake for 8 to 10 minutes, or until lightly browned. Cool on sheets for 3 to 4 minutes, then transfer to wire racks to cool completely.

Trail Mix Macaroons

*Makes 24
large macaroons*

When the "health seekers" came to California in the late 1800s, they discovered the dry climate of the Palm Springs area as the spot for healing waters, sunshine, and rejuvenation. Hollywood discovered the area in the 1920s and 1930s, and it became a popular playground and escape from the craziness of the studios. No trip to the desert is complete without visiting Hadley Fruit Orchards, which has been in business since 1931. Their original rustic roadside stand eventually became the biggest store of its kind in the country and developed into a multimillion-dollar retail, catalogue, and online business. Hadley's claims it was the first to introduce packaged trail mix, as a snack for hikers in the area. I am sure the Nature Boys inspired that idea.

Canola cooking spray

½ cup raw almonds

¼ cup raw sunflower seeds

¼ cup raw pumpkin seeds

2 cups dried unsweetened shredded coconut (don't use the moist sweetened kind)

½ cup dried cranberries, finely chopped

4 egg whites, at room temperature

Pinch of fine sea salt

1 cup sugar

4 ounces good-quality bittersweet chocolate

Preheat the oven to 325°F. Line a baking sheet with parchment paper and spray with canola spray.

In a food processor, process the almonds, sunflower seeds, and pumpkin seeds until they are finely ground, but don't make flour out of them. Place them in a medium bowl with the coconut and dried cranberries.

In a freestanding heavy-duty electric mixer, or in a bowl using a handheld mixer, whip the egg whites and salt at medium speed until foamy and opaque. Increase the speed to high and add the sugar in a slow stream down the side of the bowl, beating until stiff and shiny. Remove from the machine and fold in the coconut mixture. Drop by small scoops or rounded spoonfuls onto prepare baking sheets and form each macaroon into mounds with moistened fingers. Bake for 15 minutes, or until golden brown.

When the macaroons are cool, melt the chocolate in a small metal bowl or double boiler over simmering water. Dip the bottom of each macaroon into the melted chocolate and place on a baking sheet lined with parchment paper. Let the chocolate harden and serve.

Silky Chocolate Chip Cookies

Makes about
4 dozen cookies

I developed these cookies when I started to work for Silk Soymilk, one of my favorite healthy ingredients. Silk was founded by Steve Demos, whom many regard as the king of the natural food industry, since he built Silk into the best-selling single natural food brand in history. In this recipe, the soymilk replaces the eggs traditionally used in a chocolate-chip cookie recipe. I have served these cookies backstage at Farm Aid, at the House of Representatives in Washington, D.C., at the Sundance Film Festival, and at numerous Hollywood events. Make sure you serve these cookies warm with ice-cold glasses of Silk.

2¼ cups unbleached all-purpose flour

1 teaspoon baking soda

½ teaspoon fine sea salt

1 cup unsalted butter

½ cup light brown sugar

½ cup sugar

¼ cup vanilla or plain soymilk

1 teaspoon pure vanilla extract

12 ounces semisweet chocolate chips

2 ounces bittersweet chocolate, chopped

Position two racks close to the center of the oven and preheat the oven to 350°F. Line two baking sheets with parchment paper.

In a medium bowl whisk together the flour, baking soda, and salt.

With a freestanding heavy-duty electric mixer, or in a bowl with a hand-held mixer, cream together the butter, brown sugar, and sugar until creamy. Slowly add in the soymilk and vanilla, beating well.

Add the flour mixture to the creamed butter with a rubber spatula and mix gently until the flour is blended and the dough holds together. Fold in the chocolate chips and chopped chocolate.

Drop by rounded teaspoons onto prepared baking sheets. Bake at 350°F for 8 to 10 minutes. Cool on sheets for 3 to 4 minutes, then transfer to wire racks to cool completely.

Chai-Spiced Cookies

Makes about 4 dozen cookies

The oldest health food store in operation in Los Angeles is Jones Grain Mill, which opened in 1925 inside the Grand Central Market, an L.A. landmark still standing today. One day, while Mrs. Jones was working in a little coffee shop, she found a gristmill in the back of the store. She ground some whole-wheat flour for biscuits, and the results were so good that she decided to go into business. Business got so good that they eventually opened a Beverly Hills location, which included a restaurant and a tropical juice bar patronized by Marlene Dietrich and other film stars. Their food catalogue from the 1930s included recipes using whole-wheat pastry flour, which works great in these cookies. In those days, the flour was freshly ground in the shop.

1⅔ cups whole-wheat pastry flour
1 teaspoon ground ginger
1 teaspoon ground cinnamon
⅛ teaspoon ground cloves
¼ teaspoon ground cardamom
⅛ teaspoon freshly ground black pepper
¼ teaspoon fine sea salt
1 teaspoon baking soda
1 cup unsalted butter
⅓ cup packed dark brown sugar
¼ cup pure maple syrup
2 tablespoons vanilla or plain soymilk
Sugar for rolling the cookies

Position 2 racks toward the center of the oven and preheat to 350°F. Line two baking sheets with parchment.

In a medium bowl whisk together the whole-wheat pastry flour, ginger, cinnamon, cloves, cardamon, pepper, salt, and baking soda.

With a freestanding heavy-duty electric mixer or in a bowl with a hand-held mixer, cream together the butter, brown sugar, and maple syrup until creamy. Beat in the soymilk.

Add the dry mixture to the creamed mixture with a rubber spatula and mix gently until the flour is blended and the dough holds together. Wrap the dough in plastic and place in the refrigerator for 1 hour to chill. Sprinkle some sugar over a baking sheet. Form the dough into walnut-size balls and roll in the sugar. Place on the prepared baking sheets and bake for 8 to 10 minutes. Cool on sheets for 3 to 4 minutes, then transfer to wire racks to cool completely.

Strawberry-Lavender Goat's Milk Gelato

Makes about 1 quart

ossip diva Rona Barrett broke many stories during her career. But it wasn't until she scooped everyone on the Elvis Presley–Priscilla Beaulieu marriage and Cary Grant–Dyan Cannon divorce that Hollywood really began to take notice of "Miss Rona." These days, Miss Rona spends her time creating unique recipes using fresh lavender grown on her California certified organic farm. In 2001 she launched Miss Rona's Lavender, using lavender herbs in all her products. A portion of her profits goes to charitable causes. Lavender flowers add an amazing flavor to this ice cream, and you can buy dried lavender from Miss Rona for making the custard.

1 pint strawberries, hulled and cut into ¼-inch slices

¼ cup lavender or other varietal honey

½ teaspoon fresh lemon juice

2 tablespoons Grand Marnier

2¼ cups whole goat's milk, or 1 cup heavy cream and
    1¼ cups whole milk

2 teaspoons dried lavender flowers

6 large egg yolks

⅓ cup sugar

1½ teaspoons pure vanilla extract

In a medium bowl combine the strawberries, honey, lemon juice, and Grand Marnier. Stir to combine and refrigerate for at least several hours, or overnight.

Meanwhile, heat the goat's milk in a small saucepan over medium heat until scalding. Turn off the heat and add the lavender flowers. Let steep for 15 to 20 minutes. Meanwhile, using a freestanding heavy-duty electric mixer or in a bowl using handheld beaters, beat the egg yolks and sugar together until thick and pale yellow, 2 to 3 minutes.

Strain the milk and reheat it until it reaches 175°F on an instant-read thermometer. Reduce the heat to low and add about a quarter of the milk mixture to the yolks in a very thin stream, stirring constantly, until well blended. Transfer the yolk mixture to the saucepan and cook over low heat, stirring constantly, until the mixture thickens enough to coat the back of a spoon and reaches a temperature of 180°F. Don't let it boil. Remove from the heat and strain into a bowl. Add the vanilla. Let cool to room temperature, then refrigerate overnight. I usually make the custard and strawberries the day before and refrigerate them overnight, since they need to be completely cold to churn properly.

Strain the liquid from the berries. Puree half of the berries in a blender or food processor and add to the custard. Pour into an ice cream or gelato machine and mix according to the manufacturer's directions, adding the remaining berries during the last 2 minutes of mixing. Freeze according to the manufacturer's directions.

Avocado–Green Tea Gelato

*Makes about
1 quart*

Two hundred and fifty feet above Hollywood Boulevard is Yamashiro, a Japanese castle perched on a hill. The Bernheimer brothers built Yamashiro as a private mansion in 1911 to house their priceless collection of Asian treasures. After they died, in the late 1920s, it became the 400 Club, a private club for the Hollywood elite, where screen legends Lillian Gish, Bebe Daniels, and Ramón Novarro socialized during Hollywood's Golden Age. Yamashiro was used as the site for filming of the Oscar-winning 1957 movie *Sayonara,* starring Marlon Brando, James Garner, and Ricardo Montalban. Movies are still filmed and Hollywood parties still happen at Yamashiro, and their restaurant serves Cal-Asian cuisine and green tea ice cream.

2 cups plain soymilk

6 egg yolks

⅓ cup sugar

⅓ cup mild honey such as acacia

1 teaspoon pure vanilla extract

1 ripe Hass avocado, peeled, pitted, and mashed (about 1 cup)

2 tablespoons fresh lemon juice

2 tablespoons green tea powder (matcha)

Heat the soymilk in a small saucepan over medium heat until scalding. Meanwhile, using a freestanding heavy-duty electric mixer or in a bowl using a hand-held mixer, beat the egg yolks, sugar, and honey together until thick and pale yellow, 2 to 3 minutes.

Add about a quarter of the soymilk mixture to the yolks in a very thin stream, stirring constantly, until well blended. Transfer the yolk mixture to the saucepan and cook over low heat, stirring constantly, until the mixture thickens enough to coat the back of a spoon and reaches a temperature of 180°F on an instant-read thermometer. Don't let it boil. Remove from the heat and strain into a bowl. Add the vanilla. Let cool to room temperature, then refrigerate overnight to cool completely.

Just before you are ready to make the gelato, puree the avocado, lemon juice, and green tea powder together in a food processor. Transfer to a bowl and cover with plastic wrap. Chill in the freezer for 15 minutes, then add to the custard, mixing well. Pour into an ice cream or gelato machine and freeze according to the manufacturer's directions.

Chocolate Jack Daniel's Soy Gelato

Makes about 1 quart

The first time I had Chocolate Jack Daniel's ice cream was at Spago, in Hollywood, a restaurant that will go down in history as one of the legendary Hollywood haunts. I will never forget the time I met Frank Sinatra in the dining room—what a thrill. Spago founder Barbara Lazaroff is the best party thrower I know. She made that dining room sizzle! When you are making gelato with soymilk it is necessary to add some additional fat—like the semisweet chocolate here—otherwise you will end up with a sorbet. The whiskey is an option, and since alcohol doesn't freeze it keeps the gelato smooth and creamy. If you make it without the alcohol, let the gelato sit for 5 to 10 minutes out of the freezer to soften. All it takes is one small scoop of this gelato to make me happy.

6 ounces semisweet chocolate

1 ounce bittersweet or bitter chocolate

2 cups plain soymilk

6 egg yolks

¼ cup sugar

3 to 4 tablespoons Jack Daniel's whiskey

¼ cup soymilk creamer

1 teaspoon vanilla extract

Chop the chocolate into 2-inch pieces. In a stainless-steel bowl placed over a pot of simmering water, melt the chocolate. Don't let the water touch the bottom of the bowl. Turn off the heat and let stand over the warm water until ready to use.

Heat the soymilk in a small saucepan over medium heat until scalding. Meanwhile, using a freestanding heavy-duty electric mixer or in a bowl using a handheld mixer, beat the egg yolks and sugar together until thick and pale yellow, 2 to 3 minutes.

Heat the soymilk until it reaches 175°F on an instant-read thermometer. Reduce the heat to low and add about a quarter of the soymilk mixture to the yolks in a very thin stream, stirring constantly, until well blended. Transfer the yolk mixture to the saucepan and cook over low heat, stirring constantly, until the mixture thickens enough to coat the back of a spoon and reaches a temperature of 180°F. Don't let it boil. Remove from the heat and strain into a bowl. Add the melted chocolate, Jack Daniel's, soymilk creamer, and vanilla. Let cool to room temperature, then refrigerate overnight.

Pour the mixture into an ice cream or gelato machine and freeze according to the manufacturer's directions.

Maté Chocolatté Truffles

Makes 18 truffles

I have catered events with lots of famous guest lists, but I was beside myself when I found out that Dr. Andrew Weil was going to attend a fundraising dinner I catered for the Organic Center for Education and Promotion. The Organic Center is a cause I personally support, since their mission is to research and provide information on the benefit of organically grown foods. Dr. Weil is the one who tells Oprah and Larry King about herbs and alternative medicine, and no one in the history of the natural foods movement can take his place. I was so happy he liked these truffles, which were part of a four-chocolate dessert plate I created for the evening. The plate also included mini versions of the Sundance Chocolate Torte (page 252), Silky Chocolate Chip Cookies (page 266), and Chocolate Jack Daniel's Soy Gelato (page 271).

8 ounces good quality semi-sweet chocolate, chopped into 2-inch pieces

2 bags Guayaki brand Maté Chocolatté flavored tea

½ cup soymilk creamer or plain soymilk

Toasted chopped almonds, coconut, cocoa powder, or finely grated semisweet chocolate for rolling

In a double boiler or medium stainless-steel bowl placed over a pot of gently simmering water, melt the chocolate. The water should not touch the bottom of the bowl. Turn off the heat and let stand over warm water until ready to use.

Place the tea bags in a coffee cup or teacup. In a small saucepan, scald the creamer. Pour the creamer over the tea bags and let steep for four minutes.

Strain the creamer from the tea bags and whisk into the melted chocolate. Pour the mixture into a shallow 9-inch glass pie dish and refrigerate for at least one hour, or until firm.

Using the small-scoop side of a melon baller, scoop out the truffles one by one, forming 1-inch balls. Knock the melon baller against the corner of a work surface to release the truffle, and form into a ball with your hands. Place on a plate lined with parchment or wax paper and freeze for 15 minutes.

When they are all done, roll in a topping of your choice. Keep refrigerated until ready to serve, but give them a few minutes out of the refrigerator before serving to bring out the flavor.

12

Beetle Juice

JUICES, SMOOTHIES, AND TONICS

Fresh-squeezed juice makes a great start to any meal. The film world has had a passion for juices dating back to at least 1936, when Hansen's Natural (still in business) was delivering fresh juices to the film studios. *California Health News* reported in 1941 that Bing Crosby loved coconut-grapefruit juice, Bette Davis liked parsley, and *Peter Pan* star Mary Martin liked carrot juice.

Manual and electric vegetable juicers did not become available for home use until the early 1930s. Otto Carque wrote about juicing in his book *Rational Diet* (1923) and said, "Fresh vegetable juice, made by grinding the vegetables in a food chopper, and pressing the pulp through cheese cloth, has a great therapeutic value and may often be used in infant feeding." In the early 1920s, Gayelord Hauser first drank fresh vegetable juices in Czechoslovakia at the Carlsbad Sanatorium, where they picked organic vegetables for their hand-cranked juice each morning.

Gayelord Hauser and Paul Bragg imported the first hand-cranked juicers to America in the early 1930s, since electric juicers had not yet been designed for home use. Canned juices were being made by Hain Pure Foods in 1933, and by the time the home version of the electric juicer began appearing in the late 1930s, juicing had become the talk of the town. By the 1940s, juice bars were thriving on Hollywood Boulevard and Hauser's "Beauty Cocktails" were all the rage among social sets and film stars.

Before the invention of the blender, shakes were made with a rotary beater or with stand mixers at soda fountains. The first milkshake machines were developed by Hamilton Beach in 1911, which led to the development of the blender. Bandleader and radio star Fred Waring helped develop and market one of the first blenders, which he originally named the Miracle Mixer, and which then became the Waring Blendor. Waring was known for making the first frozen daiquiris in the blender, but he also was the man behind the woman who developed the first "smoothees."

Hollywood had its own blender, called the "Hollywood Liquefier" and print ads for the appliance began showing up in *California Health News* in 1937. The ad stated that many "famed stars," including Spencer Tracy and Tyrone Power, were using the "beautiful Hollywood machine." Once blenders were available, protein drinks became popular in the 1950s with bodybuilders down at Muscle Beach. *Los Angeles Times* beauty editor Lydia Lane often reported on the stars' favorite protein drinks, many patterned after Adelle Davis's Tiger's Milk, a dreadful-sounding mixture of milk, fruit juice, wheat germ, brewer's yeast, and powdered milk.

Indio Date Shake

Ninety-five percent of America's dates are grown near Indio, in California's Coachella Valley, which is made up of nine towns, including Palm Springs. Since the 1920s, Hollywood has been flocking to the valley's hot springs for rejuvenation and relaxation. After World War II, Kirk Douglas and Frank Sinatra built homes in the area and Bob Hope was appointed honorary mayor of Palm Springs. The *Los Angeles Times* first mentioned date shakes in 1932, and they are still the most popular drink served at the annual Date Festival in Indio.

¾ cup plain soymilk

1 banana, sliced into 1-inch pieces and frozen

3 Medjool dates

¼ teaspoon pure vanilla extract

2 ice cubes

In a blender combine the soymilk, banana, dates, vanilla, and ice cubes. Blend until smooth and creamy.

Orange–Green Tea Smoothie

One of the earliest written soy shake recipes appeared in 1936 in *La Sierra Recipes* by Dorothea Van Gundy, who pioneered soy foods way before they were mainstream. My friend Beth Ginsberg, whose catering clients include Michael Chiklis and Christina Applegate, perfected green tea–infused soy shakes in her *Taste for Living Cookbooks*. Beth is definitely part of Hollywood's healthy history—she was the original chef at Mrs. Gooch's delis, the creator of the original Naked Juice and Salads, and the chef at the now defunct 442 Restaurant, where regulars included Madonna, k.d. lang, and Ben Stiller. Beth and I have recently teamed up as the cochefs of the new Eaturna, featuring freshly prepared and packaged natural foods to take out.

NOTE: Acai is a fruit from the rainforest that contains more antioxidants than blueberries, strawberries, or red wine. Sambazon brand acai can be found at natural food stores.

  1¼ cups plain or vanilla soymilk
  1 banana, sliced into 1-inch pieces and frozen
  1 package frozen Sambazon acai
  ¼ cup frozen orange juice concentrate
  1 teaspoon pure vanilla extract
  ½ to 1 teaspoon green tea powder (matcha), or powder from 1 to 2 capsules
    of green tea
  ¼ teaspoon finely grated orange zest
  1 tablespoon orange blossom honey (optional)

In a blender combine the soymilk, banana, acai, orange juice concentrate, vanilla, green tea powder, orange zest, and honey, if using. Blend until smooth and creamy.

Pomegranate-Mango Smoothie

Serves 2

Pomegranates have been considered nature's elixir since the days of King Tut, but only in Hollywood could pomegranate juice once have been the official juice of the Emmys. Hollywood's reigning "Cleopatra" of pomegranates is Lynda Resnick, who grows the Wonderful pomegranate variety to make juice for her company, Pom Wonderful. When the fruit is in season, garnish the top of the smoothie with a few of the tiny seeds, called aerials.

★ Fred Waring (1900–1984) ★

Fred Waring has three stars on Hollywood Boulevard, one each for radio, movies, and television. Waring was a famous bandleader, showman, and film star, who also happened to be a dreamer and entrepreneur. Waring didn't invent the blender, but he was the man who put it on the map, in true Hollywood fashion.

One night in 1936, Frederick Osius walked into Waring's dressing room after he finished a broadcast in New York with his band, the Pennsylvanians. Osius had been one of the original founders of Hamilton Beach, a company that in 1911 had filed a patent for a standing drink mixer, the kind that was used in soda fountains. Osius brought Waring an emulsifying gadget still in its initial stage, which he claimed would "revolutionize people's eating habits." Waring was interested and eventually decided to help Osius with ideas, money, and marketing. A friend at Chrysler Corporation secretly helped him get the Miracle Mixer in working order.

Waring was ready to take his new gadget on the road with the band with a simple concept—show everyone the machine and what they could make with it. Waring decided to use all of his show-business connections to promote the blender. He made drinks backstage everywhere he played, and in May 1938, the Miracle Mixer became the Waring Blendor (the new name was Fred's idea).

In 1938, Waring brought his blender to home economist Mabel Stegner and asked her to create blender recipes that weren't just drinks and cocktails. Mabel's first book was a small one entitled *Recipes to Make Your Waring-Go-Around* (1940), which contained the first smoothie recipes, under the name "Milk Smoothees." In addition to smoothies, the small book contained recipes for Fruit Nectars, Vitamin-Full Health Cocktails, Cakes, Desserts, Entrées, Griddle Cakes, Omelets, Soups, and Salad Dressings. When Stegner wrote *Electric Blender Recipes* in 1952, she dedicated the book to Fred Waring and thanked James Beard and *Good Housekeeping* magazine, both early users of the Waring Blendor. In her book she tells how Waring brought her the blender in 1938, and asked her what else she could make with it besides daiquiris and vegetable drinks. In this book, she includes more "Milk Smoothee" recipes and says that a "milk smoothee" "is the name we have given to a milk beverage blended with fruit, ice, and even ice cream." Ever since the late 1960s, smoothies have been as common as milkshakes, and today they are big business.

1½ cups pomegranate-mango juice

1 medium banana, cut into 1-inch pieces and frozen

1 medium mango, peeled, cut into chunks, and frozen

1 teaspoon flaxseed oil

2 teaspoons spirulina powder

In a blender combine the pomegranate-mango juice, banana, mango, flaxseed oil, and spirulina powder. Blend until smooth and creamy.

Boysenberry Yogurt Smoothie

Serves 2

In 1967, Twentieth Century Fox made a sequel to the secret-agent spoof *Our Man Flint* (1966), called *In Like Flint,* starring James Coburn. The plot revolved around a society of Amazon-type women who used a health resort as a front for their mission of taking over the planet. Since the movie had a health-oriented theme, P.R. whiz Leo Pearlstein suggested a health-food bar for the set filled with natural treats like honey, boysenberries, certified raw milk, and prunes. The publicists loved it, and the foods received national coverage, particularly in the movie magazines.

7 ounces (about 1½ cups) frozen boysenberries, blackberries, or blueberries

1 cup berry-flavored soy or dairy yogurt drink

1 to 2 tablespoons acacia honey, to taste

½ cup fresh orange juice

In a blender combine the berries, soy yogurt drink, honey, and juice. Blend until smooth and creamy.

Strawberry-Wheatgrass Daiquiri

Serves 2 to 3

Fred Waring of Waring Blendor fame was not a drinker, so his first blended drinks were banana milkshakes and concoctions made from fruits, vegetables, nuts, and anything else available. When Fred heard that his friend Rudy Vallee's favorite new drink was a frozen strawberry daiquiri, he decided to make one for him in his new toy.

Before Frank Sinatra and Elvis, there was Rudy Vallee, who performed on stage, starred in films and was a huge radio star. Back in pre-blender days, a handmade daiquiri took a bartender 10 to 15 minutes to make. Fred whipped one up for Rudy in a minute, and Rudy was sold. He became Fred's first "salesman," and soon every bartender in the country wanted a Waring Blendor.

¼ cup cold water

⅓ cup light honey such as acacia or orange blossom

⅓ cup fresh lime juice

2 packages frozen Sambazon acai (see page 278)

4 frozen hulled strawberries, preferably organic

1 ounce fresh wheatgrass juice

Fresh strawberries for garnish

In a blender combine the water, honey, lime juice, acai, strawberries, and wheatgrass juice. Blend until smooth and creamy. Pour into glasses and garnish with a fresh strawberry.

Beauty Cocktail

*Makes 1 large
or 2 small servings*

As West Coast editor for Bernarr Macfadden's *Physical Culture,* and for his "Pikes Peak at the Stars" column for *Let's Live* magazine, Arnold Pike told America about all the fresh juices and other healthy foods the "stars" were eating. His column eventually became a television show called *Viewpoint on Nutrition,* and for over twenty-eight years he interviewed many health experts and celebrities, including Carol Burnett, Arnold Schwarzenegger, and Shirley MacLaine. Pike credits Gayelord Hauser as being the man who converted him from "2 cents plain (seltzer water) to carrot juice."

6 medium carrots, peeled and ends trimmed
1 hothouse cucumber, peeled and ends trimmed
2 stalks celery
1 large apple, cut into quarters, seeds and core removed
Two ½-inch slices fresh ginger

Juice the carrots, cucumber, celery, apple, and ginger in an electric juicer. Serve immediately.

Hedda Vegetable Hopper

*Makes 1 large
or 2 small servings*

In 1944, Gayelord Hauser was the guest of honor at Lady Mendl's Villa Trianon in Versailles. For lunch he served fresh vegetable juices to twelve of the world's best-known women, including the Duchess of Windsor. The centerpiece was made of fresh vegetables, and sitting next to them was the only electric juicer in France. Once Gayelord Hauser made juicing glamorous, companies like Hain Pure Foods were selling more carrot juice than ever.

★ Hain Pure Foods ★

Harold Hain opened his first health food store in downtown Los Angeles on October 17, 1926. Hain's first branded products included health mayonnaise, pure mountain honey, nut butters, and bran. The store had a mill that ground whole-grain flours and cereals daily, and grocery deliveries were ten cents. By 1933 the company had a large laboratory and manufacturing plant in Los Angeles, canning carrot, cabbage, and other vegetable juices, pressing fruit juices, and making nut butters. The factory had a vacuum dehydrator for drying vegetables, modern equipment for food manufacturing, and a kitchen that produced Hain Health Candies. During that time, Hain was also making a product called Hain Vegetable Accessory Reducing Food, a weight-loss product promoted by local actresses and dancers. Hain was so diversified that during the war Harold Hain made energy bars for the army.

Hain retired in 1953 and sold the company for $100,000 to cousin George Jacobs. Jacobs grew the company by filling his station wagon with products and sales tools, traveling the country promoting and selling. Some of his new products included skin creams made of avocado oil, the first expeller-pressed vegetable oils in clear bottles, wheat germ oil, cosmetics, and breath mints.

Hain went Hollywood in 1958 by going into a partnership with Jimmy Fidler, a Hollywood gossip monger and radio-show host who wrote "Jimmy Fidler's Hollywood" column for the *Los Angeles Times*. Fidler also played himself in three movies and hosted a television show in the early 1950s called *Hollywood Opening Night*. Fidler had a passion for natural foods and packaged some Hain products as the Hollywood Brand, which still exists today. Since those days, the company has changed hands several times and has grown tremendously. Today, known as the Hain-Celestial Group, they are the largest natural food conglomerate in the industry and own many of the best natural food brands, including Garden of Eatin' and Health Valley, both founded in Los Angeles. Hain-Celestial still makes some of the original Hain products, including packaged carrot juice, vegetable broth, mayonnaise, stone-ground flours, candies, nut butters, expeller-pressed oils, and sea salt.

6 Roma tomatoes, cut in half

I large carrot, peeled

2 cups spinach leaves

½ bunch watercress

I small handful fresh parsley leaves

½ bell pepper

I small red beet, scrubbed well

Juice the tomatoes, carrot, spinach, watercress, parsley, pepper, and beet in an electric juicer. Serve immediately.

Passion Fruit Cooler

Serves 4

*L*os Angeles–based Chef Milani had a food line, television and radio shows, and acted in sixteen movies, including *To Have and Have Not* (1944), with Lauren Bacall and Humphrey Bogart. Milani ran the kitchen at the Hollywood Canteen, which was founded by Bette Davis and John Garfield in 1942. The Canteen was a place for servicemen to go and see famous faces perform, make sandwiches, and wash dishes. A movie of the same name was made in 1945, starring Bette Davis, with Chef Milani playing himself. The plot revolves around two GIs on sick leave who spend three days in Los Angeles, hanging out nightly at the Hollywood Canteen. In one scene they go to the juice bar at the Third and Fairfax Farmers Market and buy some passion fruit juice, hoping it will do wonders.

3 fresh passion fruit

¼ cup fresh lime juice

2½ cups pineapple juice

I tablespoon Hawaiian white honey or other mild variety

I cup pomegranate juice

Cut open the passion fruit and scoop the pulp into a blender. Blend with the lime juice, pineapple juice, and honey until smooth. Strain through a sieve and add the pomegranate juice. Serve over ice.

Pineapple-Ginger Cooler

Serves 2

In 1934, Gayelord Hauser was promoting his "beauty cocktails" made from various fruit and vegetable juices. His influence stretched across the entire city, and juice bars opened in Beverly Hills, Hollywood, and downtown in the Grand Central Market. Along with Hauser, Paul Bragg was one of the first to bring them to the movie studios, demonstrating to actors how to make fresh juices. In 1936, Bragg said that many "film notables" were taking their fresh juices to the film studio and drinking their lunch instead of eating it. One of the best places to buy fresh juice in L.A. is the Beverly Hills Juice Club, located in West Hollywood. Owner Dave "The Juiceman" Otto is known for his amazing juice combinations, like Apple Lemon Double Ginger and Hot Tomato Tonic.

1- to 2-inch piece fresh ginger, peeled and chopped
½ pineapple, peeled and chopped to fit in the juicer
1 apple, cored and seeded
2 cucumbers, peeled and cut to fit in the juicer
12 to 15 fresh mint leaves

Juice the ginger, pineapple, apple, cucumbers, and mint in an electric juicer. Serve over ice.

Flaxseed Lemonade

*Makes about
1 quart*

In the 1920s, Sunkist promoted lemons for eating and for their healthful properties, and was the first national advertiser to mention vitamins in advertising. A recipe for Flaxseed Lemonade appeared in *How We Cook in Los Angeles* (1894) and in an early Sunkist promotional pamphlet, with the claim that it was good for colds. Actress Claire Windsor helped promote lemonade for Sunkist in the early 1920s. Windsor was a big star in her day; she dated Charlie Chaplin, danced with Valentino, and was a frequent guest at William Randolph Hearst's castle in the Golden Days.

> 1 quart water
> 1-inch slice fresh ginger
> 2 tablespoons whole flaxseeds
> ¼ cup fresh lemon juice
> ¼ cup orange blossom or sage honey

Place the water and ginger in a blender, cover, and blend for 30 seconds, or until the ginger is finely chopped. Place the blended ginger and flaxseeds in a 2-quart saucepan and bring to a boil. Boil for 1 minute, then remove from the heat and strain. Add the lemon juice and honey. When I feel a cold coming on, I add some liquid echinacea. Drink hot or cold.

Maté-Ginger Tonic

*Makes about
1 quart*

In the 1930s, the healthy beverage of choice was the Hollywood Cup, a coffee substitute made from California figs and barley. Seems fitting, since the area now known as Hollywood was built on former fig orchards and barley fields. Today it's all about maté tea, a drink I was introduced to by a friend known as El Maté, who promotes maté tea drinks at parties and film premieres. El Maté and I first created this drink for an event during Oscar week that featured yoga, organic food, and spa treatments. Our guests included Daryl Hannah, whose sincere support of organic food and environmental issues inspires me all the time.

I quart water
8 herbal maté tea bags
2 ounces liquid ginger elixir
Lemon wedges for serving

Bring the water to a boil in a kettle. Pour over the tea and let steep for 10 minutes. Strain and add the ginger elixir. Serve hot or cold, with lemon wedges.

Soya Chocolate

Serves 3 to 4

Hot chocolate was a popular drink with the Spanish Mission Padres when chocolate was brought from Mexico on trading ships. Aztec Emperor Montezuma supposedly drank fifty cups of chocolate, long known as an aphrodisiac, every day before visiting his harem of 600 women. Chocolate-themed movies, like *Charlie and the Chocolate Factory* (2005) and *Chocolat* (2000), are always hits, and they leave me desperate for chocolate treats like this one. Refrigerating the leftovers turns it into a light, creamy pudding.

2¾ cups plain soymilk
¼ cup soymilk creamer
I whole green cardamom pod
2 cinnamon sticks
I whole vanilla bean, split
5 ounces bittersweet chocolate, grated

3 to 4 tablespoons mild honey

¼ cup fat-free liquid egg substitute or 1 fresh egg

Pinch of ancho chile powder or cayenne pepper (optional)

In a medium-size, heavy saucepan heat the soymilk and soy creamer on low until hot but not bubbling. Turn off the heat and add the cardamom pod, cinnamon sticks, and vanilla bean. Cover and let sit for 10 minutes. Strain the milk mixture, then pour it back into the pan. Turn the heat back on to medium-low and whisk in the grated chocolate and honey.

In a small bowl beat the liquid egg product. Add 1 tablespoon of the chocolate mixture to the beaten egg and whisk well. Slowly stir the egg mixture into the chocolate. Whisk the hot chocolate 1 to 2 minutes, or until thickened, and serve immediately. Add the ancho chile powder, if using.

Black Pepper–Ginger Latte

Serves 4 to 6

I first learned about ginger tea from Gurmukh, author of *Bountiful, Beautiful, Blissful* (2003) and Hollywood's favorite prenatal yoga teacher. Gurmukh was the reason I moved to Los Angeles, back when I wanted to be a yoga teacher. When Gurmukh was pregnant, the only exercise classes for moms-to-be were at Jane Fonda's Workout. Inspired by Jane, Gurmukh began to teach prenatal yoga to expectant mothers like Madonna, Cindy Crawford, and Reese Witherspoon. Gurmukh's latest gift to Hollywood is her "spiritual village" called Golden Bridge, which includes yoga classes, healing treatments, and a vegetarian café. Ginger tea can help relieve morning sickness during pregnancy, and I like to drink it when I'm fighting off a cold.

2½ quarts water

8 ounces unpeeled fresh ginger, sliced ¼ inch thick

½ teaspoon whole black peppercorns

1 quart vanilla soymilk

Place the water, ginger, and peppercorns in a 4-quart stockpot. Bring to a boil, then reduce the heat and simmer for 30 minutes. Strain.

Just before serving, return the mixture to the pot, add the soymilk, and bring it back to the scalding point.

You also can refrigerate the tea without the soymilk for up to 1 week, then add the soymilk as you make fresh cups.

Yogi Tea

Makes 2 quarts

Yogi Bhajan (1930–2004) came to Los Angeles in 1969, bringing the teachings of Kundalini Yoga and his own unique style of Indian and Ayurvedic cooking. In 1974 his students opened Golden Temple Conscious Cookery in Los Angeles. I was the chef there from 1979 to 1984, and we made Bhajan's recipe for homemade chai, called Yogi Tea. The Golden Temple was the first non-Indian restaurant chain to serve chai in America. Yogi Tea was Yogi Bhajan's trademark recipe, and in 1984 a group of his students in Los Angeles began to package Yogi Tea. Today the tea is sold worldwide in natural food and grocery stores.

You can keep the tea without the milk, refrigerated, up to one week.

2 quarts water

12 whole cloves

16 green cardamom pods

20 whole black peppercorns

5 cinnamon sticks

Eight ¼-inch slices fresh ginger

1 tablespoon black tea (optional)

1 quart plain soymilk or low-fat cow's milk

Honey

★ Swamis and Yogis ★

Ever since Swami Vivekananda came to Chicago, accepting an opportunity to represent Hinduism at Chicago's Parliament of Religions in 1893, Los Angeles and the rest of America have embraced Indian teachers of philosophy, yoga, and religion. Many of these teachers inspired their students to become vegetarians and to eat healthfully. The word "guru" is so much a part of our everyday language that it is now used to describe someone who is prominent and influential in a specific field or who starts a trend. The Sanskrit definition of guru is someone who takes you from darkness into light—in essence a spiritual teacher or leader.

One of the most famous swamis to live in Los Angeles was Paramahansa Yogananda, founder of the Self-Realization Fellowship. Paramahansa Yogananda came to this country in 1920 as the delegate from India to the Seventh Congress of Religious Liberals in Boston. In 1925 he moved to Los Angeles, and thousands attended his standing-room-only lectures at the Philharmonic Auditorium. Yogananda believed in a healthy vegetarian diet and his magazine *East-West,* which was first issued in 1926, contained diet advice and included recipes for soy foods, salads, health drinks, and vegetarian burgers. On April 8, 1951, Yogananda opened the SFR India Café at his India House compound on Sunset Boulevard. India Café was known for its mushroom burgers, Indian curries, and Calcutta croquettes. Until the café closed in 1969, it was the place to go for vegetarian cuisine in L.A.

Yogi Krishnamurti came to California in the 1920s and eventually settled in Ojai. It has been said that the California food revolution began when Krishnamurti student Alan Hooker planted a kitchen garden at his Ranch House restaurant in Ojai.

Maharishi Mahesh Yogi arrived in Los Angeles in 1959 to speak at the Masquer's Club, a private actors' club. Maharishi never opened a restaurant in Los Angeles, but his students started some of the leading organic food companies in the country. In *All You Need Is Love* (2003), Nancy Cooke de Herrera gives an account of her time with the Maharishi and the Beatles, Mia Farrow, Mike Love, and Donovan. It is the real story of how spirituality came from the East to the West.

When Congress eased Asian quota restrictions on immigration laws in 1965, Eastern teachers of all types came to Los Angeles, following Yogananda's footsteps, teaching yoga, meditation, and spirituality. The timing was perfect, as the counterculture was ready, and a whole generation was seeking spiritual direction. Like Yogananda, many of these teachers believed that a vegetarian diet was best for the body and the soul. Yogananda did it first with his India Café in 1951, and the rest followed his lead, opening vegetarian restaurants and starting the trend of vegetarian and spiritually nourishing dining. There was Muktananda's Amrit in Santa Monica, the Hari Krishnas' Govindas in Culver City, and Yogi Bhajan's Golden Temple Conscious Cookery in Los Angeles. There is an unexplainable quality to food prepared by students of yoga and meditation—I still can remember the fantastic food served at Amrit, and I am convinced that the chanting and shakti energy put a special energy into the food.

Place the water, cloves, cardamom, peppercorns, cinnamon, and ginger in a large stockpot. Bring to a boil, reduce the heat, and simmer for 45 minutes. Turn off the heat and add the black tea, if using. Let sit for 15 minutes, then strain. Return to the pot and reheat with the soymilk and sweeten with honey to taste. You can keep the tea refrigerated without the soymilk, adding the soymilk as you make fresh cups.

Resources

Foods and ingredients are available nationally in supermarkets, natural food markets, and specialty grocery stores. For convenient mail-order shopping, check out the websites that provide harder to find ethnic and organic ingredients. Also included are some useful information web sources about organic and sustainable foods and farming.

Alta Dena Certified Dairy
17637 E. Valley Blvd.
City of Industry, CA 91744
Phone: (800) 535-1369
Website: www.altadenadairy.com
Produces natural and organic dairy products.

Applegate Farms
750 Route 202 South, Third Floor
Bridgewater, NJ 08807
Phone: (866) 587-5858
Website: www.applegatefarms.com
Produces natural and organic pork, poultry, and meat products.

Begley's Best
Website: www.begleysbest.com
Makers of Ed Begley Jr.'s nontoxic biodegradable household cleaner.

Bell and Evans
P.O. Box 39
154 West Main St.
Fredericksburg, PA 17026
Phone: (717) 865-6626
Website: www.bellandevans.com
Produces natural poultry.

Bernard Jensen International
1914 W. Mission Rd., Suite F

Escondido, CA 92029
Phone: (888) 743-1790
Website: www.bernardjensen.com
Books, supplements, and vegetable seasoning.

Bobs Red Mill
5209 SE International Way
Milwaukie, OR 97222
Phone: (800) 349-2173
Website: www.bobsredmill.com
Manufacturers of stone-ground specialty flours like masa harina, whole grains, and cereals.

Bragg Live Food Products
Box 7
Santa Barbara, CA 93102
Phone: (800) 446-1990
Website: www.bragg.com
Books, organic apple cider vinegar, olive oil, and Bragg Liquid Aminos.

Brave New Shrimp
P.O. Box 160
Wilmot, AR 71676
Phone: (870) 473-2350
Website: www.bravenewshrimp.com
Produces preservative- and antibiotic-free farm-raised shrimp.

Cascade Fresh
P.O. Box 33576
Seattle, WA 98133
Phone: (800) 511-0057
Website: www.cascadefresh.com
Makers of all natural live- and active-culture yogurt and sour cream.

Coleman Purely Natural Brands
1767 Denver West Marriott Rd., Suite 200
Golden, CO 80401
Phone: (800) 442-8666
Website: www.colemannatural.com
Produces natural beef with no hormones or antibiotics.

Dagoba Organic Chocolate Company
1105 Benson Way
Ashland, OR 97520
Phone: (800) 393-6075
Website: www.dagobachocolate.com
Makers of premium organic baking chocolate.

Diamond Crystal Kosher Salt
Cargill, Inc.
P.O. Box 9300
Minneapolis, MN 55440-9300
Phone: (800) 227-4455
Website: www.cargill.com
Manufacturers of kosher salt.

Diamond of California
P.O. Box 1727
Stockton, CA 95201
Phone: (209) 467-6000
Website: www.diamondnuts.com
Cooperative of family farms for California walnuts, almonds, and other nuts.

Diamond Organics
1272 Highway 1
Moss Landing, CA 95039
Phone: (888)-ORGANIC (888-674-2642)
Website: www.diamondorganics.com
Online source for organic food and produce.

Diestel Family Turkey Ranch
22200 Lyons Bald Mountain Rd.
Sonora, CA 95370
Phone: (888)-4-GOBBLE (888-446-2253)
Website: www.diestelturkey.com
Produces free-range and organic turkey.

Earth Balance
P.O. Box 397
Cresskill, NJ 07626
Phone: (201) 568-9300
Website: www.earthbalance.net

Makers of nonhydrogenated and trans-fat-free vegetable shortenings and spreads.

Earthbound Farms/Natural Selection Foods
1721 San Juan Highway
San Juan Bautista, CA 95045
Phone: (800) 690-3200
Website: www.ebfarm.com
Grower and distributor of organic fruits and vegetables.

EcoFish
340 Central Ave.
Dover, NH 03820
Phone: (877) 214-3474
Website: www.ecofish.com
Distributes Ocean Boy organic shrimp and other environmentally sustainable seafood products.

Eden Foods, Inc.
701 Tecumseh Road
Clinton, MI 49236
Phone: (888) 441-3336
Website: www.edenfoods.com
Makers of organic green tea powder (matcha) and other organic foods.

Eggology, Inc.
6728 Eton Ave.
Canoga Park, CA 91303
Phone: (818) 610-2222
Website: www.eggology.com
Produces 100 percent pure liquid egg whites.

Emerald Organics
1241 Adams St., Suite 1127
St. Helena, CA 94574
Phone: (707) 967-1118
Produces organic salmon and other
seafood.

Environmental Media Association
10780 Santa Monica Blvd., Suite 210
Los Angeles, CA 90025
Phone: (310) 446-6244
Website: www.ema-online.org
The Environmental Media Association mobilizes the entertainment industry in a global effort to educate people about environmental issues and inspire them into action.

Florida Crystals
P.O. Box 4671
West Palm Beach, FL 33402
Phone: (877) 835-2828
Website: www.floridacrystals.com
Produces organic and natural sugar.

Follow Your Heart Natural Foods
P.O. Box 9400
Canoga Park, CA 91309
Phone: (818) 348-3240
Website: www.followyourheart.com
Makers of Vegenaise (all-natural mayonaise) and Vegan Gourmet Cheese.

Freida's
4465 Corporate Center Dr.
Los Alamitos, CA 90720
Phone: (714) 826-6100
Website: www.friedas.com

Distributes specialty produce, Asian, and Latin ingredients.

Frontier Natural Products
P.O. Box 299
3021 78th St.
Norway, IA 52318
Phone: (800) 717-4372
Website: www.frontiercoop.com
Makers of all-natural and organic spices and seasonings.

Guayakí Sustainable Rainforest Products
P.O. Box 14730
San Luis Obispo, CA 93406
Phone: (888)-Guayaki (888-482-9254)
Website: www.guayaki.com
Makers of organic yerba maté tea and organic energy drinks.

The Hain-Celestial Group
4600 Sleepytime Dr.
Boulder, CO 80301
Phone: (800) 434-4246
Website: www.hain-celestial.com
Makers of Celestial Seasonings (tea), Hain Pure Foods (crackers, cookies, condiments, chips, sugar, juice, mayonnaise), Westbrae Natural (beans and miso), Arrowhead Mills (organic specialty flours, cereals, and whole grains), DeBoles (pasta), Health Valley (soups, snacks, cereals), Imagine Foods (organic broths and soups), Garden of Eatin' (blue corn chips), Yves Veggie Cuisine (soy meats, soy cheese, veggie burgers), Hollywood (cooking oils,

mayonnaise), Walnut Acres (juices, salsa, sauces).

Horizon Organic
WhiteWave Foods Company
1990 North 57th Court
Boulder, CO 80301
Phone: (888) 494-3020
Website: www.horizonorganic.com
Producers of organic milk, juice, yogurt, cheese, butter, sour cream, cream cheese, whole cream, cottage cheese, smoothies, eggs, infant formula.

Indian Foods Company
8305 Franklin Avenue
Minneapolis, MN 55426
Phone: (952) 593-3000
Website: www.indianfoodsco.com
Online source for Indian food products.

Kashi Company
P.O. Box 8557
La Jolla, CA 92038
Phone: (858) 274-8870
Website: www.kashi.com
Makers of whole-grain cereals and crackers.

Melissa's/World Variety Produce, Inc.
P.O. Box 21127
Los Angeles, CA 90021
Phone: (800) 588-0151
Website: www.melissas.com
Distributes specialty and exotic produce, Asian and Latin foods, and soy products.

Meyenberg Goat Milk Products
Jackson-Mitchell
P.O. Box 934
Turlock, CA 95381
Phone: (800) 891-GOAT
Website: www.meyenberg.com
Producers of goat milk.

Modern Health Products/Fearn
Natural Foods
P.O. Box 09398
Milwaukee, WI 53209
Phone: (262) 242-2400
Website: www.modernfearn.com
Makers of Gayelord Hauser's Spike
and other products.

Monterey Bay Aquarium
886 Cannery Row
Monterey, CA 93940
Phone: (831) 648-4800
Website:
www.montereybayaquarium.org
Provides up-to-date information on
buying sustainable seafood.

Muir Glen Organic
General Mills, Inc.
P.O. Box 9452
Minneapolis, MN 55440
Phone: (800) 624-4123
Website: www.cfarm.com
Makers of organic canned tomatoes
and pasta sauces.

Nature's Path Foods
9100 Van Horne Way
Richmond, BC
V6X1W3, Canada
Phone (888) 805-9505

Website: www.naturespath.com
Makers of crispy brown rice cereal and
other whole-grain cereals.

New Chapter
22 High Street
Brattleboro, VT 05301
Phone: (800) 543-7279
Website: www.newchapter.info
Makers of organic supplements, green
tea capsules, and ginger elixirs.

Newman's Own Organics
246 Post Road East
Westport, CT 06880
Website:
www.newmansownorganics.com
Makers of chocolate wafer cookies,
chocolate bars, and other organic
foods.

Niman Ranch
1025 E. 12th St.
Oakland, CA 94606
Phone: (866) 808-0340
Website: www.nimanranch.com
Produces natural beef, pork, and lamb
with no hormones or antibiotics.

nSpired Natural Foods
1850 Fairway Drive
San Leandro, CA 94501
Phone: (510) 346-3860
Web site: www.nspiredfoods.com
Makers of Tropical Source chocolate
chips and Maranatha nut butters.

Organic Farming Research
Foundation
P.O. Box 440

Santa Cruz, CA 95061
Phone: (831) 426-6606
Website: www.ofrf.org
Provides information on the improve-
ment and adoption of organic farming
practices.

Organic Prairie Family of Farms
Organic Valley Family of Farms
Phone: (888) 444-6455
Website: www.organicprairie.com
Produces organic meat and pork
products.

Organic Vintners
1628 Walnut Street
Boulder, CO 80302
Phone: (800) 216-3898
Website: www.organicvintners.com
Distributors and sellers of organic
wine.

Petaluma Poultry
2700 Lakeville Highway
Petaluma, CA 94955
Phone: (800) 556-6789
Website: www.petalumapoultry.com
Produces natural and organic poultry.

Pom Wonderful
11444 West Olympic Blvd., Suite 210
Los Angeles, CA 90064
Phone: (800) 577-7881
Website: www.pomwonderful.com
Growers and makers of pomegranate
juice and fresh pomegranates.

Purely Organic
Website: www.purelyorganic.com
Phone: (877) 201-0710
Importer of organic varietal honey and
other organic foods.

Raised Right
P.O. Box 10
Fredericksburg, PA 17026-0010
Phone: (717) 865-2136
Website: www.raisedright.com
Producers of organic poultry.

Redmond RealSalt
P.O. Box 219
Redmond, UT 84652
Phone: (800) 367-7258
Website: www.realsalt.com
Makers of all-natural mineral sea salt
and kosher sea salt.

Redwood Hill Farm
5480 Thomas Rd.
Sebastopol, CA 95472
Phone: (707) 823-8250
Website: www.redwoodhill.com
Producers of goat cheese and goat
yogurt.

Rona Barrett Lavender Company
P.O. Box 1620
Santa Ynez, CA 93460
Phone: (805) 688-8887
Website: www.missronaslavender.com
Growers of dried lavender and makers
of lavender products.

Rudi's Organic Bakery
3640 Walnut Street, Unit B
Boulder, CO 80301

Phone: (877) 293-0876
Website: www.rudisbakery.com
Makers of organic spelt breads and
other whole-grain breads.

Sambazon
927 Calle Negocio, Suite J
San Clemente, CA 92673
Phone: (877) 736-2296
Website: www.sambazon.com
Produces acai products.

San-J International
2880 Sprouse Drive
Richmond, VA 23231
Phone: (804) 226-8333
Website: www.san-j.com
Makers of organic tamari.

Seafood Choices Alliance
731 Connecticut Ave. NW, 4th Floor
Washington, DC 20009
Phone: (866) 732-6673
Website: www.seafoodchoices.com
Sustainable seafood shopping and
information.

Seapoint Farms
2183 Fairview Road
Costa Mesa, CA 92627
Phone: (888) 722-7098
Website: www.seapointfarms.com
Makers of frozen edamame and other
edamame-based products.

Seeds of Change
Phone: (888) 762-7333
Website: www.seedsofchange.com
Organic seeds, gardening tools, and
organic foods.

Shelton's Poultry
204 N. Loranne
Pomona, CA 91767
Phone: (909) 623-4361
Website: www.sheltons.com
Producers of natural and organic
poultry.

Silk Soymilk
WhiteWave Foods
Phone: (303) 443-3470
Website: www.silkissoy.com
Makers of soymilk, soy yogurt,
soymilk creamer, tofu, tofu tenders,
and tempeh.

Soyfoods Center
P.O. Box 234
Lafayette, CA 94549-0234
Phone: (925) 283-2991
Website: www.soyfoodscenter.com
Information and publishing com-
pany—the world's best source of
information on soyfoods and soy
history.

Spectrum Naturals
133 Copeland St.
Petaluma, CA 94952
Phone: (707) 778-8900
Website: www.spectrumorganics.com
Makers of organic oils, mayonnaise,
vinegars, and organic
nonhydrogenated vegetable
shortening.

Sunkist Growers. Inc.
P.O. Box 7888
Van Nuys, CA 91409
Website: www.sunkistgrowers.com
A cooperative association of California
and Arizona citrus growers.

Sun-Maid Raisins
13525 South Bethel Ave.
Kingsburg, CA 93631
Phone: (800) 786-6243
Website: www.sunmaid.com
California-based grower-owned
cooperative.

Sun Organic Farm
411 S. Las Posas Rd.
San Marcos, CA 92078
Phone: (888) 269-9888
Website: www.sunorganic.com
Online source for chia seeds and other
organic products.

Thai Kitchen
30315 Union City Blvd.
Union City, CA 94587
Phone: (800) 967-THAI
Website: www.thaikitchen.com
Makers of preservative-free and or-
ganic coconut milk, chile paste, and
fish sauce.

The O'Mama Report
Website: www.theorganicreport.org
Founded by the Organic Trade Association to provide consumer information on organics.

The Organic Center
Website: www.organic-center.org
Founded by the Organic Trade Association to provide information on the
scientific benefits of organic products
and production methods.

Tumaro's Gourmet Tortillas
5300 Santa Monica Blvd., Suite 311
Los Angeles, CA 90029
Phone: (323) 464-6317
Website: www.tumaros.com
Makers of flavored tortillas and
snacks.

Vann's Spices
6105 Oakleaf Ave.
Baltimore, MD 21215
Phone: (800) 583-1693
Website: www.vannsspices.com
Makers of non-irradiated and
chemical-free spices and spice blends.

Vita Spelt Products/Purity Foods
2871 W. Jolly Rd.
Okemos, MI 48864

Phone: (517) 351-9231
Website: www.purityfoods.com
Producers of organic spelt flours,
pastas, and other spelt products.

Waring Products
314 Ella T. Grasso Ave.
Torrington, CT 06790
Phone: (800) 4-WARING
Website: www.waringproducts.com
Manufacturer of the Waring Blender,
juicers, and other kitchen equipment.

Wholesome Sweeteners
8016 Highway 90A
Sugar Land, TX 77478
Phone: (281) 490-9582
Website:
www.wholesomesweeteners.com
Produces organic and natural sugars
and molasses.

Yogi Tea
2545 Prairie Rd.
Eugene, OR 97402
Phone: (800) Yogi-Tea
Website: www.yogitea.com
Makers of herbal and chai-spiced teas.

References

Anderson, Jean. *The American Century Cookbook*. New York: Clarkson Potter, 1997.

Assistance League of Southern California. *The Palatists Book of Cookery*. Hollywood, CA: Citizen-News Company, 1933.

Bassett, Norman W. *Best of Let's Live*. Los Angeles: Oxford Industries, 1967.

Baur, John E. *The Health Seekers of Southern California, 1870–1900*. San Marino, CA: The Henry E. Huntington Library, 1959.

Beard, James. *Hors d'Oeuvre and Canapés with a Key to the Cocktail Party*. New York: M. Barrows, 1940.

Beck, Neill, and Fred Beck. *The Farmers Market Cookbook*. New York: Henry Holt and Co., 1951.

Belle, Frances P. *California Cook Book*. Chicago: Regan Publishing Corp, 1925.

Beverly Hills Woman's Club. *Fashions in Foods in Beverly Hills*. Beverly Hills, CA: Beverly Hills Woman's Club, 1931.

Bieler, Henry G. *Food Is Your Best Medicine*. New York: Random House, 1965.

Bieler, Henry G., and Sarah Nichols. *Dr. Bieler's Natural Way to Sexual Health*. Los Angeles: Charles Publishing, 1972.

Boots, Gypsy. *The Gypsy in Me!* Camarillo, CA: Golden Boots Co., 1993.

Boots, Gypsy, and Jerry Hopkins. *Bare Feet and Good Things to Eat*. Hollywood, CA: Virg Nover Printer, 1965.

Bragg, Paul C. *Live Food Cook Book and Menus*. Hollywood, CA: Live Food Products Co., 1930.

———. *The Miracle of Fasting*. Burbank, CA: Health Science, 1966.

———. *Paul Bragg's Health Cookbook*. New York: Alfred A. Knopf, 1947.

———. *Paul C. Bragg's Personal Health Food Cook Book and Menus*. Burbank, CA: P. C. Bragg, 1935.

Brown, Helen Evans. *A Book of Appetizers*. Los Angeles: Ward Ritchie Press, 1958.

———. *Helen Brown's West Coast Cook Book*. Boston: Little, Brown, 1952.

———. *Holiday Cook Book*. Boston: Little, Brown, 1952.

Brown, Helen Evans, and James Beard. *The Complete Book of Outdoor Cookery.* Garden City, NY: Doubleday, 1955.

Brown, Helen Evans, with William Templeton Veach. *A Book of Curries and Chutneys.* Los Angeles: Ward Ritchie Press, 1963.

Bruce, Scott, and Bill Crawford. *Cerealizing America: The Unsweetened Story of American Breakfast Cereal.* Boston: Faber and Faber, 1995.

California Fig Institute. *California Dried Figs.* California Fig Institute, 1939.

California Health News magazine archives, 1933–1941.

California Walnut Growers Association. *To Win New Cooking Fame, Just Add Walnuts.* Los Angeles: California Walnut Growers Association, no date.

Callahan, Genevieve. *The New California Cook Book.* New York: Bonanza Books, 1955.

———. *Sunset All-Western Cook Book.* Stanford, CA: Stanford University Press, 1933.

Carberry, James F. *Our Daily Bread. Wall Street Journal,* January 21, 1971.

Carque, Otto. *Natural Foods: The Safe Way to Health.* Los Angeles: Carque Pure Food Co., 1925.

———. *Rational Diet.* Los Angeles: Times-Mirror Press, 1923.

Carson, Gerald. *Cornflake Crusade.* New York: Rinehart and Co, 1957.

Church, Simpson M.E., and the Ladies Social Circle. *How We Cook in Los Angeles.* Los Angeles: Commercial Printing House, 1894.

———. *Los Angeles Cookery.* Los Angeles: Mirror Printing and Binding House, 1881.

Crocker, Betty. *Vitality Demands Energy.* Minneapolis: General Mills, 1934.

Cummings, Bob. *Stay Young and Vital.* Englewood Cliff, NJ, 1960.

Daniels, Bebe, and Jill Allgood. *282 Ways of Making a Salad.* London: Cassell & Co., 1950.

Davis, Adelle. *Let's Eat Right to Keep Fit.* New York: Harcourt, Brace and World, 1954.

Deutsch, Ronald M. *The New Nuts Among the Berries.* Palo Alto, CA: Bull Publishing Company, 1977.

Fisher, M. F. K. *The Art of Eating.* New York: Macmillan, 1990.

Fulton, E. G. *Vegetarian Cook-Book.* Mountainview, CA: Pacific Press Publishing, 1904.

Gooch, Sandy. *If You Love Me, Don't Feed Me Junk!* Reston, VA: Reston Publishing, 1983.

Goodan-Jenkins Furniture Company. *Hollywood's Famous Recipes of the Movie Stars.* Los Angeles: Goodan-Jenkins Furniture Company, 1932.

Goodwin, Betty. *Hollywood Du Jour.* Santa Monica: Angel City Press, 1993.

Gottfried, Martin. *Nobody's Fool: The Lives of Danny Kaye.* New York: Simon & Schuster, 1994.

Hamilton, Dorothy and Maxwell. *What Cooks in Hollywood.* Chicago: Disabled Veterans Service Foundation, 1949.

Harbhajan Singh Khalsa, Yogiji. *Foods for Health and Healing.* Pomona, CA: K.R.I. Publications, 1983.

Harlan, Kenneth, and Rex Lease. *What Actors Eat—When They Eat.* Los Angeles: Lyman House. 1939.

Hart, Bet, and Jean Anderson. *Hollywood News—How the Stars Eat and Exercise. Ladies' Home Journal,* July 1961.

Hauser, Gayelord. *Be Happier, Be Healthier.* New York: Farrar, Straus and Young, 1952.

———. *Eat and Grow Beautiful.* New York: Tempo Books, 1936.

———. *The Gayelord Hauser Cook Book.* New York: Coward-McCann, 1946.

———. *Gayelord Hauser's New Guide To Intelligent Reducing.* New York: Farrar, Straus and Young, 1955.

———. *Harmonized Food Selection.* New York: Tempo Books, 1930.

———. *Look Younger, Live Longer.* New York: Farrar, Straus, 1951.

———. *New Health Cookery.* New York: Tempo Books, 1930.

Herrara, Nancy Cooke de. *All You Need Is Love*. San Diego: Jodere Group, 2003.

Hooker, Alan. *New Approach to Cooking*. Ojai, CA: Ranch House Restaurant, 1966.

Howard, Jane. "Earth Mother to the Foodists." *Life,* October 22, 1971.

Internet Movie Database, www.imdb.com.

Jarvits, Janet. *An Introduction to Helen Evans Brown and Her Library*. Pasadena, CA: Weather Bird Press, 2003.

Jensen, Dr. Bernard. *Foods That Heal*. New York: Avery Publishing Group, 1988.

———. *Vital Foods for Total Health*. Los Angeles: Dr. Bernard Jensen Enterprises, 1950.

Jones, Dorothea Van Gundy. *The Soybean Cookbook*. New York: Gramercy Publishing, 1963.

Kellogg, Mrs. E. E. *Every-Day Dishes and Every-Day Work*. Battle Creek, MI: Modern Medicine Publishing Co., 1897.

Kennedy, Gordon. *Children of the Sun*. Ojai, CA: Nivaria Press, 1998.

Lager, Mildred. *Food Facts*. Acton, CA: Stonehurst, 1935.

———. *The Useful Soybean: A Plus Factor in Modern Living*. New York: McGraw-Hill Book Co., 1945.

LaLanne, Jack. *Foods For Glamour*. Englewood, NJ: Prentice-Hall, 1961.

———. *The Jack LaLanne Way to Vibrant Good Health*. Englewood, NJ: Prentice-Hall, 1960.

Let's Live magazine archives, 1942–1975, Franklin Publications, Los Angeles.

Levenstein, Harvey. *Paradox of Plenty*. New York: Oxford University Press, 1993.

Los Angeles Times. *Los Angeles Times Economy Cookbook Number Five*. Los Angeles: Times- Mirror Co., 1917.

———. *Los Angeles Times Cookbook Number Four*. Los Angeles: Times Mirror Co., 1911.

———. *Los Angeles Times Cookbook Number Two*. Los Angeles: Times Mirror Co., 1905.

Lovegren, Sylvia. *Fashionable Food*. New York: Macmillan, 1995.

Lovell, Phillip Dr. *Diet for Health By Natural Methods*. Los Angeles: Times-Mirror Press, 1927.

Lurie, Karen. *TV Chefs: The Dish on the Stars of Your Favorite Cooking Shows*. Los Angeles: Renaissance Books, 1999.

Mariani, John F. *The Dictionary of American Food and Drink*. New York: Hearst Books, 1994.

Mariposa [Mariposa Hayes]. *Hollywood Glamour Cook Book*. Miami: Glamour Publications, 1940.

Marks, Susan. *Finding Betty Crocker*. New York: Simon & Schuster, 2005.

Marmorstein, Gary. "Dear Doctor Lovell." *Los Angeles Herald,* March 23,1986.

Max, Peter, and Ronwen Proust. *The Peter Max New Age Organic Vegetarian Cookbook*. New York: Pyramid Books, 1971.

Mcfadden, Bernarr. *Weakness Is a Crime*. Syracuse, NY: Syracuse University Press, 1991.

Medrich, Alice. *Chocolate and the Art of Low-Fat Desserts*. New York: Warner Books, 1994.

Mendelson, Anne. *Stand Facing the Stove*. New York: Henry Holt and Co., 1996.

Milliers, G. W. *Servants and Stars*. Hollywood, CA: G. W. Milliers, undated (circa 1930s).

Paddleford, Clementine. *How America Eats*. New York: Scribner's, 1960.

Pearlstein, Leo. *Celebrity Stew*. Los Angeles: Hollywood Circle Press, 2002.

Penny, Prudence. *Coupon Cookery: A Guide to Good Meals Under Wartime Conditions of Rationing*. Hollywood, CA: Murray & Gee, 1943.

Peters, Lulu Hunt. *Diet and Health, with Key to the Calories*. Chicago: Reilly and Lee Co., 1922.

Pike, Dr. Arnold. *Viewpoint on Nutrition*. Hollywood, CA: Newcastle Books, 1973.

Price, Mary, and Vincent. *A Treasury of Great Recipes*. New York: Ampersand Press, 1965.

ProQuest Historical Newspapers. *Los Angeles Times,* 1881–1987.

———. *The New York Times,* 1851–2001.

————. *The Washington Post,* 1877–1988.

Reardon, Joan. *Poet of the Appetites: The Lives and Loves of M. F. K. Fisher.* New York: North Point Press, 2004.

Reich, Egon. *An Unusual Life.* Costa Mesa, CA: Egon Reich Publishing, 2003.

Renaud, Helena. *Cook Book of the Stars.* New York: Grosset & Dunlap, 1941.

Richter, Vera. *Mrs. Richter's Cook-Less Book.* Los Angeles: Los Angeles Service and Supply Co., Eutropheon, 1925.

Rodale, J. I. *Health Secrets of Famous People.* Emmaus, PA: Rodale Books, 1961.

Rombauer, Irma. *The Joy of Cooking.* New York: Bobbs-Merrill, 1935, 1943, 1951.

————. *Streamlined Cooking.* New York: Bobbs-Merrill, 1939.

Rose, Marla Matzer. *Muscle Beach.* New York: St. Martin's Griffin, 2001.

Sansum, Dr. W. D. *The Normal Diet.* St. Louis, MO: C.V. Mosby Co., 1930.

Smith, Andrew. *The Oxford Encyclopedia of Food and Drink in America.* New York: Oxford University Press, 2004.

Source Foundation. *The Source Restaurant Recipes and Source Family.* Kilauela, HI: The Source Foundation, 2004.

Stenger, Mabel. *Electric Blender Recipes.* New York: M. Barrows and Co., 1952.

Swanson, Gloria. *Swanson on Swanson.* New York: Random House, 1980.

Szekely, Deborah. *Vegetarian Spa Cuisine from Rancho La Puerta.* Escondido, CA: Rancho La Puerta, 1990.

Székely, Edmond Bordeaux. *The Golden Door Book of Beauty and Health.* Englewood, NY: Prentice-Hall, 1961.

Thomas, Anna. *The Vegetarian Epicure.* New York: Random House, 1972.

Underkoffler, Renee Loux. *Living Cuisine: The Art and Spirit of Raw Food.* Avery, 2003.

Voltz, Jeane and Burks Hamner, eds. *The L.A. Gourmet.* Garden City, NY: Doubleday, 1971.

Wallace, David. *Lost Hollywood.* New York: St. Martins Press, 2001.

Waring Corporation. *Recipes to Make Your Waring-Go-Round.* New York: The Waring Corporation, 1940.

————. *340 Recipes for the New Waring Blendor.* New York: Waring Products Corporation, 1947.

Waring, Virginia. *Fred Waring and the Pennsylvanians.* Urbana, IL: University of Illinois Press, 1997.

Wenner, Paul. *Gardencuisine.* New York: Simon & Schuster, 1997.

Whorton, James C. *Crusaders for Fitness.* Princeton, NJ: Princeton University Press, 1982.

Wiener, Joan. "New Food Freaks." *Seventeen,* March 1972.

Wyman, Arthur Leslie. *Chef Wyman's Daily Health Menus.* Los Angeles: Wyman Food Service, 1927.

Yergin, Daniel. "Let's Get Adelle Davis Right—Supernutritionist." *New York Times Magazine,* May 20, 1973.

Zaslavsky, Nancy. *Meatless Mexican Home Cooking.* New York: St. Martin's Press, 1997.

Zimbalist Jr., Efrem. *My Dinner of Herbs.* New York: Limelight Editions, 2003.

Zinkin, Harold. *Remembering Muscle Beach.* Santa Monica: Angel City Press, 1999.

Index